BEQUEST MANAGEMENT FOR CHARITABLE ORGANIZATIONS

M. Jasmine Sweatman, B.A. (Hon.), LL.B., TEP, LL.M.

Canadian Centre for Philanthropy ™
Le Centre canadien de philanthropie ᴹᶜ

Bequest Management for Charitable Organizations
© LexisNexis Canada Inc. 2003
June 2003

All rights reserved. No part of this publication may be reproduced, stored in any material form (including photocopying or storing it in any medium by electronic means and whether or not transiently or incidentally to some other use of this publication) without the written permission of the copyright holder except in accordance with the provisions of the Copyright Act. Applications for the copyright holder's written permission to reproduce any part of this publication should be addressed to the publisher.

Warning: The doing of an unauthorized act in relation to a copyrighted work may result in both a civil claim for damages and criminal prosecution.

Members of the LexisNexis Group worldwide

Canada	LexisNexis Canada Inc, 75 Clegg Road, MARKHAM, Ontario
Argentina	Abeledo Perrot, Jurisprudencia Argentina and Depalma, BUENOS AIRES
Australia	Butterworths, a Division of Reed International Books Australia Pty Ltd, CHATSWOOD, New South Wales
Austria	ARD Betriebsdienst and Verlag Orac, VIENNA
Chile	Publitecsa and Conosur Ltda, SANTIAGO DE CHILE
Czech Republic	Orac sro, PRAGUE
France	Éditions du Juris-Classeur SA, PARIS
Hong Kong	Butterworths Asia (Hong Kong), HONG KONG
Hungary	Hvg Orac, BUDAPEST
India	Butterworths India, NEW DELHI
Ireland	Butterworths (Ireland) Ltd, DUBLIN
Italy	Giuffré, MILAN
Malaysia	Malayan Law Journal Sdn Bhd, KUALA LUMPUR
New Zealand	Butterworths of New Zealand, WELLINGTON
Poland	Wydawnictwa Prawnicze PWN, WARSAW
Singapore	Butterworths Asia, SINGAPORE
South Africa	Butterworth Publishers (Pty) Ltd, DURBAN
Switzerland	Stämpfli Verlag AG, BERNE
United Kingdom	Butterworths Tolley, a Division of Reed Elsevier (UK), LONDON, WC2A
USA	LexisNexis, DAYTON, Ohio

National Library of Canada Cataloguing in Publication

Sweatman, M. Jasmine (Marion Jasmine), 1965-
    Bequest management for charitable organizations / M. Jasmine Sweatman.

Includes index.
ISBN 0-433-44161-5

    1. Charitable uses, trusts, and foundations--Canada. 2. Nonprofit organizations---Canada.
I. Title.

HV105.S94 2003   346.71'064   C2003-902462-8

Printed and bound in Canada.

To Michelle O., Linda P. and Pauline W.
for your inspiration and friendship.

With love to Wayland, Matthew, Oliver, Emma and Calum.

About the Author

M. Jasmine Sweatman, B.A. (Hon.), LL.B., TEP, LL.M., is a partner at the Toronto office of Miller Thomson LLP. Her practice focuses on issues related to fiduciary obligations, trusts and estates, with emphasis on protecting charitable interests. She has a particular focus on advising charities on bequest management and gift planning. Ms. Sweatman is an active member of, and frequent speaker for, the Law Society of Upper Canada, the Ontario Bar Association, The Advocates Society, the Canadian Association of Gift Planners and the Society of Trusts and Estate Practitioner. She has written articles for the *Estate, Trust and Pensions Journal* on estate administration and litigation. She is also the author of the textbook *Guide to Powers of Attorney*.

Foreword

If you work at a charity, bequest management is, ironically, a task you inherit. At most charities, it is a side-of-the-desk function, relegated to the finance department, or more recently at larger organizations, the gift planner. You learn by doing: reading files, talking to lawyers and trust officers, and making mistakes. While charities are growing in sophistication, there are still few resources that address the estate administration needs of charities. Until now.

Jasmine Sweatman's *Bequest Management for Charitable Organizations* is the first Canadian book I am aware of that addresses the estate administration process from the charity's perspective. It is a tremendously welcome resource. Charities approach bequest administration differently than trustees and solicitors. Having a step-by-step discussion of the bequest management process, with specific information for Ontario, Alberta and British Columbia, should help charities get the practical knowledge they need to uphold their fiduciary responsibilities.

The emphasis is practical. This book contains definitions of terms, simple descriptions of the process, a clear explanation of estate accounting, clarity on timing and fees, and information about different asset classes and types of beneficiaries. It also has an exceptionally useful case study, which puts the theory into sobering practice. Reading this book has taught me, once again, the key issues at stake. I can see it saving The Hospital for Sick Children Foundation money and taking us to a higher level of professionalism. Whether you are an old pro or a rank beginner, it is hard to ask for a better resource.

Malcolm D. Burrows, CFRE
Director, Development & Gift Planning
The Hospital for Sick Children Foundation, Toronto

Preface

The management of bequest by charitable organizations has been an ongoing process for a long time as the generosity of Canadians in leaving gifts to charities in their estate plan has been unfaltering. That passage of time, however, has seen the growth in the complexity of estate administration and, in particular, the development of the sometimes unique position of the charitable beneficiary. For bequest management to be practiced in an effective and efficient manner at a charitable organization, whether small or large, internal structure and support needs to be in place. The intent of this text, developed from a popular in-house seminar, is to offer understanding and guidance into the process from the vantage point of the charitable beneficiary. To that end, this book was written with that focus in mind, although it is hoped that advisors of charitable organizations will also find this reference useful. I trust that this book will serve as a useful reference text and guide.

I would like to acknowledge the contributors of key sections of this book by Deborah L. Campbell (Chapter 5 and case study), Sandra Enticknap (British Columbia) and Dragana Sanchez-Glowicki (Alberta). Without their addi-tions, this book would not have been as practical or national in scope. In addition, I would like to thank those to whom this book is dedicated for their unwavering support in turning the idea of spreading the word about effective bequest management to charitable organizations into the written word.

When writing on a topic such as bequest management, it is important to review and refresh. I hope that this reference will meet that purpose and that all of its readers find it useful as you either provide advice to clients during the administration of an estate, or engage in the process of administering bequests for your organization.

M. Jasmine Sweatman
May 2003

TABLE OF CONTENTS

About the Author v
Foreword vii
Preface ix

Chapter 1: Introduction and Definitions 1
    What is an Estate? 1
    What is a Will? 1
    What is a Codicil? 2
    What Happens if There is No Will (or Testamentary Document)? 2
    What is a Testator and Testatrix? 3
    What is a Beneficiary? 3
    What is an Estate Trustee? 3
    What is a Trustee? 4
    What is a Personal Representative? 4
    What is an Administrator? 4
    What is an Attorney? 4
    What is a Trust? 5
    What is Probate? 5
    What is a Certificate of Appointment? 6
    What are the Basic Steps in Administering an Estate? 6
    What is a Charitable Beneficiary? 6
    Additional Definitions 7

Chapter 2: Estate Administration 11
    Ontario 11
    Steps 11
        Funeral 11
        Meeting with Solicitor 12
        Intestacy 13
    Testamentary Documents 14
        Typed or Holographic 14
        Codicil 16
        Appointment of Estate Trustee 16
        Documentation 18
    Administration of the Estate 19
    Probate 20
    Division of Labour 23

Table of Contents

The Charitable Beneficiary 26
Liabilities 30
Advertising for Claims...31
Income Taxes..32
Intermediate Stage...33
Winding up the Estate..37
Alberta 37
Identification of Executor/Administrator/ Personal Representative......38
    Personal Representative's Conflict of Interest 40
    Bonds...40
    Duties 41
Notice to Creditors and Claimants 42
Applications For Grants Of Probate And Administration..............44
    Necessity for Obtaining a Grant 44
    Information Collection...47
    Fees for Grants..47
    Intestate Succession Act 48
Notices Under the Surrogate Rules 51
    Notice to a Specific Bequest Beneficiary 51
    Notice to a Residuary Beneficiary 51
    Notice to Deceased Persons 52
    Missing Persons..52
    Convicts 53
    Minor Persons 53
    Unborn Beneficiaries 53
    Dependent Adults 53
Service of Notices Under The Surrogate Rules 54
Notice of Rights Under The Dependants Relief Act.......................54
    Notice to Spouse...55
    Notice to Children..56
Notice Under The Matrimonial Property Act 57
    Notice to Spouse...57
Applications For Advice and Directions...58
Rectification and Construction/Interpretation of Wills 60
British Columbia 61
Intestacy 61
Typed or Holographic...63
Appointment of Executor 64
Documentation..64
Probate 65
Charitable Beneficiary 67

Chapter 3: Legal Fees, Compensation, Taxes, Releases And Costs 69
Ontario 69
Legal and Professional Fees 70
Solicitor Acting as Estate Trustee 72
Compensation 74
Pre-taking Compensation..80
Income Taxes..81
Releases and Indemnity...85
  Release...85
  Indemnity 90
Costs in Estate Proceedings...92
Alberta 93
Personal Representative's Compensation......................................93
  Entitlement to Compensation...93
  Amount of Compensation...94
Out-of-Pocket Expenses..98
Pre-Taking Compensation and Out-of-Pocket Expenses.............98
Legal Fees...99
  Estate Administration 99
  Form of Solicitor's Account 104
  Assessing the Solicitor's Account 104
Costs in Estate Litigation..105
British Columbia 107
Compensation 108
Costs in Estate Proceedings...109

Chapter 4: Estate Accounting..111
Ontario 111
Purpose 113
Timing 113
Compelling a Passing of Accounts...114
Format 116
Procedure 117
Statement of Original Assets 119
Statement of Capital Receipts...121
Statement of Capital Disbursements 121
Statement of Revenue Receipts 122
Statement of Revenue Disbursements...122
Statement of Investment Account 122
Cash Summary...124
Statement of Unrealized Original Assets 124

Statement of Trustees' Investment 125
Statement of Outstanding Liabilities 125
Statement Of Estate Trustee's Compensation 125
Release and Indemnity 126
Formal Passing of Accounts 126
"Over the Counter" 126
Charities' Perspective 128
Auditing Estate Accounts 130
Reviewing Testamentary Documents 130
General Review 133
Response to the Account Review 133
Auditing Trust Company Accounts 133
Alberta 134
Requirement to Account 135
Preparation of Accounts 136
Procedures for Passing Accounts 139
Informal Accounting and Releases 139
Court Application Dispensing with a Formal Passing of Accounts 140
Court Application for a Formal Passing of Accounts 142
British Columbia 145
Compelling a Passing of Accounts 146
Format 147
    Statement of Investment Account 147
    Statement of Unrealized Original Assets 148
Formal Passing of Accounts 148

Chapter 5: Case Study 153
Case Study: Estate of Mary Sophia Young aka the Good,
    Bad & the Ugley 154
Trustee Letter 155
Last Will and Testament of Mary Sophia Young 156
Statement of Estate Accounts (Flawed Version) 161
Case Study Commentary (Flawed Accounts) 185
Commentary: Legal Accounts 189
Sample Letters From Attorney 190
Case Study Commentary (Corrected Accounts) 209
Statement of Estate Accounts (Corrected Version) 215

Chapter 6: Estate Litigation and Management 243
Ontario 243
Introduction 243

Types of Estate Proceedings 244
"Lost" Will 244
Interpretation of Testamentary Instruments 245
The *Cy-près* Doctrine 245
Will Challenges 251
Proper Execution 252
    Typed or Processed Wills 252
    Holograph Wills 254
Will Challenges 254
    Age and Testamentary Capacity 254
    Suspicious Circumstances/Due Execution 256
    Undue Influence 257
    Fraud 258
Claims Against the Estate by Spouses, Dependants,
    and Neighbours 258
    Spousal Election 259
    Dependant Support or Relief Claims 260
    Services Rendered Claims 261
Steps in an Estate Action 264
Notification 265
    Orders for Assistance 265
    Order to Accept or Refuse the Appointment 266
    Order to Beneficiary Witness 267
    Order to Former Spouse 267
    Order to File Statement of Assets 267
    Order for Further Particulars 268
    Order to Pass Accounts 268
    Notice of Commencement of Proceedings 268
    Formal Proof of Testamentary Instrument 269
    Objection to Issuing a Certificate of Appointment 269
    Revocation of Certificate of Appointment 270
    Return of Certificate of Appointment 270
Application or Motion for Directions 271
    Notice of Appearance 273
    Submitting One's Rights 273
    Estate Trustee During Litigation 274
    Interlocutory Procedures 275
    Production of Documents 275
    Examination for Discovery 276
    Resolution – Settlement or Trial 277
    Mediation 277

Pre-Trial and Trial 279
Appeal 280
The Players 280
    Estate Trustee 280
    Minors, Unborns and Unascertaineds 281
    Mentally Incapable Persons 281
    The Beneficiary 282
    Costs in Estate Litigation 282
Impact and Consequences of the Estate being in Litigation 286
    Impact on Beneficiaries 286
Conflict of Interest 287
    Charities' Perspective and Response 288
Factors to Consider 289
Alberta 295
Introduction 295
Appointment of a Personal Representative to Handle
    Estate Litigation 295
Contested Claims Procedure 297
Evidence And Corroboration In Estate Litigation 299
    Examinations for Discovery 300
Involvement of Beneficiaries in Estate Litigation 300
    Settlement of Claims 300
Costs in Estate Litigation 301
Applications Pursuant to the Dependants Relief Act 301
    Introduction 301
    Claims Under the Dependants Relief Act 302
    Who May Make a Claim Under the Dependants Relief Act 303
    Procedure/Forum and Initiating Documents for Claims
        Under the Dependants Relief Act 306
    Limitation Periods 306
    Effect of Agreements, Waivers and Releases on
        Dependants Relief Act Claims 307
Matrimonial Property Act 307
    Who May Make a Matrimonial Property Act Claim 308
    Definition of Spouse 309
    Assets Subject to a Matrimonial Property Act Claim 309
    Debts 310
    Relationship of Dependants Relief Act and Matrimonial
        Property Act Claims, Dower and Intestacy 310
    Time Limitations 312
    Procedure 312

    Estate Distribution in Light of a Matrimonial Property
        Act Claim 312
British Columbia 313
Introduction 313
Dependant Support or Relief Claims in British Columbia 313
Steps in an Estate Action in British Columbia....................................313
Procedures before the Grant 314
    Citations 314
    Caveats 315
Procedures After the Grant 316
    Proof in Solemn Form 316
    Mediation 317
Pre-Trial and Trial 318
Costs in Estate Litigation 319

Appendix 1: Estate Checklist — Bring Forward Form 321
Appendix 2: Receipt by Legatee 323
Appendix 3: Estate Audit Checklist 325

Index 335

Chapter 1

INTRODUCTION AND DEFINITIONS

This chapter introduces the subjects of estates and trusts by providing a sampling of definitions of the most common terms encountered in estate matters.

WHAT IS AN ESTATE?

When a person dies, becomes incapable, or bankrupt, the property he or she holds, whether real or personal, is called his or her estate. Real property includes real estate and anything fixed on that real property, such as a piece of land with a house on it. Personal property includes everything else, such as furniture, jewellery, and any intellectual property.

Only the deceased's interest in real or personal property forms part of his or her estate. For example, if the deceased owned a one-half interest in the family cottage, only that one-half interest forms part of his estate. If the cottage had a mortgage on it, then the value of the one-half interest would be the value less one-half of the mortgage.

An estate is all the property of which a testator or an intestate had power to dispose by will, otherwise than by virtue of a special power of appointment, less the amount of funeral, testamentary and administration expenses, debts and liabilities and succession duties payable out of the estate on death.

WHAT IS A WILL?

A Will is the most common form of testamentary document. It is a legal document that names the person or persons the testator or testatrix wants appointed as estate trustee, sets out the scheme of distribution of the estate and provides powers that enable the estate trustee to administer the estate.

The authority of the estate trustee comes from the Will itself and is effective the moment the testator or testatrix dies. Proof of his or her authority is granted by the court later through a Certificate of Appointment.

A Will is valid if certain requirements are met. The document must represent the free will of the testator or testatrix and the testator or testatrix must have the legal ability to make a Will. In other words, a Will must not have been created under the undue influence of another person, procured by fraud or made at the time that the testator or testatrix lacks testamentary capacity. The document must also have been executed properly. In Ontario, if a Will is holographic, or totally written in the hand of the testator or testatrix, then only the testator's or testatrix's signature at the end of the document is required. There is no need for witnesses. If typed or word processed, then not only must the testator or testatrix sign the document at the end, but the signature must also be witnessed by two persons who do not have an interest in the Will.

WHAT IS A CODICIL?

A Codicil is a form of testamentary document which is typically used when the testator or testatrix already has a Will, but wants to make minor changes, such as changing the estate trustee, or adding or deleting legacies. If the changes are significant or numerous, then it is recommended that a new Will be executed. The same validity and execution requirements apply to a Codicil as to a Will.

WHAT HAPPENS IF THERE IS NO WILL (OR TESTAMENTARY DOCUMENT)?

If there is no Will or other testamentary document, then the person is considered to have died intestate. A statute (in Ontario, the *Succession Law Reform Act*),[1] will dictate who becomes a beneficiary of the estate and what share of it they will receive. This is dictated by the Table of Consanguinity. Charitable organizations are not part of this intestacy scheme. This means that the only way (other than *in memoriam* gifts which are gifts made in the memory of the deceased and not necessarily directly from the deceased) a charitable organization can receive a gift

---

[1] R.S.O. 1990, c. S.26.

from an estate is to be named a beneficiary in the deceased's Will or other testamentary document.

This distinction is very significant when a Will is being challenged. If that challenge is upheld, and there are no prior valid Wills, or if there is a valid prior Will under which the charity is not a beneficiary, then that prior Will becomes the last Will of the deceased, and, in either case, the charity will receive nothing.

WHAT IS A TESTATOR AND TESTATRIX?

A person who makes a Will, Codicil or testamentary instrument is called a testator, if male, and a testatrix, if female. Once the testator or testatrix dies, he or she is called the deceased.

WHAT IS A BENEFICIARY?

A beneficiary is a person or organization who receives a benefit or gift from the estate of the deceased. Where there is a valid Will, the beneficiaries will be the individuals named in the Will. A beneficiary has certain rights and obligations (which will be discussed later in this book).

WHAT IS AN ESTATE TRUSTEE?

In Ontario, the estate trustee (formerly called an executor, if male, or executrix, if female), is the person responsible for administering the estate of the deceased. He or she is appointed by the testator and will carry out directions and instructions and distribute property according to the Will's provisions. The estate trustee holds the assets of the deceased for the benefit the beneficiaries. In British Columbia, this person is called an executor; in Alberta, personal representative. An estate trustee can be an individual, such as a family member, close friend or lawyer of the deceased; or can be a corporation or professional estate trustee, such as a trust company. There can be more than one estate trustee, although usually not more than three, as that would be practically cumbersome.

If the deceased died with a valid Will, then the estate trustee will administer the estate in accordance with the Will. This kind of estate trustee is formally called an "Estate Trustee with a Will". If the deceased died without a valid Will, then an estate trustee called an "Estate Trustee Without a Will", administers the estate in accordance with the intestacy rules.

WHAT IS A TRUSTEE?

A trustee is a person who holds property for the benefit of the beneficiaries of the trust. Where the trust is testamentary in nature, typically, the estate trustee becomes the trustee of that trust once it is established. There is no official transfer paperwork that signifies this change in roles — it is more like the person switches "hats". It is also possible for a testator to appoint different or additional persons other than the estate trustee as trustees.

WHAT IS A PERSONAL REPRESENTATIVE?

A personal representative is the person who administers the estate of the deceased. It is another name for estate trustee.

WHAT IS AN ADMINISTRATOR?

An administrator is a person appointed by the court to administer the estate of the deceased. Typically, this name is given to those who are administering the estate without a will. The Court usually appoints the closest surviving relative as the administrator, although that decision should be guided by whether the Court feels that that relative will act in the best interests of the estate. There is no statute which provides a hierarchy of potential appointees, but, generally, the Courts look first to the spouse, followed by children, grandchildren, parents, siblings and then more distant relatives.

WHAT IS AN ATTORNEY?

In Canada, an attorney is a person who has been given the authority or power by another person to act on his or her behalf during his or her lifetime. Typically, a person is appointed attorney for personal care or for property (in Ontario, this is called a continuing power of attorney), and makes those decisions for the grantor of the power of attorney when the grantor becomes incapable. If acting under a power of attorney, the authority or power to act ends immediately upon the death of the grantor. More frequently, an estate may be faced with a claim by the attorney for compensation for services rendered to the deceased.

WHAT IS A TRUST?

A trust is created when a person (the trustee) holds property for the benefit of another person or organization (the beneficiary). Legal ownership of the property rests with the trustee and equitable ownership rests with the beneficiary. A trustee must act in the best interests of the beneficiaries in accordance with the terms of the trust and the law. A trustee is considered a fiduciary and cannot use the trust property for his or her own use, must act prudently and with skill, and cannot act in conflict with his or her position as trustee. A trustee is entitled to be compensated from the assets of the trust for his or her efforts.

There are different types of trusts, including *inter vivos* and testamentary trusts. An *inter vivos* trust, a trust created between the living, is intended to take effect during the lifetime of the person who created it. A testamentary trust is intended to take effect only on the death of its settlor.

There can be more than one trustee and more than one beneficiary. There can also be different kinds of beneficiaries. For example, a trust can be set up such that a person receives the income from the capital of the trust during his or her lifetime (called the life tenant or income beneficiary), and another person or organization receives the capital of the trust when the life tenant dies (called the capital beneficiary). A common example is where the testator names his spouse, the life tenant and charitable organizations as the capital beneficiaries. In such a case, in certain circumstances, it may be possible to wind up the trust in the lifetime of the life tenant.

WHAT IS PROBATE?

The term "probate" refers to the obtaining of Court proof of the appointment of the estate trustee or administrator. Once probate is obtained, the estate trustee can satisfy any third party queries as to his or her authority to act as estate trustee, and, in turn, third parties can rely on the appointment and begin to deal with the person as estate trustee. In order to obtain probate, the estate trustee must file certain documents with the court and the estate must pay an estate administration tax or probate fee. The fee is based on the value of the estate for probate purposes.

WHAT IS A CERTIFICATE OF APPOINTMENT?

In Ontario, the Court grants certificates, called Certificates of Appointment to formally appoint the estate trustee as the administrator of the estate. By issuing the certificate, the Court confirms the validity of the Will. While the authority of the estate trustee to act comes from the Will itself, and is effective the moment the testator or testatrix dies, proof of his or her authority comes from the court by way of this certificate.

The receipt of a Certificate of Appointment is also known as "getting probate". In the past, the certificate was called "Letters Probate". Now, when there is a Will, the grant is called a "Certificate of Appointment of an Estate Trustee with a Will" and where there is no Will (*i.e.*, the deceased died intestate), the grant is called a "Certificate of Appointment of an Estate Trustee without a Will".[2]

WHAT ARE THE BASIC STEPS IN ADMINISTERING AN ESTATE?

Regardless of whether or not there is a Will, the steps involved in administering an estate are essentially the same. The difference rests in the distribution. The Will dictates who receives what, when. If there is no Will then, in Ontario, the *Succession Law Reform Act*, establishes the scheme of distribution.

Simpliciter, the first thing that must be done is to determine what is and what is not part of the estate. Once that is done, the assets must be gathered and realized; debts (including income taxes) must be paid — the estate is then distributed and subsequently, wound up. During this process, each of the estate trustee, solicitor for the estate and the beneficiaries have distinct and different obligations and roles to play (which will be discussed further in this book).

WHAT IS A CHARITABLE BENEFICIARY?

A charitable beneficiary is a beneficiary under a Will who is also a charity. As a charitable beneficiary, a charity has the same rights and obligations as any other beneficiary; however, its fiduciary obligations impose a greater burden than that of an individual beneficiary in certain circumstances. Further, at times, there is an erroneous public perception that such a difference does exist.

---

[2] These Certificates are set out in Rules 74.04 and 74.05 of the Ontario *Rules of Civil Procedure*, R.R. 1990, Reg. 194.

ADDITIONAL DEFINITIONS

Bequest: Personal property given by Will. A gift of a certain item is called a specific bequest.

Bond: Except where otherwise provided or Court ordered, anyone who is appointed to administer a person's estate must give a bond (security) to the Court as part of the appointment.

Certificate of Appointment of Estate Trustee With a Will: An instrument, granted by an Ontario Court giving authority to an estate trustee to carry out the provisions of a person's Will. Formerly known in Ontario as Letters Probate, Letter of Administration or Letters of Administration With a Will.

***Cestui Que*:** A beneficiary; beneficial owner of trust property.

Children's Lawyer (Office of the): In Ontario, formerly called the Office of the Official Guardian. The law of Ontario calls upon the Children's Lawyer to assist the Courts and others in authority, such as executors and trustees, to deal with the property right interests of children. The purpose of the law is to make sure that the investments of children are safe and secure.

This office is unique to Ontario, however, similar jurisdiction is held in Alberta by the Public Trustee and in British Columbia by the Public Guardian and Trustee.

Deed: A document signed, sealed and delivered through which an interest, property or right passes.

Devise: A disposition or gift by Will.

Estate Trustee During Litigation: An administrator appointed to administer the estate by the Court during the estate's litigation.

Estate Trustee With a Will: An executor or an administrator who is appointed to administer a person's estate in accordance with the provisions of the person's Will.

Estate Trustee Without a Will: An administrator. A person who administers a person's estate in accordance with the intestacy legislation (as there is no Will).

Holdback: The amount retained (usually after an interim distribution of estate assets) by the estate trustee to satisfy the remaining or potential liabilities of the estate, such as income taxes.

Holograph Will: A Will written entirely in the testator's own hand.

Inter Vivos: Done while the donor is living.

Intestacy: The condition or state of dying without a valid Will.

Issue: Descendants, including a descendant conceived before and born alive after the person's death.[3]

Joint Tenancy: An ownership situation created where the same interest in real or personal property is passed to two or more persons with the same rights. Each interest enjoys a right of survivorship which means upon the death of the person with an interest, the survivor is entitled to the whole property, *i.e.*, called a right of the survivorship.

Lapse: To fail. When a gift fails (for whatever reason) it will go into residue as if the gift had never been made.

Legacy: A specific gift to a beneficiary by Will (called a "bequest" to charity).

Legatee: A person who is named in a Will to receive a bequest or legacy. A residuary legatee is a person designated to receive the residue of the estate. A specific legatee is a person who is to receive specific property under the Will. A legatee can also be called a beneficiary.

Life Tenancy/Tenant or Life Estate: An estate held only for the duration of a specific person's life. A life tenancy is created, for example, by the words "to Jane for life". In this case, Jane has an interest in the estate for the duration of her life (if she is alive upon the testator's death).

---

[3] See the *Succession Law Reform Act*, s. 1(1).

Upon Jane's death, her interest ceases. This is in contrast to a residual interest.

Next-of-Kin: The persons who are entitled to share in the estate of the deceased under the rules of intestacy. These rules are set out in the *Succession Law Reform Act* (Ontario) and *Intestate Succession Act* (Alberta, B.C.).

Per Capita: In equal shares, one a person.

Per Stirpes: "By roots" or "by stocks". When used in the context of a gift to issue, it means that the gift will be distributed within each stirpe according to generation such that the generations of descendants represent their ancestors and take the share to which those ancestors would have been entitled had they survived until the distribution date.

Public Guardian and Trustee (Office of the): In Ontario, formerly the Office of the Public Trustee. In B.C., this person is also called the Public Guardian and Trustee. In Alberta, the person is called the Public Trustee. The Public Trustee represents a variety of interests in estate litigation, including the estate of deceased persons, incapable persons and absentees. The Public Trustee has an independent role that is in addition to (not in substitution or as representative of) that of a charitable beneficiary in proceedings affecting charitable interests or charitable property. The Public Trustee has a supervisory function over charities.

Quantum Meruit: These words come from the Latin and mean "as much as he deserves." In the estate context when a claim is made for services rendered to the deceased for which there is no agreement as to the amount of compensation, the Court will satisfy the *quantum meruit* claim by awarding reasonable remuneration for the services rendered. It is an equitable remedy.

Residue: The part of the estate remaining after all debts, expenses, taxes and specific bequests or legacies have been satisfied.

Right of Survivorship: This principle relates to the effect of death where property is jointly held. For example, if Jane and Peter own a house jointly as tenants in common, then upon the death of Jane the house passes to Peter automatically by right of survivorship. The same would hold true for money in a jointly held bank account. Note, that if the house was owned equally by Jane and Peter as tenants in common, then upon the death of Jane the ownership of the property is severed. Peter retains his half interest in the house, and Jane's estate becomes the "owner" of the other half.

Sui Juris: Of one's own right, without disability.

Tenancy in Common: An ownership condition created when there are words of severance; unequal sharing may be created. Each "tenant" may independently dispose of his or her share by will.

Testate: Having executed a Will.

Testator: A person making a Will or a person who has died leaving a Will. If female, called a testatrix.

Title: A vested right or title, something to which the right is already acquired, though the enjoyment may be postponed.

Chapter 2

ESTATE ADMINISTRATION

ONTARIO

This section discusses the process of administering an estate in Ontario. The discussion will focus on situations where there is a valid Will that governs the estate's administration, and the named estate trustee is willing and able to carry out his or her duties as estate trustee.

The administration of an estate begins at the testator's death. The steps involved in administering an estate depend in large measure on how well the deceased, during his or her lifetime, planned for death. A well thought out and up-to-date plan should lead to an easy and smooth administration, whereas, an estate governed by an out-of-date Will is often plagued with numerous issues and delays. Hence, the recommendation that everyone ensure that they have an up-to-date estate plan and Will, and review the plan every three to five years or whenever there is a significant life change, such as marriage, children, grandchildren, divorce, incapacity, and death.

STEPS

Funeral

The first step after death is usually a funeral. The responsibility of arranging the funeral rests with the named estate trustee (formerly known as "executor" in Ontario) in the testamentary documents, not the surviving family members. The decisions regarding the details of the funeral or burial rest with the estate trustee. The Will may provide direction as to the details and costs of the funeral or cremation. This is why it is frequently said that one should not keep their Will or testamentary documents in a safety deposit box — by the time the estate trustee can or does access the safety deposit box, the funeral has long since taken place.

The deceased may have also pre-arranged their funeral. If so, hopefully, the deceased has told his or her family and/or the estate trustee about the arrangements. These arrangements are governed by the contract entered into between the deceased and the funeral home. Typically, these arrangements have already been paid for and the details have been pre-selected by the deceased. This assists the estate trustee in ensuring that the funeral is the one envisioned by the deceased. If there is no named estate trustee, then arranging the funeral is the duty of the next-of-kin.[1]

Meeting with Solicitor

The next step is usually to arrange a meeting with a solicitor. This meeting between estate trustee (which can include family members) and the solicitor is to obtain advice on how to administer an estate. Unless the estate trustee is a corporate or professional trustee, most estate trustees have never undertaken the task of being an estate trustee and are often unprepared for the tasks they have to carry out.

At this meeting, the solicitor will begin with a review of any testamentary documents (*i.e.*, Will and Codicil). This is because these documents name the person who will complete the administration (*i.e.*, the estate trustee), provide the framework that directs the estate trustee and solicitor on how to complete the administration of the estate, and identify who will participate as beneficiary. Occasionally, some direction is given about estate assets and debts (*i.e.*, the forgiveness of loans to named individuals) and estate trustee compensation.

It is important that the solicitor clearly explain the administration process at this stage as, although named as estate trustee by the deceased, the deceased cannot "force" a person to act as estate trustee. The named estate trustee does have a choice: they may accept the appointment and can agree to act, or they may renounce the position. Although infrequent (most people feel a moral responsibility to accept the appointment), where the estate is insolvent or looks like it will be difficult to administer, the named estate trustee may decide to renounce.

---

[1] For further discussion, see M. Zwicker, and M.J. Sweatman, "*Who Has the Right to Choose the Deceased's Final Resting Place?*" (2002) 22 Estates, Trusts and Pension Journal.

Intestacy

If there are no testamentary documents, or if errors were made in their preparation — for example, the deceased provided no testamentary direction on how to distribute his or her estate (or part of it) — the estate (or that share) is not distributed by the testamentary document and an intestacy occurs.

The estate (or part thereof) in Ontario is then distributed in accordance with the *Succession Law Reform Act*.[2] This statute provides that the estate of an individual who dies intestate is distributed to a married (not common-law) spouse and/or relatives by blood in the following order: children, grandchildren and other descendants of the deceased; parents, grandparents and other ascendents of the deceased; siblings; nieces and nephews; and finally to other next-of-kin in equal degrees of consanguinity to the deceased. Failing anyone who fits these relationships, the estate becomes the property of the Crown pursuant to subsection 47(7) of the Act. Note that in an intestacy, a gift will never be made to a charity, as the charity is not included in the table of consanguinity.

In the case of an intestacy, the authority for an Estate Trustee Without a Will to act comes solely with the approval of the Court. The estate trustee has no power to act until and unless the grant of the Certificate of Appointment has been made. In an intestate estate, the person who is entitled to be appointed estate trustee must be a resident of Ontario. He or she is selected from the deceased's next-of-kin in accordance with the order of interest in the estate as set out in the *Succession Law Reform Act*,[3] or if the majority of the beneficiaries consent, another person can be appointed. In an insolvent estate, a creditor may be appointed to act as estate trustee. This applicant applies by way of an Application of Certificate of Appointment of Estate Trustee without a Will.

Further, the applying estate trustee, if an individual, must provide security in the form of an administrative bond.[4] The bond (*i.e.*, insurance policy) is designed to protect the estate's assets in the event the administrator steals them. The bond is usually twice the value of the

---

[2] R.S.O. 1990, c. S.26, Part II, ss. 544-47.
[3] *Ibid*. The list is as follows: spouse; children; grandchildren; great grandchildren or other descendants; parents; brothers and sisters; grandparents; uncles, aunts, nephews or nieces; collateral relatives of a more remote degree; and where no relatives are found, or there are no living relatives or only persons found to be incompetent, then the Public Guardian and Trustee.
[4] *Estates Act*, R.S.O. 1990, c. E.21, s. 35.

assets in the estate.⁵ Where the estate is worth $200,000 or less, trust companies or surviving spouses are not generally required to post a bond.⁶

TESTAMENTARY DOCUMENTS

As part of the documentary review, the solicitor will make inquiries as to the validity of the testamentary documents. The document must be valid in order to govern. A valid document is one that reflects the testator's true testamentary wishes — in that it was not procured under undue influence or at a time when the testator lacked testamentary capacity.⁷ The document must also have been properly executed.

Typed or Holographic

A testamentary document can be in two forms — typed or handwritten. A typed document, whether by typewriter or word processor, must be signed at the end by the testator in the presence of two adult witnesses, who are not named beneficiaries, in order to be valid. This means that the witnesses must be present when the document is signed and must actually see the testator sign his name. It is also prudent to have no one else in the room at the time of execution, other than the solicitor, the testator and the witnesses, in order to minimize allegations of undue influence.

One (or both) of the witnesses will also be asked to sign an Affidavit of Execution wherein they swear that they were in the presence of the other witness and the deceased when he or she signed the document. The Court will not accept a testamentary document for probate, even if executed, without the required Affidavit. This evidence of attesting accompanies the Application made by the estate trustee in order to obtain a Certificate of Appointment.

The ability to make a holograph Will, or create a valid Will by hand, is relatively recent in Ontario law, having been introduced into the *Succession Law Reform Act* in 1978. The rationale for permitting holograph Wills was to help people with limited access to lawyers or who cannot afford lawyers, people who come from holograph jurisdictions and are

---

⁵ *Ibid.*, s. 37(1).
⁶ *Ibid.*, s. 36(2).
⁷ For further discussion of testamentary capacity, see Chapter 6.

unaware of the existing Ontario law, or people who cannot execute a formal Will due to exigent circumstances.[8]

For a handwritten testamentary document (called "holographic") to be valid, it must be completely in the person's own handwriting. Where a testator uses a pre-printed Will or "will kit" and simply fills in the blanks, the document is not considered to be entirely in the testator's hand. If the testator were to re-copy a pre-printed Will by hand, this would be sufficient to constitute a holograph Will.

This type of testamentary document also needs to be signed at the end, but there is no witness requirement. In this case, the estate trustee (and the court) will need to be assured that the handwriting is that of the deceased. Assurance is provided by way of an "Affidavit Attesting to the Handwriting and Signature of a Holograph Will or Codicil" from someone who can swear that they recognize the handwriting in the document as being that of the deceased. This Affidavit accompanies the Application for a Certificate of Appointment.

Although holograph Wills enjoy relaxed formality requirements, they also raise their own set of issues, which provide a common ground for challenging these kinds of Wills. One frequent area or issue that rarely arises with a typed Will is whether the person intended the document in question to be a testamentary document. It can sometimes be difficult to discern the difference between a holograph Will and a testator's notes to himself or herself for the purpose of planning their Will, or a note to their lawyer indicating their instructions or wishes. A holograph Will, like any other testamentary document, must represent intended testamentary wishes,[9] not preliminary thoughts about the disposition of their estate, or future intentions to make or change a Will.

Due to the formality requirements, such as proper execution, that must be present in order for the document to be considered a valid testamentary document, where there is any suggestion that these requirements were not followed, a challenge will likely be mounted. In this case, the party seeking to propound the will, usually the estate trustee, bears the onus of due execution. Once this onus has been discharged, a presumption that the Will is valid arises.

---

[8] *Bennett v. Gray*, [1958] S.C.R. 392.
[9] *Re Kinahan* (1981), 9 E.T.R 53 (Ont. Surr. Ct.).

Codicil

It is not uncommon for a person to want to make changes to their Will at a later date. If the changes are relatively minor, then the existing Will can be modified by a further testamentary document called a Codicil. A Codicil will not be used when the testator wants to make major amendments. In this case, a new Will is executed. A Codicil sets out the specific provision in the Will which the testator wishes to amend, and indicates that that provision is to be deleted and replaced with the substituted amendment. A Codicil, like a Will, can be holographic or typed. The validity issues and execution requirements are the same as with a Will. A testator can execute more than one Codicil, in which case they are named sequentially. A testator can also have a holographic Codicil and a typed Will or *vice versa*.

Whenever a beneficiary such as a charity, has a right under a testamentary instrument — contingent or absolute — a complete copy of the testamentary document should be given to the charity, whether or not probate is being sought. Where there is a valid Codicil, its terms will add or modify the provisions of the prior existing Will. Therefore, it is important for a beneficiary to ensure that he, she or it has the complete package of all valid testamentary instruments (*i.e.*, the Will and any and all Codicils).

Appointment of Estate Trustee

At this first meeting, the solicitor will also discuss the appointment process. The person named as estate trustee has the choice of agreeing to act or renouncing the appointment. The person may, by the time of death, be unwilling or unable (*i.e.*, for example, due to their incapacity or death) to act. This is why it is recommended that an alternative or secondary estate trustee be named in a Will, just in case the primary estate trustee cannot act. If the testator names more than one primary estate trustee, then all named estate trustees have this choice. The surviving estate trustee (if he or she agrees) will act alone.

In Ontario, there are few legal requirements for being an estate trustee. He or she must be at least 18 years of age, mentally competent, not an undischarged bankrupt and neither criminally responsible for the death of the deceased nor in prison. Although there is no legal requirement that the estate trustee reside in Ontario, it is a recommended practice to appoint someone who lives in the area as this makes it easier to administer the estate. Further, if the estate trustee does not reside in

Ontario, then the Court will insist that a bond be posted before the Certificate of Appointment is issued.

If the first named estate trustee renounces, then the alternatively named person next in line has priority and the same choice. If the alternatively named estate trustee agrees to act, then they become the estate trustee just as if they had been named the primary estate trustee. If the alternatively named estate trustee also renounces his or her appointment, then, in Ontario, the *Estates Act*[10] sets out the order of appointment. The appointment of anyone in a subsequent class will only be permitted if all preferential applicants renounce their right to be appointed and if the interests of the beneficiaries together represent a majority consent to the appointment.

In Ontario, if no specific provision is made for the replacement of a retiring estate trustee or for the remaining estate trustee or trustees to act alone, then resort is made to the *Trustee Act*[11] and the court's inherent jurisdiction to deal with these matters.

As a beneficiary, a charity will be advised of the potential appointment of someone other than the named (primary or alternate) estate trustee usually by letter from the estate solicitor setting out the circumstances and usually requesting consent to the appointment. Upon receipt of such a request, the charity should consider it carefully. Sufficient information, such as the person's relationship to the deceased, age, relevant experience, residence and confirmation that the person agrees to act, should be given (or asked for if not provided at first instance). In certain circumstances, the issue of compensation should also be discussed. A charity should also consider asking the estate solici-tor to confirm that he or she recommends the person for the position.

A charity should ensure that it has as much information about this person as possible. Obviously, the person was not chosen by the deceased for the position, and a charity does not want to be in a position at the end of the administration where it has agreed to the appointment of the person as estate trustee and it turns out that they do not perform satisfactorily. A charity will often not know anything about the person except what has been told to them. As a precaution, a charity may agree to the suggested person, but should indicate that its agreement is based on the information and recommendation of the estate solicitor, and that the charity assumes that the person has been advised of and understands his or her duties as estate solicitor.

---

[10] R.S.O. 1990, c. E.21, s. 29.
[11] R.S.O. 1990, c. T.23.

Sometimes a charitable beneficiary may be asked to take on the appointment.[12] This request should be considered carefully, as charities are not in the business of administering estates. It can be a thankless task with the potential for liability exposure. A preferred course is to see whether there is a family member, friend, lawyer or trust company who could take on the appointment. In the right circumstances (*i.e.*, simple assets, known liabilities, the organization is the sole beneficiary, uncomplicated administration), a charity could agree to act as estate trustee. With such a request, the guidance of a solicitor should be sought.

Documentation

After the solicitor has explained the appointment procedure and the appropriate person agrees to act, the solicitor will prepare the necessary documents. The appointment of an estate trustee by the Court is completed when the required documentation (including beneficiary consents or renunciations of previous trustees) is filed and court approval is obtained.

It should be pointed out that, in Ontario, there are other Certificates of Appointment other than a Certificate of Appointment of Estate Trustee with or without a Will. The other certificates include:

- a Certificate of Appointment of Succeeding Estate Trustee with a Will (Rule 74.06, Form 74.21) — used when a new trustee or an additional trustee needs to be appointed when, for example, the estate trustee dies during the administration of the estate;
- a Certificate of Appointment of Succeeding Estate Trustee without a Will (Rule 74.07, Form 74.24) — used when the administrator of the estate dies leaving a partially administered estate;

---

[12] As well, a charity may be asked to be the named estate trustee at the time that the deceased prepared their Will. This is relatively frequent where the person has no family or no close family, does not want to burden their friends or distrusts lawyers and/or trust companies. Often, the person is leaving their estate to charity. In this case, if the circumstances are appropriate, a charity can be named. Typically, an officer position would be named, such as the secretary of the organization at the time of the person's death rather than a particular person. Flexibility should also be built into the appointment to allow the Board of Directors to designate a person to act as estate trustee if the person in the named position at the time is unable or unwilling to act as estate trustee. At the time of making the application for the Certificate of Appointment, a certified resolution of the Board of Directors would also have to be filed.

- a Confirmation of Resealing of Appointment of Estate Trustee (Rule 74.08, Form 74.27) — used when a grant has been given by Court in the commonwealth outside Ontario;
- a Certificate of Ancillary Appointment of Estate Trustee with a Will (Rule 74.09, Form 74.27) — used when a grant has been given by a non-commonwealth Court; and
- a Certificate of Appointment of Estate Trustee during Litigation (Rule 74.10, Form 74.30) — granted when an estate is in litigation and the assets need to be preserved and the estate managed during the litigation.

If the Court receives no objections to the application, it will issue a Certificate of Appointment of Estate Trustee with a Will (Form 74.13).

Once appointed, the estate trustee may not resign unless the Court approves the resignation. The approval process is by way of application to the Court and is usually accompanied by an application to pass accounts.

ADMINISTRATION OF THE ESTATE

At this first meeting, the solicitor should also outline the steps involved in administering an estate. In the administration of a non-contentious estate, an estate trustee or estate solicitor must:

- review the testamentary documents, if any;
- explain the administration process and roles of the various players;
- obtain an overview of the assets and liabilities of the deceased;
- apply for a Certificate of Appointment if deemed necessary;
- conduct an inventory of assets;
- open an estate bank account;
- make a list of liabilities and determine whether to advertise for creditors;
- begin and maintain records of all transactions;
- realize (*i.e.*, gain control and secure) the assets (depending on the directions, if any, set out in the Will);
- pay debts;
- pay legacies (if any);
- report to beneficiaries on regular basis as required;
- answer beneficiaries' questions as arise;
- prepare income tax returns as necessary;
- distribute estate;
- prepare and pass accounts if and as necessary;

- obtain Clearance Certificate; and
- manage testamentary trust and/or wind-up estate.

After meeting with the solicitor, the estate trustee and the family will have a better idea of what must be done to administer an estate. It should be made clear at this stage who is going to do what and how that decision can impact compensation down the road. The issue of compensation and legal fees are discussed in detail in Chapter 3.

PROBATE

If it has been determined that a Certificate of Appointment or probate is needed, then the next step is for the solicitor (or, more typically, his or her law clerk) to prepare the application for the Certificate of Appointment.

Unless the testamentary documents, themselves, suggest otherwise, they speak from the moment of death. The named estate trustee is authorized to act as the estate's representative from the moment of death. However, in order to provide assurance to third parties whom the estate trustee might be dealing with, such as financial institutions, an estate trustee will "apply for probate". Probate is achieved by applying for a Certificate of Appointment (as described above). When that application is accepted, the court will issue a Certificate of Appointment of Estate Trustee with a Will.

Probate (or the Certificate) is not mandatory (as the authority to act flows from the testamentary documents, not the Certificate). For example, probate is not required when the deceased's assets are held jointly by the deceased and someone else and there is a right of survivorship. For the definition of right of survivorship, see Chapter 1, "Additional Definitions".

Despite this fact, obtaining probate is a very common practice as financial institutions usually require the Certificate of Appointment before they will take instructions from the estate trustee. In Ontario, probate is always required by stock transfer agents where the deceased held shares which need to be transferred or sold. Although probate may not be required for all estate assets if one asset requires probate (*i.e.*, stocks) then all of the estate's assets must be probated. In other words, the value of the estate for probate purposes would be all of the assets of the deceased that fall into the estate to be probated, not just the value of the assets that require probate. It is for this reason (and others) that it is becoming more frequent for a person, as part of his or her estate plan, to execute two Wills (called multiple Wills) at the same time — one Will dealing with those assets which require probate, the other dealing with the assets that do not require probate. While this may reduce probate fees, unless the plan is thought out carefully, it may also create an estate with insufficient assets to pay the debts of the estate and legacies. In this case, the estate trustee is dealing with an insolvent estate and a different set of rules.

An estate is insolvent if its assets, when realized, cannot pay the funeral, testamentary and administrative expenses and all the debts and liabilities of the deceased in full. Such estates may be administered in accordance with the federal *Bankruptcy and Insolvency Act*[13] or provincial legislation. In Ontario, the *Trustee Act*[14] provides that the creditors are to be paid on a *pari passu* (pro rata) basis. In British Columbia, the *Estate Administration Act*[15] provides a specific order in which the debts are to be paid.

By issuing the Certificate of Appointment, the court authenticates the estate trustee's appointment and confirms that the estate trustee has the authority to represent the estate. Such a grant applies in all parts of Ontario.

In Ontario, Rule 74 of the *Rules of Civil Procedure* (Court Rules) sets out the procedure for obtaining a Certificate of Appointment of Estate Trustee with a Will (formerly Letters Probate) and other Court grants. First, the application form must be completed. Form 74.4 deals with an estate trustee who is an individual, while Form 74.5 deals with an estate trustee who is a corporation, such as a trust company.

The material that must accompany the application form is set out in Rule 74.04, and includes the following:

- The original Will and every Codicil.
- An Affidavit of Execution of the Will and every codicil if the documents are typed, or an affidavit attesting to the authenticity of the handwriting and signature, if holographic.
- A renunciation (Form 74.11) by every living person named in the Will or Codicil as estate trustee who has not joined in the application but is entitled to do so.
- If the applicant is not named as the estate trustee in the testamentary documents, a majority of the persons who are entitled to share in the

---

[13] R.S.C. 1985, c. B-3.
[14] R.S.O. 1990, c. T.23, s. 50.
[15] R.S.B.C. 1996, c. 122, s. 101.

distribution of the estate must file consents to his or her appointment.
- The security required by the *Estates Act*.[16]
- A cheque for the payment of the estate administration tax (probate fee) payable to the Minister of Finance.
- An Affidavit of Service of Notice (Form 74.6) indicating that all interested persons (*i.e.*, the named beneficiaries) have been notified of the application by receiving a copy of the Notice of an Application for a Certificate of Appointment of Estate Trustee with a Will (Form 74.7) and accompanying documents. "All interested persons" may include the Children's Lawyer where there are children or potentially unknown or unborn beneficiaries, or the Public Guardian and Trustee where there is an incapable person and that person has no guardian.

Anyone who has an interest in the estate should receive a copy of the application. If the gift to charity is a specific gift or legacy, then, technically, only the page that references the gift needs to be provided with the application (although there is no harm in giving a complete copy). Where, however, the gift is of the residue (remaining estate), then the complete Will must be provided.

It is prudent for the beneficiary to always get a complete copy of the Will, regardless. There is no harm in asking — once the application is filed with the court, the Will becomes a public document. In this case, if the estate solicitor or estate trustee refuses to provide the complete Will, once an application is made, anyone can search the court file and obtain a copy of the testamentary documents for a small fee.

In order to complete the application materials, the estate trustee will be required to do an inventory and valuation of all assets as of the date of death. This valuation will be used to determine the appropriate tax payable. In Ontario, the only debt that an estate trustee can apply against the assets valued for the purposes of probate is the value of any outstanding mortgage against real property. Other capital expenses such as funeral expenses and income taxes cannot be deducted.

In Ontario, this tax is called the estate administration tax (formerly known as probate fees) and calculated on the value of the estate at the date of death at the rate of $5 for every $1,000 of estate value for the first $50,000, and at the rate of $15 per every $1,000 of estate value over

---

[16] Section 21.

$50,000.[17] As an example, the tax on an estate valued at $230,000 for probate purposes would be calculated as follows:

First	$ 50,000	$ 250 ($ 5 x $50,000/1000)
Remaining	$180,000	$2,700 ($15 x $180,000/1000)
Total Tax		$2,950

It is sometimes difficult to completely determine the assets during the initial stages of administration. Where the exact value cannot be ascertained at the time of the application, the estate trustee can file an undertaking with the court agreeing to provide the further particulars and balance of the tax payable when known.

The Application is filed in the judicial county where the deceased resided. At this point, the documents become available to the public and can be searched.

DIVISION OF LABOUR

Although this does not always happen, the estate solicitor should explain what expectations the beneficiaries will have of the estate trustee, as well as the roles of the estate trustee and estate solicitor early on in the administration of the estate. The roles of the estate solicitor and estate trustee and their corresponding duties are different and distinct.

Generally speaking, the duties of an estate trustee include the responsibility to ascertain the deceased's assets, debts and to administer the estate. Estate trustees are fiduciaries who act not for themselves but, for the beneficiaries. Although they are entitled to receive compensation for their efforts, they must act selflessly and always in the best interests of the beneficiaries. Estate trustees are absolutely obliged to administer the deceased's assets in accordance with the testamentary documents or as directed by a court, on behalf of the beneficiaries.

The following duties or rules of conduct have evolved for an estate trustee. He or she:

- must act prudently, honestly and with the appropriate level of skill (*i.e.*, the standard of care expected from a corporate or professional trustee is considerably higher than that expected of an inexperienced layperson);

---

[17] As set out in the *Estate Administration Tax Act, 1998,* S.O. 1998, c. 34, Sched., s. 2.

- must follow the directions contained in the governing document or documents (unless unlawful) or the intestacy rules;
- must treat all beneficiaries with an even hand unless otherwise directed;
- may not delegate his or her authority to make decisions in connection with the administration of the trust property to another;
- may not personally profit as a trustee or from his or her dealings with the trust property or the beneficiaries;
- may not place themselves in, or act or perceive to be acting in conflict with the best interests of the beneficiary as directed;
- must keep and maintain records and produce accounts on reasonable notice; and
- must not unreasonably delay the estate's administration.

The circumstances of the particular estate will determine whether the estate trustee has unreasonably delayed the administration of the estate or the settling of the deceased's affairs. While there is no hard and fast rule as to what constitutes unreasonable delay, the usual practice is to allow an estate trustee an "executor's year" in which to determine the assets, realize them, pay the debts and make an interim distribution, if appropriate.

The executor's year is a nominal year and a common law concept (in the sense that a judge will allow a "reasonable" time to administer an estate and one year has traditionally been seen as a reasonable amount of time).[18] Depending on the circumstances, estate trustees should be encouraged to make a distribution as soon (and as much) as possible. A charity can encourage and request that the estate trustee do this, but should be aware that because of this "executor's year", an estate trustee may not be inclined to make an interim distribution until the year is up. In any event, in an uneventful estate administration, at a minimum, a charity should expect an interim distribution once the year has passed.

Accordingly, a beneficiary can expect that an estate trustee will do the following:

- make funeral arrangements;
- retain a solicitor for advice;
- locate, inventory, value and secure the assets; and ensure adequate insurance coverage is in place as required;
- determine and provide addresses for all beneficiaries;

---

[18] *Nielsen v. Nielsen Estate*, [1990] B.C.J. No. 1186 (B.C.S.C.).

- discuss any potential adverse claims against the estate by possible dependants with estate solicitor;
- determine the debts of the deceased and pay them after contestation and settlement as necessary;
- obtain investment advice regarding transfer or sale of assets;
- file tax returns, pay taxes owing and obtain appropriate tax clearance;
- distribute assets as directed by Will or by the rules governing intestate succession;
- invest assets for establishment of any testamentary trusts;
- maintain proper accounting records and prepare periodic estate accounts detailing estate administration for beneficiaries' information and review; and
- report to beneficiaries as required.

The duties of an estate solicitor are principally to advise the estate trustee; prepare legal documents; advertise for creditors; arrange for settlement of creditor's claims, if required; and generally protect the interests of the estate trustee. The estate solicitor does not represent the interests of the beneficiaries. If a dispute arises, a beneficiary should consult and, if necessary, retain his or her own solicitor.

In the event that the estate trustee also happens to be a solicitor, the beneficiaries are entitled to insist that the solicitor make a very clear distinction in his or her professional accounts between services rendered as estate solicitor and those rendered as estate trustee. In practice, it is not uncommon for an estate trustee to defer the majority of the work required to administer an estate to a solicitor. The solicitor and client or clients should discuss this in order to clearly understand the implications of this perhaps improper delegation. At a minimum, the solicitor should segregate the actions undertaken as solicitor and those performed on behalf of the estate trustee.[19] In the latter case (as discussed in more detail in Chapter 3), charges for services performed by the solicitor on behalf of the estate trustee for estate trustee's duties should be applied to reduce the estate trustee's compensation.

Accordingly, the estate solicitor's duties are to:

- determine the last testamentary document(s) — check for Codicils and/or the existence of holograph Wills or Codicils;
- read and, if necessary, interpret the Will — check for Affidavit of Execution (and arrange for the execution of the affidavit, if missing);

---

[19] *Re Schroeter Estate* (2001), 57 O.R. (3d) 8 (S.C.J.).

- meet with the estate trustee(s) to review estate assets and Will to determine if probate application is necessary;
- obtain all information and particulars regarding assets and beneficiaries, as necessary to complete application for Certificate of Appointment;
- prepare application for Certificate of Appointment and other documentation required for execution by the estate trustee(s), serve and file the document with the appropriate court office;
- prepare legal documents for asset re-registration or redemption including powers of attorney, notarial copies of Certificate of Appointment and declarations of transmission;
- arrange for real estate conveyance and/or registration of documentation required to pass title to beneficiary(ies);
- advertise for creditors and arrange settlement of any creditors' claims, if needed;
- assist the estate trustee with the preparation of estate accounts;
- arrange for the passing of the estate accounts, if necessary;
- assist the estate trustee with the preparation of all income tax return(s);
- advise with respect to income tax returns, holdbacks/non-resident tax liability and necessity for final tax clearance certificate; and
- prepare release for execution by beneficiary(ies).

THE CHARITABLE BENEFICIARY

At this stage, there are anticipatory steps which a charitable beneficiary should consider undertaking. Sometimes a charity is aware before the person's death of the intention to benefit by Will. It may even have a copy of a Will on file. If so, that copy should be compared with the Will received as part of the Application for Certificate of Appointment.

If a copy of a Will has been previously provided to the charity by the deceased, then it should be compared to the one sent as there may be a difference. In *University of Manitoba v. Sanderson Estate*,[20] a husband and wife entered into a written agreement to execute mirror Wills and not to revoke the Wills during their joint lives or after the death of one of them. Under these mirror Wills, each had a respective life interest with the residue going to the university. The university had fortunately been given a copy of the written agreement and the Wills. The wife died, and thus,

---

[20] (1998), 155 D.L.R. (4th) 40 (B.C.C.A.), rev'g. (1996), 17 E.T.R. (2d) 78 (B.C.S.C.).

by the right of succession, the husband received all her property and the Will was not probated. The husband made a new Will that included several bequests to relatives. After he died, the relatives brought claims against the estate that eventually settled on a *quantum meruit* basis.

The British Columbia Court of Appeal held that the joint property and the net residue of the husband's estate were impressed with a constructive trust in favour of the university. However, would the university have been as successful if it had not had copies of the agreement and Wills?

Sometimes, the charity is not made aware of the person's death. This situation is when a list of expectancies (including the age of the donor) is helpful. It may be appropriate to arrange to have obituaries reviewed on a regular basis — maintaining a record of prospective donors and their families and keeping in touch with them on a periodic basis allows charities the added benefit of being able to get in touch with families when a death does occur. It will not seem as strange for a family member to receive a call from a charity inquiring about a family member if there has been regular contact in the past. Of course, quite often, unexpected bequests just arrive in the mail.

Typically, a charity receives notification of its interest when served with the Notice of Application for Certificate of Appointment of Estate Trustee with a Will. This notice should attach the whole or relevant portion of the testamentary documentation. If only part of the testamentary documentation is provided (*i.e.*, just the clause indicating the beneficiary's interest), and the beneficiary wishes to see the complete document, a request can be made to the estate solicitor, or once the Certificate of Appointment is issued, a copy can be obtained from the Court.

Upon receipt of the Notice of Application, a charitable beneficiary should make a record of the relevant information regarding this particular bequest — for example, the type of bequest, any conditions connected with the bequest, timing issues (such as a life interest) and whether the bequest is acceptable to the charity[21] should be summarily recorded. It is

---

[21] This speaks to the need for a current gift acceptance policy in that the gift should not only be consistent with that policy, but also not contrary to public policy. As stated by the Ontario Court of Appeal in *Canada Trust Co. v. Ontario (Human Rights Commission)* (1989), 38 E.T.R. 1, 74 O.R. (2d) 481 (C.A.), at O.R. 495:

> The freedom of an owner of property to dispose of his or her property as he or she chooses is an important social interest that has long been recognized in our society and is firmly rooted in our law… That interest must, however, be limited by public policy considerations.

…

helpful if this information is kept stapled to the back of the front cover of the file for easy reference. Colour coded files are also helpful. For example, one colour would be used where the charity is receiving a legacy, another colour for outright residual bequests, and a third colour where the charity is a residuary beneficiary after a life tenancy. For the definition of life tenancy, see Chapter 1, "Additional Definitions". This review can be a "goldmine".[22]

The collected information should also be recorded in a tickler or bring forward system, and a decision should be made at this time as to when the charity should expect further communication from the estate trustee or estate solicitor. Again, this will depend on the nature of the estate and bequest. By having a tickler system, the estate is put on a timeline to allow effective monitoring of the administration of the estate on a regular basis. A sample bring forward form can be found in Appendix 1.

It should be stressed that at this early stage, a charity should take the time to review the materials and assess the situation to the extent possible. Simply filing the materials and not responding or simply acknowledging receipt of the materials is not enough. It is expected and assumed by a donor that a charity will approach the bequest with professionalism and ensure that all steps are taken to protect the gift.

Like a trustee, a charity is answerable for its activities and disposition or use of its property. It is subject to the supervisory equitable jurisdiction of the court and the provisions of certain statutes such as the *Trustee Act*, the *Charitable Gifts Act*,[23] and the *Charitable Accounting Act*.[24] Accordingly, the directors are under a fiduciary obligation since a charity's fundamental obligation is to deal with the funds it obtains from the public (including deceased persons) for strictly charitable purposes.[25]

A charity is entitled to make its presence known. There are a variety of responses that a charity should consider at this stage — that first communication is critical. It creates first impressions with the estate

---

[A] trust [that is] premised on these notions of racism and religious superiority contravenes contemporary public policy. The concept that any one race or any one religion is intrinsically better than any other is patently at variance with the democratic principles governing our pluralistic society in which equality rights are constitutionally guaranteed and in which the multicultural heritage of Canadians is to be preserved and enhanced.

[22] See N. van Bentum, CFRE, "Your Bequest Files: A Neglected Goldmine", in *Gift Planning in Canada* (Mar/Apr. 2002).
[23] R.S.O. 1990, c. C.8.
[24] R.S.O. 1990, c. C.10.
[25] *Ontario (Public Trustee) v. Toronto Humane Society* (1987), 27 E.T.R. 40, 60 O.R. (2d) 236 (H.C.J.).

trustee and estate solicitor and starts the tickler system and may also begin the paper trail that may be needed down the road.

As well, a beneficiary should be told (to the extent possible) the value of their interest or the value of the estate. The value of the estate may not necessarily be the value stated on the Application for a Certificate which is simply the value of the estate for probate purposes. Further, this value of the assets in the estate accounts is the value as of the date of death (although this may give a reasonable idea) and may not, where the estate is invested, reflect current market values. Finally, liabilities are not noted on the application. Accordingly, at this stage a charity should consider asking for this information.

At this stage, some sample responses (or variations therein) include:

"Thank you for your letter advising us of our interest in this estate. On behalf of Charity X please pass on our condolences to the family of Ms. Y."
"We would appreciate being advised the expected value of Ms. Y's gift."
"We would also appreciate being told how long the estate trustee expects it will take to administer the estate, when they expect to make a distribution, and in what amount."
"Although we understand administering an estate takes time, we would appreciate being told when the estate trustee expects to deliver an accounting."

With this kind of detailed questioning set out in the beginning, it is fairly easy to follow-up. The salient information required by a charity is recorded in the early correspondence and the follow-up can also refer back to this correspondence.

Where the bequest is residuary following the death of a life tenant, it is helpful to know the age of the life tenant. This information helps a charity estimate when the gift will crystallize. This is not an easy question to ask (even if not to the life tenant directly) as offence can be taken. It may also make the charity look "greedy". There is, however, eventually an appropriate time to ask the question — usually down the road, once the trust is in place. There are also ways to create the opportunity to ask the question, yet another reason to maintain a relationship and keep in reasonable contact with the estate solicitor or estate trustee.

Above all, remember to use common sense. The caveat remains — consider the "public relations" aspect of the communications. Also, it is important to remember the public perception. Not all lawyers or members of the public are aware themselves of the role of a charitable beneficiary and may assume (for example, when the response is "You are biting the hand that feeds you" or "You are only in this Will because I put you there") that the charity should not be asking such questions. It is important to remain sensitive to this factor even if the perception is incorrect. If this is the overwhelming reaction, then the safest course is pick up the phone and explain the charity's fiduciary responsibilities. Do not stop asking the questions, but do not presume error until the question is answered. Finally, sometimes a discussion lawyer-to-lawyer helps clear the air, an example of how the retaining of counsel may be worthwhile.

The benefit of taking the time to consider the estate and drafting the appropriate response is that the estate trustee and, perhaps, even more importantly, the estate solicitor, are made aware that the charity is paying attention and is sophisticated. This shows that the charity is communicating its expectations.

LIABILITIES

Before the estate trustee is in a position to distribute any estate assets, the debts and other liabilities of the deceased must be determined and settled. After collecting the assets of the deceased, the first duty of the estate trustee is to attend to the payment of the debts and liabilities of the deceased. An estate trustee has a fiduciary duty to protect the interests of the creditors.[26]

In Ontario, the *Estates Administration Act*[27] provides guidance as to the debt burden that various estate assets bear. Generally speaking, unless the contrary intention appears in the Will, the assets comprising the residue of the estate, whether real or personal property, are proportionally liable for the payment of debts.

The payment of legacies is also considered a "debt" of the estate. Under common law, an estate trustee cannot be compelled to pay a legacy before the end of one year from the date of death even if the Will states otherwise.[28] However, it is the practice to speak of an "executor's year" and the courts attach importance to this timing. Interest will be payable if there is delay. Note that this practice of waiting before distributing does not mean that an estate trustee operating under a Will is precluded from

---

[26] *Ontario (Attorney General) v. Ballard Estate* (1995), 6 E.T.R. (2d) 311 (Ont. Gen. Div.).
[27] R.S.O. 1990, c. E.22.
[28] *Nielsen v. Nielsen Estate*, [1990] B.C.J. No. 1186 (B.C.S.C.); *Re Livingston Estate*, [1922] 2 W.W.R. 408 (Man. K.B.).

paying legacies or making an interim distribution to residuary beneficiaries within the first year if the circumstances are right.

Beyond the usual liabilities such as bill payment and income taxes, there are other, sometimes significant, claims. In Ontario, these claims can include the spousal election, dependant support claims, claims for services rendered and other creditor claims. A detailed discussion of these claims is found in Chapter 6.

ADVERTISING FOR CLAIMS

Given the significance of these claims, a prudent estate trustee will advertise for claims against the estate.[29] Nova Scotia, Prince Edward Island and Saskatchewan all have legislation requiring estate trustees to give notice to all person or persons having a claim against the estate. No such legislative requirement exists in Ontario, Alberta or British Columbia.

A prudent estate trustee will advertise before the debts and legacies are paid, unless that is not required under the circumstances, such as where the estate trustee is also the sole beneficiary. If the decision is made to advertise, it should be done in accordance with the statutory requirements[30] in order to ensure the protection from liability. Where no specific legislative process exists, the principles for advertising have developed from the English law. In Ontario and British Columbia, there is no prescribed form[31] (unlike Alberta, which has prescribed Form NC34). As there are no formal requirements,[32] the process of advertising for creditors usually involves the insertion of a carefully worded notice in a publication that is circulated in the area where the deceased lived. If the deceased carried on a business, the notice would also be circulated wherever the business was conducted. Normally the notice is published three times, providing a deadline for filing claims and an address for further information. It can be an expensive process.

The effect of advertising for creditors means that an unpaid creditor who appears after the deadline set out in the notice has no remedy

---

[29] *Trustee Act*, s. 53, which is intended to protect trustees against claims of creditors and others having claims against the estate who, after due notice, fail to register their claims: *Re Driscoll*, [1948] O.W.N. 124 (H.C.).

[30] For example, in British Columbia, the process is set out in the *Trustee Act*, R.S.B.C. 1996, c. 464, s. 38.

[31] *Stewart v. Snyder* (1898), 30 O.R. 110 (K.B.), aff'd. (1900) 27 O.A.R. 423 (C.A.).

[32] Some guidance is provided by *Re Furik Estate*, [1993] O.J. No. 1689 (Gen. Div.); *Re Ashman* (1907), 15 O.L.R. 42 (H.C.); *Re Daubeny* (1902), 1 O.W.R. 773 (H.C.); and *Re Egan Estate*, [1994] O.J. No. 84 (Gen. Div.).

against the estate trustee if there are insufficient assets to pay the claim. Therefore, where an estate trustee has properly advertised, the estate may be distributed anytime after the time set out in the advertisement and the estate trustee will not be personally liable for any subsequent claims (other than for income tax) as long as the estate trustee had no actual or constructive knowledge of the claim.[33] In this case, the creditor's recourse is to demand payment and/or sue the estate with the result that the estate trustee will, in turn, demand that the beneficiaries return the monies received from the estate. The success rate of this kind of demand will depend on the circumstances.[34]

INCOME TAXES

As the saying goes, nothing in life is certain except death and taxes. The greatest liability of an estate can be the payment of outstanding income taxes. There are various returns that must or can be filed. This liability can represent a significant debt to the estate, especially where there are no charitable beneficiaries.

The estate trustee is responsible for ensuring that all income taxes are paid. Under section 159 of the *Income Tax Act*,[35] the estate trustee is jointly and severally liable with the "taxpayer" (*i.e.*, the deceased and his or her estate) for any taxes owing, to the extent of the estate assets in the possession or control of the estate trustee.[36] A detailed discussion of the income tax liability is found in Chapter 3.

In summary, in Ontario, the more common deadlines at the beginning stage of an estate administration include:

- Election under section 5 of the *Family Law Act*[37] (to take under the Will or under section 5 of the Act) — must be filed within six months of date of death. Surviving spouse should have independent legal advice before signing election.

---

[33] *Commander Leasing Corp. v. Aiyede* (1983), 4 D.L.R. (4th) 107 (Ont. C.A.).
[34] *Cronan Estate v. Hughes*, [2000] O.J. No. 4491 (S.C.J.) (QL), *per* Haley J. In this case, the estate trustee was successful in part because the insufficient holdback was based on a "mistake of fact" and there were no "countervailing equities" in preventing the beneficiaries from refunding part of the funds received from the estate.
[35] R.S.C. 1985, c. 1 (5th Supp.).
[36] *Ibid.*, s. 159(1)(a)(i).
[37] R.S.O. 1990, c. F.3.

- Dependant Support Application under the *Succession Law Reform Act* — must be filed within six months of grant of Certificate of Appointment of Estate Trustee with (or without) a Will.
- Notices of Objection (caveats) registered against Certificate of Appointment contesting Will — restricts granting of Certificate of Appointment without notice being given to person filing the notice of objection. A Notice of Objection expires three years after it is filed and may be withdrawn by person filing notice at any time.[38]
- Cautions (to prevent the vesting of land in the beneficiaries) — must be registered within three years of death and remain in force for a further three years.
- Income Tax Returns — returns for years prior to death, the returns are due six months from date of death. The year of death return is due the later of six months following the date of death or April 30 of the year following the date of death. The estate trust returns must be filed annually 90 days after the estate's year-end.

INTERMEDIATE STAGE

After the payment of funeral, testamentary expenses, costs of administration, debts and legacies, the remaining estate is called the "residue". As soon as the debts are paid, the estate trustee holds the estate in trust (hence the use of the title trustee) to convert and divide the remaining assets among those residuary beneficiaries entitled under the Will. Whatever is "left over" after the making of the Will by lapse, invalid disposition or otherwise, falls into residue. Once the residue is ascertained, it should be distributed (in large part), or if an ongoing trust as provided by the Will, invested.

It is at this intermediate stage that a residuary beneficiary should be given a status report, and, quite often, even receives the first set of accounts for review. If it is an outright distributable estate, what typically remains outstanding before the estate can be wound-up is the approval of the accounts, the Clearance Certificate from the Canada Customs and Revenue Agency (CCRA) and the final distribution to the residuary beneficiaries. If there is an ongoing administration situation, such as where a trust is established under the Will, then this intermediate stage will focus on the administration of the trust and ensuring that an even hand is maintained between the different classes of beneficiaries.

---

[38] For further discussion, see Chapter 6.

The charitable beneficiary continues to have a role to play at the intermediate stage of the administration of the estate. As a beneficiary, a charity is entitled to ask for information regarding the administration of the estate, including status reports. The timing of these requests will vary depending on the nature of the estate. At a minimum, a status report should accompany every interim distribution, and on a regular basis (*i.e.*, every six months) with respect to ongoing trusts.

In Ontario, any person with a financial interest in the estate, such as a charitable beneficiary, also has the right to request the assistance of the court when requests for information are ignored or not satisfactorily answered. These options, which are discussed in more detail in Chapter 6, are very effective. Also effective is information sharing among the various charitable beneficiaries working together to present a united front.

A charity should also be advised when a request for the tax Clearance Certificates has been made. By advising that the request has been made, a charity will know that the administration is effectively concluded and that the estate trustee will be winding up the estate once the Certificate is received. The charity will also know that obtaining the Certificate will take time and it will need to be patient. However, at this time, a charity should check to see whether there is the possibility of making a further interim distribution.[39] At this stage, especially if there are charitable beneficiaries, there should be no further taxes payable and the holdback (see Chapter 1, "Additional Definitions") maintained for the purposes of winding up the estate should be a minimal amount. The rest of the estate should be distributed.

During this intermediate stage, residual beneficiaries should also expect to receive an estate accounting that details the assets, liabilities and transactions relating to the estate for the preceding period. Generally, the first accounting should be delivered for the period covering the first 12 to 18 months after the date of death. Preparing a set of accounts is relatively straightforward and should not take a long time to put together if the estate trustee is organized and has kept records. Subsequent accounts for ongoing estates are usually provided every three to five years depending on the size of the estate. Each subsequent accounting should carry forward the information from the end of the previous accounting period.

Legatees (beneficiaries who get a fixed amount or a legacy) have no interest in the continued administration of the estate *per se*. All that they

---

[39] If an interim distribution has not yet been made at this time, the charity should insist on one or insist on a reasonable explanation as to why one has not been made.

are interested in is receiving that fixed amount. Accordingly, they do not participate in reviewing accounts.

The accounts come in different forms.[40] The beneficiaries can also be asked to informally approve the accounting. This procedure avoids the need for a formal passing of accounts. Regardless of the format, a beneficiary should review the accounts shortly after receiving them as there are time frames that affect the ability to make objections. Not only do the accounts provide basic crucial information regarding the administration of the estate, typically, an interim distribution is made at the same time. If so, a charitable tax receipt will be issued when that distribution is received. The estate trustee will also usually ask for a release from the beneficiaries for the period in question.[41]

A charity is required to protect the deceased donor by monitoring the estate administration, asking questions, pursuing instincts, retaining counsel as appropriate and properly reviewing estate accounts. Depending on the circumstances, it may be necessary to work with the other departments within the charity and review policies to ensure compliance. This communication should be proactive in order to avert potential issues or to be prepared to respond when an issue arises.

At this stage, the nature of the gift should be examined closely. An area of particular importance during an administration is any real property. In Ontario, under the *Estates Administration Act*, the real and personal property of the deceased is vested in the estate trustee in trust to pay debts and to be distributed.[42]

To remove any doubts about the estate trustee's ability to deal with the real property for those purposes, the *Estates Administration Act* provides that the real property remains vested in the personal representative for a period of three years from the death of the deceased.[43] After three years, the property vests in the "persons beneficially entitled" (as determined by the Will or intestacy rules), unless a caution has been registered against the property.[44] A caution delays the vesting for another three years from the date of registration and can be renewed for another three years before it expires.[45] For example, if the estate trustee determines that the property must be sold in order to discharge the estate's liabilities, he or she may pre-empt the vesting of the property in the beneficiaries by

---

[40] For a more detailed discussion, see Chapter 4.
[41] For a discussion as to the timing of the release with a distribution cheque, see Chapter 3.
[42] Section 2.
[43] *Ibid.*
[44] *Ibid.*, subs. 9(1).
[45] *Ibid.*, subs. 9(6).

registering a caution that would contain an affidavit (with appropriate consents) stating that it is necessary to sell the real property.

Environmental concerns are rising. Of increasing significance is the issue of environmental liability when the estate has a property that is or may be environmentally compromised. Ontario has a tough environmental legislative scheme that imposes strict liabilities for environmental contamination on "persons responsible".[46] By definition, "persons responsible" can include owners, occupiers or anybody who has management or control over the source of the contamination.[47] There is no exclusion for anybody who "owns" in a fiduciary capacity notwithstanding that a fiduciary, for example an estate trustee, "owns" the property simply because of their office and has never had any involvement with the property or has not contributed to the problem. A fiduciary, accordingly, could be liable simply by holding title to the asset, or by simply assuming responsibility for administering the estate.

For charities, the risk is great. The existence of commercial or business property, especially, should raise a red flag and due diligence questions should be asked. The risk is potentially so great that consideration may have to be given by the charity to renounce its interest in the estate.

Sometimes, prior to a distribution, a charity is asked whether they would consider receiving their gift in another form, other than contemplated by the Will. It could be that the estate has a significant holding in appreciated stocks such that donating them *in specie* could result in significant tax savings, yet the Will states that the charity is to receive cash. In this case, whether this substitution is permitted is legally governed by the Will. Quite frequently, the general provisions of the Will contain a clause that permits the estate trustee to make this substitution. In this case, as the power exists in the Will, then the fact of substitution is permitted. Whether it is acceptable to the charity depends on its gift acceptance policy and the circumstances (*i.e.*, such as the type of stock). Further, a charity must ensure that the substitute transaction nets it the same amount as it was entitled to in the Will. Certainly, receiving cash is the simplest and if that is what is contemplated, and the alternative is too complicated, a charity is entitled to say "No thanks, please just deliver the cash." If in doubt, consult a solicitor.

It is worth emphasizing at this stage that it is not uncommon for beneficiaries of an estate to, perhaps, mistakenly believe that the solicitor

---

[46] *Environmental Protection Act*, R.S.O. 1990, c. E.19.
[47] *Ibid.*, s. 1.

for the estate also acts on their behalf. It is important to remember that the solicitor's duty is to represent the interests of the estate trustee, not those of the beneficiary. In the event of a disagreement, the beneficiaries are expected to obtain their own legal counsel. In the appropriate case, the costs will (in whole or in part) be borne by the estate.

WINDING UP THE ESTATE

Near the end of the estate's administration, there are further considerations for the charitable beneficiary. In Ontario, it is not uncommon for an immediately distributable estate to take over a year to administer. As stated, once the estate trustee is in a position to wind up the estate, he or she should provide the beneficiaries with an accounting detailing estate assets, expenses and investments.

When the administration is essentially complete, a tax Clearance Certificate will be requested from the CCRA. The estate trustee should apply for the Clearance Certificate once all tax returns have been filed and assessed (or re-assessed) and any additional assessment is paid. The estate trustee applies to obtain a Clearance Certificate, as they are personally liable for any unpaid taxes, interest or penalties under the *Income Tax Act*. Once the Clearance Certificate is issued, the CCRA cannot assert a claim for unpaid taxes, interest or penalties.

As a last step, a final set of accounts will be delivered for approval. A final distribution is usually made of all or part of the holdback. With the receipt of the final distribution and the signing of the release (see Chapter 3 for further discussion), the administration of the estate is usually (absent fraud) over.

It is at this point that a charity is finally in a position to receive the balance remaining under the estate and confirm acceptance by issuing a charitable tax receipt (and release) together with whatever may be appropriate in the circumstances, such as a letter of thanks to the family.

ALBERTA[48]

The administration of an estate in Alberta is similar but not identical to that in Ontario. This section highlights the differences. When administering an Alberta estate, an executor should use the Legal Education

---

[48] This section and the other Alberta discussions were contributed by Dragana Sanchez-Glowicki, Miller Thomson (Edmonton).

Society of Alberta's (LESA) Alberta Surrogate Forms Manual as it contains all of the forms specified in the Alberta Rules of Court (Surrogate Rules).[49] Where reference is made to one of the Alberta Surrogate Forms (for example, NC 7), the form can easily be found in the LESA Alberta Surrogate Forms Manual.

IDENTIFICATION OF EXECUTOR/ADMINISTRATOR/ PERSONAL REPRESENTATIVE

As in Ontario, one of the first tasks of the named personal representative in the administration of an estate is to ascertain whether there is a valid Will which appoints one or more personal representatives. If an original Will is located, and the deceased appointed a personal representative, the named personal representative will likely need to apply to the Alberta Court of Queen's Bench (Surrogate Matter) for a Grant of Probate. If the deceased failed to appoint a personal representative in the Will, or the appointed personal representative refuses to act, or has died and there is no alternate personal representative named, or if a Will cannot be found, it will be necessary to ascertain who is the proper individual to apply for a Grant of Administration.

Surrogate Rule 11(1) lists those persons who will be given preference to apply for a Grant of Probate, or Administration with Will Annexed in the case where a personal representative is not appointed in the Will, or the appointed personal representative in the Will refuses to act, or has predeceased the testator and an alternate has not been named. Surrogate Rule 11(2) lists those persons who will be given preference to apply for a Grant of Administration in the situation where a Will does not exist and the estate is an intestacy. Surrogate Rule 13(1) identifies the documents which need to be filed with the Court when a Will exists and either a Grant of Probate or Grant of Administration with Will Annexed is applied for. Surrogate Rule 13(2) identifies those documents which need to be filed with the Court in the case of an intestacy where a Grant of Administration is being applied for. The Surrogate Rules[50] give preference to an applicant who resides in Alberta if two or more applicants apply for a Grant of Administration. Unless a Court orders otherwise, a Grant of Administration will not be given to more than three persons at one time.[51]

---

[49] AR 130/95.
[50] Surrogate Rule 11(3).
[51] Surrogate Rule 11(4).

No person can be made to act as a personal representative of an estate. If a personal representative is appointed by a Will and does not wish to act, and so long as he or she has not intermeddled in the estate, he or she may renounce his or her appointment as personal representative by signing a Form NC 12 (Renunciation of Probate).[52] By renouncing, the personal representative is forever giving up all of his or her rights and entitlements to administer the estate. However, if the named personal representative wishes to reserve the right to administer the estate at some time in the future, he or she should sign an NC 13 (Reservation of Right to Apply for a Grant of Probate).[53]

Reserving the right to apply for probate may be appropriate where a person resides out of the jurisdiction, or prefers not to act initially for reasons such as illness, or efficiency. If an alternate personal representative is named in the Will, he or she would apply for probate. If a personal representative is not named in the Will, or if a Will does not exist, the person with first priority to apply to the Court for either a Grant of Probate[54] or a Grant of Administration[55] would make the appli-cation. If the person with first priority does not wish to act, he or she may also renounce by signing either a Form NC 14[56] or NC 15,[57] thereby allowing a person with equal or lower priority to apply.[58] The person that has first priority to apply but does not wish to do so may also nominate a person to apply by signing a Form NC 16.[59]

Form NC 16 is, therefore, used when a person entitled to apply for a Grant of Administration wishes to renounce in favour of another person who may either not be listed in the Surrogate Rule 11 hierarchy, or may not be the next in line in the hierarchy. The right of the person with first priority to apply for a grant is then passed to his or her nominee. If a nomination is not made and someone lower in the hierarchy wishes to apply, then a form NC 15 must be signed by all those persons named in Surrogate Rule 11(1) or Surrogate Rule 11(2) hierarchy who rank equal or higher to the proposed applicant.

---

[52] Surrogate Rule 32(1).
[53] Surrogate Rule 34(1).
[54] Surrogate Rule 11(1).
[55] Surrogate Rule 11(2).
[56] Renunciation of Probate.
[57] Renunciation of Administration.
[58] Surrogate Rule 32(3).
[59] Surrogate Rule 33.

Personal Representative's Conflict of Interest

It is also important to assess whether or not any conflict of interest is apparent or may arise in the administration of the estate. Is the personal representative named in the Will, or the person who is applying for a grant in a conflict of interest or potential conflict of interest if he or she assumes the responsibility of a personal representative? For example, a spouse of the deceased will be in a conflict of interest if he or she is the named personal representative and intends to bring an action against the estate pursuant to the *Dependants Relief Act*.[60] The spouse ought not act as personal representative and should not apply for a grant.

Bonds

The rules concerning bonding of a personal representative are contained in the *Administration of Estates Act*,[61] however, the Surrogate Rules somewhat modify the provisions in that statute. Somewhat different than Ontario, a personal representative who is a resident of Alberta is generally not required to post a bond. If the personal representative resides outside of the province of Alberta, a bond must be posted.[62] An application can be made to the Court seeking the Court's directions to dispense with the requirement of posting a bond, or to reduce the amount of the bond.[63] An Affidavit in support of such an application will also be filed with the Court.[64] A beneficiary may be asked to consent with the dispensing of the bond by a non-resident personal repre-sentative. The consent would be filed by the non-resident personal representative in support of his or her application to the Court to dispense with the bond. A beneficiary should always consider this request very carefully.[65]

Depending on the size of the estate, the Court may not be willing to grant an application to dispense with bond. Where there are two or more

---

[60] The title and chapter number of the *Family Relief Act*, R.S.A. 2000, c. F-5 were amended by the *Adult Interdependent Relationships Act*, S.A. 2002, c. A-4.5, s. 35 to the *Dependants Relief Act*, S.A. 2002, c. D-10.2. The *Adult Interdependent Relationships Act* came into force on June 1, 2003, except for s. 17 which came into force on January 1, 2003 and except for sections 26, 52, 60 and 71 which are not yet in force as of June 2003.
[61] R.S.A. 2000, c. A-2, s. 5.
[62] Surrogate Rule 28(1).
[63] Surrogate Rule 29(1).
[64] Form NC 17.
[65] Form NC 18.

personal representatives, and one resides in the Province of Alberta, a bond will generally not be required.[66]

If a personal representative is required to post a bond, the bond must be from an insurer licensed under the *Insurance Act*[67] to provide guarantee insurance.[68]

A bond is usually for an amount equal to the gross value of the estate in Alberta, and if the Court orders, less any amount distributable to the personal representative as a beneficiary of the estate.[69]

Duties

As in Ontario, the personal representative has numerous and extensive duties depending on the assets that form the estate. These duties range from basic duties to the legal duty to dispose of the deceased's remains in a suitable manner. The personal representative is also required to pay out the funeral expenses from the deceased's estate prior to all other liabilities being paid, and, therefore, must ensure that the funeral expenses are not excessive in relation to the size of the estate.

As in Ontario, the duties of a personal representative include:

(a) retaining a lawyer to advise on the administration of the estate, to apply for a grant from the Court or to bring any necessary matter before the Court;
(b) protecting any estate assets by taking valuable papers, cash, and securities into custody;
(c) ensuring that all property is properly secured;
(d) collecting the estate assets either before or after issuance of a grant;
(e) arranging with a bank, trust company or other financial institution for a list of the contents of a safety deposit box;
(f) determining the full nature and value of property and debts of the deceased as at the date of death and compiling a list, including the value of all land and buildings and a summary of outstanding mortgages, leases and other encumbrances;
(g) providing for protection and supervision of vacant land and buildings;

---

[66] Surrogate Rule 28(2)(*b*).
[67] R.S.A. 2000, c. I-3.
[68] Surrogate Rule 28(3).
[69] Surrogate Rule 28(4).

(h) arranging for the proper management of the estate including taking control of property and selling property;
(i) advising any joint tenancy beneficiaries of the death of the deceased;
(j) examining existing insurance policies, advising insurance companies of the death and placing additional insurance, if necessary;
(k) determining the names and addresses of those beneficially entitled to the estate property and notifying them of their interests;
(l) advising any designated beneficiaries of their interests under life insurance or other property passing outside the Will;
(m) applying for any pensions, annuities, death benefits, life insurance or other benefits payable to the estate, including any federal or provincial government pension and death benefits;
(n) opening an estate account with a bank for the purpose of distributing the liquid assets of the estate in accordance with the provisions of the Will;
(o) arranging for the payment of debts and expenses owed by the deceased and the estate, and contesting or settling any debts if not satisfied that alleged debts are legitimate;
(p) determining whether to advertise for claimants, checking all claims and making payments as funds become available;
(q) taking the steps necessary to finalize the amount payable if the legitimacy or amount of a debt is in issue;
(r) instructing a lawyer in any litigation involving the estate;
(s) dealing with pre and post-death tax matters;
(t) administering any continuing testamentary trusts or trusts for minors;
(u) preparing the personal representative's account, a proposed compensation schedule, a proposed final distribution schedule, and accounting of the beneficiaries of the estate; and
(v) distributing the estate in accordance with the Will.

NOTICE TO CREDITORS AND CLAIMANTS

The personal representative will likely be advised to issue a notice to creditors and claimants. Section 37 of the *Administration of Estates Act* allows an estate to be distributed provided that the notice provisions contained in the Surrogate Rules have been adhered to, and any claims filed against the estate have been resolved. If the personal representative chooses not to issue a notice to creditors and claimants, and distributes the estate, he or she will be personally liable to a legitimate creditor.

Surrogate Rule 38 states that for estates valued at $100,000 or less, the notice of creditors and claimants is to be published in a local newspaper. If the estate is over $100,000, two publications, separated by not less than six days, are necessary. A local newspaper means a newspaper in the area in which the deceased lived or, if the deceased lived outside of Alberta, in the area where the significant amount of the assets are found. The form of notice is found in Form NC 34.

A personal representative's decision as to whether or not to advertise for creditors and claims will be based on such factors as the degree of his or her personal involvement in the deceased's finances prior to death, how complicated the deceased's affairs were and the nature of the beneficiaries. Where the personal representative is the sole beneficiary of the estate, and has handled the deceased's affairs for a number of years prior to the deceased's death, it may not be necessary to advertise for creditors and claimants. In such a situation, the personal representative would likely know whether the deceased had any creditors and/or claimants and can assess the risk of not advertising.

A claimant must notify the personal representative of their claim not more than 30 days after the date on which the last notice is published in the local newspaper. If the personal representative has advertised in accordance with Surrogate Rule 38, he or she may distribute the estate after the deadline given in the publication notice, as long as no claims have been brought forward. Any claims that have been brought forward would be assessed and a determination made as to whether or not they are legitimate. If a personal representative has actual and/or constructive notice of a claim or creditor and does not assess the claim, he or she will be responsible to the legitimate creditors. However, if the personal representative has no such notice, he or she will not be liable. Creditors who advise the personal representative of their claim after the advertisement deadline, but before the claim is statute-barred, can still enforce their claim against the estate, albeit, only against the property still held in the hands of the personal representative. The creditor cannot enforce their claim against estate property that has been previously distributed.[70]

---

[70] The Surrogate Court Rules set out the procedure for making a claim against an estate in Part 2, Contentious Matters, Division 5. The appropriate forms which ought to be used by a claimant when asserting a claim against the estate are referenced in Surrogate Rules 95 and 96 of Part 2, Division 5.

APPLICATIONS FOR GRANTS OF PROBATE AND ADMINISTRATION

Necessity for Obtaining a Grant

Surrogate Rule 10 specifies the types of grants that are available. The necessity for obtaining a grant is determined by the nature and/or value of the assets which form the estate. As in Ontario, it is not always necessary to obtain a grant from the Court, however, it is always necessary to obtain a grant if the deceased had real property in his or her name alone (or is a tenant in common). Generally speaking, in Alberta, it is necessary to obtain a grant in the following circumstances:

(a) when a person or institution which controls the transfer of one or more estate assets requires a grant in order to transmit and transfer the estate asset;
(b) when the validity of the Will is at issue;
(c) when the personal representative believes it is necessary to obtain a grant to protect himself or herself against outstanding liabilities. (For example, to start a six month limitation period for the commencement of an action pursuant to the *Dependants Relief Act* and/or the *Matrimonial Property Act*[71]); or
(d) when there is no Will in existence — in this situation, it may be necessary to obtain a Grant of Administration to confirm who the personal representative of the estate is.

The following chart sets out what several Alberta banks and financial institutions are and are not presently prepared to attend to without a Grant:

Bank	CIBC	Royal Bank of Canada	Bank of Nova Scotia	Hongkong Bank of Canada	Canadian Western Bank	Alberta Treasury Branches
1. Will money be paid out to an Executor with a Will, but without a Grant of Probate?	Yes	Yes	Yes	Yes	Yes	Yes
2. Will money be paid out directly to beneficiaries with a Will, but without a Grant of Probate?	Yes	Yes	Yes	Rarely	Yes	Yes

---

[71] R.S.A. 2000, c. M-8.

Bank	CIBC	Royal Bank of Canada	Bank of Nova Scotia	Hongkong Bank of Canada	Canadian Western Bank	Alberta Treasury Branches
3. Maximum amount that will be paid out without a Grant of Probate.	$100,000 *Over $100,000 requires Head Office approval.	Branch limits vary between $10,000 and $50,000.	$25,000 *$25,000 to $100,000 with approval of Vice-President's office.	$10,000	$3,000	$40,000
4. Will money be released if there is no Will and no Grant of Administration?	Yes	Yes, up to $5,000	Yes	Rarely	Yes	Yes
5. If yes, who will the money be released to?	Next-of-kin	Beneficiaries	Beneficiaries	Spouse	Next-of-kin	Beneficiaries
6. Expenses that can be directly paid out of the deceased's Bank Account prior to or without a Grant being issued, provided a receipt is produced:						
• Funeral Home	Yes	Yes	Yes	Yes	Up to $3,000	Yes
• Cemetery Costs	Yes	Yes	Probably	Yes	Maybe	Yes
• Catering for Funeral	No	Yes	No	No	No	Yes
• Flowers	No	Yes	No	No	No	Yes
• Mortgage Payments	Generally no	Generally no	Probably	Maybe	No	Yes
• Property Taxes	Generally no	Yes	Probably	Maybe	No	Yes
• Rent	Generally no	Generally no	Probably	Maybe	No	Yes
• Utility Payments	Generally no	Yes	Probably	Maybe	No	Yes
• Loan Payments	Generally no	Generally no, but possibly	Doubtful	No	No	Yes
• Child/Spousal Support	Generally no	Possibly	Doubtful	Probably	No	Yes
• Charge Card Debts	Generally no	Generally no, but possibly	Doubtful	No	No	Yes
7. Are these policies the same throughout Alberta?	Yes	Yes	Yes	Yes	Yes	Yes
8. Does each branch manager have discretion to vary these policies?	Yes	Yes/or area manager	Yes	Yes	Yes	Head Office only

Bank	CIBC	Royal Bank of Canada	Bank of Nova Scotia	Hongkong Bank of Canada	Canadian Western Bank	Alberta Treasury Branches
9. What is the limit of Canada Savings Bonds that can be redeemed without a Grant?	$20,000	Depends on circumstances	$25,000 *Up to $75,000 in limited circumstances	$10,000	$40,000	No limit
10. Can Alberta Capital Bonds be redeemed in the same amounts?	N/A	Yes	N/A	Yes	N/A	Yes

* The Bank of Montreal and Toronto Dominion Bank were not prepared to release their information.

Financial Institution	Wood Gundy	Levesque Securities	HongKong Bank	Midland Walwyn	Scotia McLeod	TD Greenline	Nesbitt Burns
11. May Shares be sold without a Grant if it is an existing account?	Yes	No	No	No	Yes	Yes	Yes
12. Maximum amount allowed to be sold under these circumstances.	$25,000	N/A	N/A	N/A	$25,000	At least $4,000	$40,000
13. What documents are required?	1. Notarized copy of Will 2. Notarized copy of Death Certificate 3. Internal forms 4. Letter of direction from the Executor	N/A	N/A	N/A	1. Notarized copy of Will 2. Notarized copy of Death Certificate 3. Letter of direction from the Executor	1. Notarized copy of Will 2. Notarized copy of Death Certificate 3. Letter of direction from Executor signed by the beneficiaries as well	

* Canada Trust indicated that it does not have a firm policy, and the Royal Trust and Capital City Savings did not provide a response.

Information Collection

The best way to obtain all of the necessary information to prepare the application for a grant is to complete an estate checklist (provided by the personal representative's solicitor). A thorough checklist is indispensable as it ensures that no essential information is overlooked. During the information collection process, it is very important to ensure that the Will is an original, that it is the deceased's last Will, that it is still in force and has not been revoked, and that the Will conforms to all of the formal requirements for Wills as set out in the *Wills Act*.[72]

As in Ontario, the *Wills Act* allows for holographic Wills in Alberta[73] or Wills made wholly in the handwriting of the testator and signed only by him or her. A holographic Will is valid without attestation or signature of a witness.

Fees for Grants

The Surrogate Rules set out the (very reasonable) costs of obtaining grants in Alberta. The Rules state:

> 1(1) For issuing grants of probate or letters of administration or resealing grants, excluding trusteeship but including one certified copy of the document, where the net value of property in Alberta is
>
> | | |
> |---|---|
> | (a) $10 000 or under | $ 25 |
> | (b) over $10 000 but not more than $25 000 | 100 |
> | (c) over $25 000 but not more than $125 000 | 200 |
> | (d) over $125 000 but not more than $250 000 | 300 |
> | (e) over $250 000 | 400 |
>
> (2) This section applies to all grants of probate and letters of administration issued on or after February 25, 2000 and the grants resealed on or after February 25, 2000.[74]

---

[72] R.S.A. 2000, c. W-12.
[73] *Ibid.*, s. 7.
[74] Schedule 2, Rule 1.

Intestate Succession Act

If a Will does not exist and an executor or executrix is required to apply for a Grant of Administration, the distribution of the estate will be governed by the rules set out in the *Intestate Succession Act*.[75]

Until recently, only the survivor of a legally married couple qualified as a spouse pursuant to section 1 of the *Intestate Succession Act*. Recent common law decisions in the Alberta Courts have recognized the common law spouse of an intestate deceased person to have a claim pursuant to the *Intestate Succession Act*. These common law spouses include heterosexual and same sex couples. On May 14, 2002, this recognition was included in the *Intestate Succession Act* by virtue of the *Intestate Succession Amendments Act*.[76]

The Act also defines an "adult interdependent partner" as

...a person, including a minor, who lived with the intestate in a conjugal relationship, outside marriage,

(i) for a continuous period of not less than 3 years immediately before the intestate's death, or
(ii) [for] some permanence immediately before the intestate's death, if there is a child of the relationship by birth or adoption.[77]

The recently amended *Intestate Succession Act* distributes an intestate's estate as follows:

(a) If the intestate dies leaving a spouse (meaning a person he or she is married to at the time of death), but no children, his or her estate will go to the spouse (section 2).
(b) If the intestate died leaving no surviving spouse, but is survived by an adult interdependent partner, the surviving adult interdependent partner is treated as if they were the surviving spouse and takes the whole estate, or shares in the estate with the intestate's children (see (d)(iii) or (iv) below) if there are surviving children (section 3.1).
(c) If the intestate dies leaving both a surviving spouse and a surviving adult interdependent partner, the surviving spouse will not get any part of the estate, and the surviving adult interdependent partner will be treated as the surviving spouse and take the whole estate, or

---

[75] R.S.A. 2000, c. I-10.
[76] S.A. 2002, c. 16.
[77] *Intestate Succession Act*, s. 1.

shares in the estate with the intestate's surviving children (see (d)(iii) or (iv) below), if there are surviving children (section 3.2).

(d) If the intestate dies leaving a spouse or adult interdependent partner and children:

- (i) if the net value of the estate does not exceed $40,000, then the entire estate goes to the spouse or adult interdependent partner (section 3(1)(a));
- (ii) if the net value of the estate exceeds $40,000, the spouse or adult interdependent partner is entitled to the first $40,000 (section 3(1)(b));
- (iii) if the net value of the estate exceeds $40,000 and the intestate dies leaving a spouse or adult interdependent partner and one child, one-half of the residue of the estate (that is, the value of the estate less all of the debts and the $40,000 preferred share) goes to the spouse or adult interdependent partner and the other half of the residue goes to the child (section 3(3)(a));
- (iv) if the net value of the estate exceeds $40,000 and the intestate dies leaving a spouse or adult interdependent partner and more than one child, one-third of the residue in the estate goes to the spouse or adult interdependent partner and the balance is divided equally among the children. Therefore, the spouse or adult interdependent partner will receive $40,000 plus one-third of the residue. The children will divide the amount of estate remaining equally among them (section 3(3)(b));
- (v) if one of the children has died during the intestate's lifetime and had children of their own (the intestate's grandchildren), those grandchildren would "step into the shoes" of their parent and equally divide the share their parent would have received if their parent had been alive (section 3(4)).

(e) If the intestate dies leaving no spouse, no adult interdependent partner and no children, then the intestate's mother and father will receive the estate in equal shares, and if only one of them is alive, then the sole surviving parent will receive the whole of the estate (section 5).

(f) If the intestate dies leaving no spouse, no adult interdependent partner, no children, mother or father, then the intestate's brothers and sisters will receive the estate in equal shares, and if one of the brothers or sisters has died before the intestate, their children will "step into the shoes" of the parent and take or divide the share their parent would have received if the parent had been alive (section 6).

(g) If the intestate dies leaving no spouse, no adult interdependent partner, no children, mother or father, or brother or sister, then the estate will go to the intestate's nieces and nephews in equal shares (section 7).
(h) If the intestate dies leaving no spouse, no adult interdependent partner, no children, mother, father, brother or sister, niece or nephew, the estate will be distributed equally among the intestate's next of kin or equal degree of blood relationship to the intestate (section 8).
(i) If the intestate dies leaving absolutely no lineal heirs, the estate will go to the Crown in Right of Alberta pursuant to the *Ultimate Heir Act*.[78]

In 1991, the Alberta common law was changed by the *Family and Domestic Relations Statutes Amendment Act*.[79] This Act amended the *Intestate Succession Act* to include children born outside a marriage.[80] Section 1(b) of the *Intestate Succession Act* now defines "issue" as "all lineal descendants, whether born within or outside marriage of the ancestor". In addition to conferring rights upon a child born outside of marriage, the amendments to the *Intestate Succession Act* caused by the *Family and Domestic Relations Statutes Amendment Act* also conferred rights upon both of the child's biological parents. Each now has a claim on their child's estate, whether or not the child was born within the marriage. Thus, a child's biological father may now benefit from the child's estate if the child died without a Will.

Section 72(1) of the *Child Welfare Act* states that:

> 72(1) For all purposes, when an adoption order is made, the adopted child is the child of the adopting parent and the adopting parent is the parent and guardian of the adopted child as if the child had been born to that parent in lawful wedlock.[81]

Adoption, in essence, severs the child's familial links with its biological parents and a new legal relationship is created between the adoptive parents and the adopted child. On an intestacy, the adopted child, therefore, has no claim on their biological parents' estate, nor does a biological parent have a claim on their natural child's estate.[82]

---

[78] R.S.A. 2000, c. U-1, s. 2.
[79] S.A. 1991, c. 11.
[80] *Ibid.*, subs. 3(1).
[81] R.S.A. 2000, c. C-12, s. 72(1).
[82] *Re Matthews Estate*, [1992] 1 Alta. L.R. (3d) 198 (Q.B.).

Stepchildren who have not been adopted by the deceased will not inherit on an intestacy.[83]

NOTICES UNDER THE SURROGATE RULES

The Surrogate Rules provide that certain notices must be given to beneficiaries (pursuant to a Will or the *Intestate Succession Act*) and to persons who may have a right under the *Family Relief Act* and/or the *Matrimonial Property Act*, some of which are highlighted below.

Notice to a Specific Bequest Beneficiary

On either an Application for a Grant of Probate or a Grant of Administration, all of the beneficiaries of the estate must be identified on Form NC 6. Beneficiaries who are entitled to a specific bequest only are required to be given notice in the form of an NC 20 which will provide a description of the bequest and may also include a copy of the relevant section of the Will which sets out the specific bequest. A specific bequest beneficiary is not technically entitled to a complete copy of the Will nor the application for the grant.

Notice to a Residuary Beneficiary

Beneficiaries who share in the residue of the estate are given notice.[84] This notice indicates the percentage, or fractional share, of the residue of the estate that each residuary beneficiary is entitled to receive. A copy of the application for the grant, which includes a complete copy of the Will, and a list of the estate assets and debts, must also accompany this Notice.[85]

Where a deceased died intestate, the beneficiaries are given notice.[86] This type of notice indicates the nature of the interest in the estate and the application for the grant, which includes a complete list of the estate assets and debts, is also sent to the beneficiary along with the notice form.[87]

---

[83] *Naples v. Martin Estate* (1986), 23 E.T.R. 288 (B.C.S.C.).
[84] Form NC 19.
[85] Surrogate Rule 26(2).
[86] Form NC 21.
[87] Surrogate Rule 26(2).

Surrogate Rule 27 provides that if a personal representative knows of the existence of a particular beneficiary, but does not know the identity or address of the beneficiary, he or she will file, along with the application, an affidavit in the form of an NC 25. This affidavit advises the Court of the inquiries made to ascertain the beneficiary's whereabouts and all attempts made to find the beneficiary, and that the personal representative is undertaking to advise the Court that he or she will provide the clerk of the court with a written notice of the beneficiary's whereabouts as soon as the beneficiary is ascertained and/or found. The Public Trustee will also be served with this notice.[88]

Notice to Deceased Persons

The Surrogate Rules do not specifically deal with the procedure for giving notice where a beneficiary has predeceased the testator, and the gift has not lapsed. However, notice is normally sent to the personal representative of the estate of the deceased beneficiary if one has been appointed or is known. If the personal representative of the estate is unknown or cannot be located, notice is typically given to the Public Trustee pursuant to section 4(c) of the *Public Trustee Act*.[89] Section 4(c) states that the Public Trustee may act as custodian of the property of a deceased person. If an individual died intestate, and there is no appointed personal representative of the estate but the individual's heirs are known, notice may also be given to the heirs.[90]

Missing Persons

Section 6 of the *Administration of Estates Act* provides that if a missing person is interested in the estate, a copy of the complete application and notice should be sent to the office of the Public Trustee. Section 1(e) of the *Public Trustee Act* defines a missing person as a "person who, after reasonable inquiry, cannot be found and whose present place of abode is unascertainable".

---

[88] The Court has the discretion to issue the grant even if the NC 25 has not been filed. The Court is willing to exercise its discretion and issue the grant so that administration may begin without any delays caused by the inability to locate or identify a beneficiary.

[89] R.S.A. 2000, c. P-44.

[90] In this situation, an applicant may also wish to apply to the Court for advice and directions respecting the form and service of the notice pursuant to Surrogate Rules 2(4) and 4. Where the gift does lapse, there is no need for a notice, but the circumstances must be explained in the application.

The personal representative is required to make an effort to locate a missing beneficiary. This might include contacting other family members or advertising in the local newspaper where the individual last lived and/or worked. As well, inquiries may be directed to government departments such as the Canada Pension Plan, Old Age Security, Child Tax Benefit and Support for Independence (Social Assistance). These departments will not provide the address or phone number of a missing individual, but will often forward a letter from the personal representative advising that they are a beneficiary in the estate and should make contact. As previously stated, all efforts made by the personal representative to find the missing person must be specified in Form NC 25.

Convicts

The *Public Trustee Act* and the *Administration of Estates Act* have both been amended, such that convicts must be served in the usual manner.

Minor Persons

Section 6 of the *Administration of Estates Act* provides that where an application is made for a grant, and a beneficiary or person interested in the estate to which the application pertains is a minor or was a minor at the date of death, a copy of the application must be sent to the public trustee together with notice required under the Surrogate Rules using Form NC 24.1.

Unborn Beneficiaries

If an unborn child is interested in an estate, notice will be given to the Public Trustee. Subsection 4(j) of the *Public Trustee Act* allows the Public Trustee to act as trustee of the estate of an unborn child if no one has been appointed and the unborn child has or may have property vested in him or her or is contingently entitled to property. With consent, the Public Trustee will act for this limited purpose.

Dependent Adults

Section 6 of the *Administration of Estates Act* provides that if a dependent adult is interested in the estate, a copy of the notice and a copy of the application must be sent to the dependent adult's trustee. If a trustee has not been appointed for a mentally incapacitated person, then arrangements must be made to have a trustee appointed. A trustee will have to be appointed because the Court will not issue a grant without this appointment. In many cases, the Public Trustee will act as a limited trustee to revive any potential claim the dependent adult may have against the estate.

Under section 6(2) of the *Administration of Estates Act*, an Application for Probate or Administration will not proceed until the Public Trustee (who has been given notice) advises the Court that they will or will not represent the dependent adult.

SERVICE OF NOTICES UNDER THE SURROGATE RULES

Service of the notice on a beneficiary may be made by registered mail, or by serving a lawyer who is authorized to accept service on behalf of that person or organization.[91] Proof of service of the notice is filed with the Court.[92] Proof of service is not necessary if that party acknowledges service of the documents. In this case, the beneficiary's acknowledgement is contained in the affidavit prepared by the personal representative on application for the grant, or on the bottom of the actual notice.[93]

If the personal representative does not file proof of service, the Court may issue a grant, but only if it is satisfied with the reason given by the personal representative for not filing the proof of service.[94]

NOTICE OF RIGHTS UNDER THE DEPENDANTS RELIEF ACT

When an individual dies leaving a spouse and a child or children, section 7(1) of the *Administration of Estates Act* may require notice to also be given under this legislation. Section 7(6) of the *Administration of Estates Act* provides that a grant is not to be issued unless the judge is satisfied that the spouse and dependent child(ren) of the deceased have been notified of their rights under the *Dependants Relief Act*. The requirement of notice may be waived if a judge is satisfied that the spouse and/or dependent child could not be found after reasonable inquiry.

The recent amendments brought about as a result of the *Adult Interdependent Relationships Act* have amended the *Dependants Relief Act*

---

[91] Surrogate Rule 26(3).
[92] See Form NC 27 and Surrogate Rule 26(4).
[93] Form NC 2.
[94] Surrogate Rule 26(5).

to provide that notice will also be given to adult interdependent partners.[95] Adult Interdependent Partners will include persons who are in relationships of interdependence. Any relationship could fall within the definition of a relationship of interdependence if it meets the test set out in Bill 30-2 which requires that the two persons involved in the relationship must have lived together for three years and share one another's lives, be emotionally committed to one another, and function as an economic and domestic unit. If two persons are in a relationship, they will be required to enter into an Adult Interdependent Partner Agreement before the relationship would be recognized as Adult Interdependent Partners. This also applies to those people who are living together and are related to each other. A person who alleges the existence of an adult interdependent relationship knowing that the relationship does not exist could be liable to damages for any loss or cost incurred in reliance of the alleged adult interdependent relationship. The person alleging in a Court proceeding that they are or were in an adult interdependent partnership also has the onus of proving the existence of the relationship.

Notice to Spouse

Section 7 of the *Administration of Estates Act* provides that if a spouse is not the sole beneficiary under the Will of the deceased,[96] the personal representative applying for a Grant of Probate or Administration is required to send a copy of the application and a notice of the rights of the dependant under the provisions of the *Dependants Relief Act* to the spouse of the deceased.

Section 7(1)(a) further provides that the spouse must be residing in Canada as at the date of the death of the deceased in order to be entitled to this notice. If the spouse is entitled to notice, then the notice is to be in Form NC 23. If the spouse is a dependant adult, this notice should be sent to the trustee of the dependent spouse's estate. If there is no trustee, it will be necessary to have a trustee appointed. In this case, the trustee's role is to represent the spouse in determining whether an application on behalf of the spouse for a greater share of the estate is warranted.

---

[95] Bill 30-2, the bill that led to the enactment of the *Adult Interdependent Relationships Act*, was passed by the Alberta Legislative Assembly on December 3, 2002. This Act amends over 68 statutes in Alberta to include an "Adult Interdependent Partner".

[96] Or under the provisions of the *Intestate Succession Act* on an intestacy.

Notice to Children

The *Dependants Relief Act* provides that a child of the deceased is a dependant if the child is "under the age of 18 years at the time of the deceased's death", or is over the age of 18 years "at the time of the deceased's death and unable by reason of mental or physical disability to earn a livelihood".[97] The rights of dependent children under this Act apply to children born inside or outside the marriage.[98]

Section 7(1)(b) of the *Administration of Estates Act* provides that a copy of the application for the grant of probate or administration and a *Dependants Relief Act* notice in Form NC 24 must be served directly on the deceased's dependant child, so long as the child was 18 years and older at the deceased's death, and "is unable by reason of a physical disability to earn a livelihood". If the child was an adult at the time of the deceased's death and is unable by reason of mental disability to earn a livelihood, a copy of the application and notice must be sent to the trustee of the estate of the adult child.[99] If there is no trustee appointed for the adult child, a judge may, having regard to the size of the estate:

> direct that a grant for probate or administration in the deceased's estate not be issued until a [trustee] of the adult child's estate has been appointed.[100]

The Court may:

> direct that the applicant or some other person apply to have a trustee of the [adult] child's estate appointed under the Dependent Adults Act.[101]

In determining whether to make such an order, the *Administration of Estates Act* directs that:

> ...the value of the estate, the circumstances of the [adult] child and the likelihood of success of an application made on the [adult] child's behalf be considered.[102]

If the deceased was survived by a child who was a minor at the time of the deceased's death, a copy of the notice and application will be sent to the public trustee and Form NC 24.1 must be used.[103] It is also typical for the notice to be sent to the minor child's trustee. Section 7 also

---

[97] R.S.A. 2000, c. A-2, s. 1(d).
[98] Ibid., s. 1(b).
[99] Ibid., s. 7(5).
[100] Ibid., s. 7(5)(a).
[101] Ibid., s. 7(5)(b).
[102] Ibid., s. 7(5); see also s. 7 of the *Dependent Adults Act*, R.S.A. 2000, c. D-11.
[103] See s. 7(4)(a) of the *Administration of Estates Act*.

requires that such a child must be a resident of Canada at the date of death of the deceased before they will be entitled to notice. If the minor child does not have a trustee, the Court will likely be consulted for directions in this regard.

NOTICE UNDER THE MATRIMONIAL PROPERTY ACT

Notice to Spouse

If the spouse of the deceased is not the sole beneficiary under the Will of the deceased,[104] a copy of the application for the grant and a notice in Form NC 22 informing the spouse of his or her rights under the *Matrimonial Property Act* will be sent to the spouse (as defined under the *Matrimonial Property Act*).[105] It is important to note that for the purposes of giving this notice, an individual may have more than one spouse. Section 6 of the *Matrimonial Property Act* provides that a matrimonial property action must be commenced within two years of the issuance of the divorce judgment. If the spouse is a dependent adult, this notice will be given to the trustee of the spouse. If there is no trustee, the public trustee will be given notice, and a trustee may have to be appointed to determine the course of action to be taken on behalf of the individual.

A judge may:

> ...dispense with the requirement that a copy of the application and notice be sent to a spouse...if the Judge is satisfied that the spouse does not have the right to make a claim under the *Matrimonial Property Act* against the estate of the deceased.[106]

This could be established by providing the Court with copies of Minutes of Settlement or a Court Order which deals with the division of matrimonial property, or, if a divorce occurred more than two years prior to death, no notices need be served.[107]

As in Ontario, the personal representative should not make any distribution within six months from the date the grant was obtained if notice was given under the *Dependants Relief Act* and/or *Matrimonial Property Act*, unless consent is obtained from the surviving spouse, or a Court Order is obtained. Any distribution in contravention of these

---

[104] Or under the *Intestate Succession Act* on an intestacy.
[105] Ibid., s. 7(2); *Matrimonial Property Act*, R.S.A. 2000, c. M-8.
[106] *Administration of Estates Act*, s. 7(3).
[107] The provisions of subs. 7(6) of the *Administration of Estates Act* should be noted (i.e., the grant shall not be issued unless the judge is satisfied that the requirements for notice of rights under the *Matrimonial Property Act* have been complied with).

statutes can leave the personal representative personally liable to the spouse.

APPLICATIONS FOR ADVICE AND DIRECTIONS

Section 60 of the *Administration of Estates Act* allows for applications to be made by the personal representative of an Estate for the opinion, advice or directions of a Judge of the Court of Queen's Bench of Alberta (Surrogate Matter) on any matter relating to the management or administration of the estate.

Surrogate Rule 4 also provides that:

> A personal representative, or a person interested in an estate may apply to the court for directions at any time.

It is appropriate to apply to the Court for advice and directions on any matter respecting the management and administration of the estate. However, the Court will not hear certain matters. For example, the Court will not determine questions of ownership. The focus of the Advice and Directions Application is to assist personal representatives in their duties by giving them advice on matters of administration which will benefit the beneficiaries, rather than resolve a dispute between various interested parties.[108]

Such an application is appropriate when, for example:

(a) The personal representative wants to construe the extent of a discretion of power.
(b) The personal representative wants to determine the beneficiary under an RRSP when there is a general revocation clause in the Will.
(c) The personal representative wants a prior designation in the plan and where no facts were in dispute.
(d) The personal representative wants to interpret the wording of a Will.

The following circumstances have been considered inappropriate for an Advice and Directions Application:

(a) to determine the appropriate time and/or price for sale of shares;
(b) for a direction as to who should be paid on intestacy; and

---

[108] The Application for Advice and Directions is commenced by way of a Notice of Motion pursuant to Surrogate Rule 58, Part 2, Division 1. The proper forms to use are Forms C1 and C2.

(c) where the legal and administrative principles were well-established and a solicitor's opinion would have provided adequate protection to the personal representative.

Surrogate Rule 6 states that such an application must be filed in the judicial district in which the deceased resided at the date of his or her death and unless the Court permits otherwise. Rule 6 goes on to say that:

> (2) If the deceased resided outside Alberta immediately before dying, an application for a grant [and any subsequent Applications for Advice and Directions] may be filed in any judicial district where the deceased had property on the date of death.

As stated previously, the personal representative generally commences such an Application,[109] however, a person interested in the estate may also commence such an application.[110]

Pursuant to Surrogate Rule 63, all such proceedings must be heard before a judge in chambers. The Court, upon hearing such an application, may receive evidence by way of affidavit or, if a prior applica-tion has been made to the Court, by way of *viva voce* evidence. The Court may also summarily dispose of the issue, direct trial of the issue, or make any other Order the Court considers necessary.[111]

Surrogate Rule 64(1)(h) is authority for the proposition that the Court has the full discretion to order costs to be paid by any party after hearing the application. The Court may even "order security for costs to be posted by any party at any stage of the proceedings" pursuant to Surrogate Rule 69. Where an Application for Advice and Directions is necessary, and is necessitated as a result of the fault of the testator, or where the application is appropriate and for the benefit of the estate or the estate beneficiaries, the Court will usually direct that costs of such an application be paid from the estate. However, this ought not to be considered a rule of thumb: In *Re Lotzkar*,[112] the Court held that the personal representative should have exercised his or her discretion since there was no serious doubt or difference of opinion, and as a result the application ought not to have been brought. The personal representative was denied his costs and penalized with costs of the other parties for making the application.

---

[109] Surrogate Rule 4.
[110] Surrogate Rule 78.
[111] Surrogate Rule 64.
[112] (1985), 66 B.C.L.R. 265 (S.C.).

RECTIFICATION AND CONSTRUCTION/INTERPRETATION OF WILLS

It is important to briefly discuss non-contentious applications other than the conventional applications for grants. The Court of Queen's Bench of Alberta (Surrogate Matter) may sit either as a Court of Probate or as a Court of Construction/Interpretation. When the Court sits as a Court of Probate, it has the jurisdiction to grant various types of probate. When the Court sits as a court of interpretation, it has jurisdiction to interpret or construe the contents of the Will.

The Court may sit as such a Court only after the Will has been approved by the Court of probate. When the Court sits as a court of interpretation, it can only interpret the words in the Will which the Court of Probate has determined validly makes up the Will. If a Will is admitted for probate without an Application for Rectification, then the words that validly make up the Will are those contained in the original document. If a Rectification Application is also brought before the Court simultaneous with the Application for Probate, and the Court grants an order rectifying the Will, then the words that validly constitute the Will are those that are contained in the Court Order granted in respect to the Rectification Application.

Therefore, if there is a problem with the words contained in the Will, such as the mistaken inclusion of certain words, often an Application for Rectification of the Will is brought simultaneously with obtaining a Grant of Probate or, in any event, before proceeding to obtain probate. Otherwise, the relief available could be restricted to the more limited jurisdiction of a Court of Interpretation to interpret the wording contained in the Will. Therefore, rectification of a Will is available only before or at the time of a Grant of Probate.

The jurisdiction for a Court of Interpretation to rectify the wording of the Will in accordance with what it determines to have in fact been the testator's Will does not extend to adding words into a Will. The jurisdiction at the Court of Probate to correct mistakes in a Will is very limited. The Court is confined only to striking out words inserted by mistake without the approval of the testator. The Court's ability to rectify a Will does not permit them to add and/or substitute words to a Will, and only provides the Court with a limited jurisdiction to delete or ignore words.

Although a Court may strike out words inserted into a Will by mistake, the Court will not strike out words that the testator intended to use, but was mistaken as to their legal effect. In effect, if the testator personally knows and approves of the language of the Will, then the language is binding on a testator. If the testator relies on a drafter, and the drafter makes an inadvertent error, then the Court can only rectify the Will to the extent that the drafter has made the error. The Court will not strike out words if the effect of striking those words would be to change the meaning of the words deliberately selected by the Testator or drafter.

The rules respecting an Application to Construe the Will are set out in the Surrogate Rules.[113] If contentious, the Application is commenced pursuant to Surrogate Rule 55 with supporting affidavit, or as part of the Formal Proof of Will Application under Surrogate Rule 75 using forms C1 and C2.[114] Such an application may not be necessary if a personal representative has ascertained all of the interested or potentially interested parties and they have consented to a particular distribution.

This application is normally made by the personal representative as it is his or her obligation to ensure that they are acting in compliance with the terms of the Will. However, a beneficially interested party other than the personal representative may also bring such an application if the personal representative is asked to do so, but refuses.

The Court documents for such an application are required to be served on all persons whose interest may be affected by the Court Order.

BRITISH COLUMBIA[115]

This Part highlights the practice, procedure and law unique to British Columbia with respect to the process of administering an estate. The differences in British Columbia estate administration from that of Ontario and Alberta relate primarily to the intestacy provisions, the validity of testamentary documents and the court procedures, forms and fees.

INTESTACY

In British Columbia, where there is an estate, or a part thereof, which is to be distributed on intestacy, the provisions of the *Estate Administration*

---

[113] Part I, Division 1.
[114] This type of application is heard in chambers. If the matter is going to take more than 10 to 15 minutes, it will be placed on the Special Chambers List where half or full days are available.
[115] This section and the other British Columbia sections were contributed by Sandra Enticknap, Miller Thomson (Vancouver).

Act[116] apply. Part 10 of this Act provides that an estate of an individual who dies intestate is distributed in a certain order. If there is a spouse and no issue, the entire estate goes to the spouse.[117] If there is a spouse and one child (or issue of a deceased child), the spouse gets a preferential share of the first $65,000, the household furnishings and an estate for life in the spousal home and then gets one-half of the residue; the child or issue of the deceased child, subject to the rights of the spouse, gets one-half of the residue.[118] If there is a spouse and more than one child (including a deceased child with issue), the spouse's share of the residue is reduced from one-half to one-third and the children (or their issue, if deceased) receive two-thirds of the residue.[119] If there is no spouse, the order is as follows: children, grandchildren and other descendants of the deceased person, parents of the deceased person, siblings, nieces and nephews and finally next-of-kin in equal degrees of consanguinity to the person.

The term "spouse" includes a person who has lived and cohabited with the person who has died intestate in a marriage-like relationship, including a marriage-like relationship between persons of the same gender, for a period of at least two years immediately before the person's death. The term children includes natural children, and adopted children but does not include stepchildren.

The person who applies to be appointed to deal with an intestate estate is called an administrator and his or her application is for Letters of Administration. The persons who are entitled to apply are generally the persons entitled to share in the estate. The administrator has no power to act until the Letters of Administration have been granted. Although the *Estate Administration Act* does not clearly set it out, priority is generally given to the person or persons having the greatest interest in the estate. Consents to such person's application to be appointed as administrator will be required from any person entitled to share in the estate who has a greater or equal right to apply.

While there is no impediment to a person who resides outside British Columbia to apply for Letters of Administration, it may be a consideration for the Court in exercising its discretionary power to appoint.

---

[116] R.S.B.C. 1996, c. 122.
[117] *Ibid.*, s. 83.
[118] *Ibid.*, subs. 85(5)(a) and s. 96.
[119] See *ibid.*, subs. 85(5)(b) and (6).

Unless all heirs or creditors of the estate are competent and consent to the administrator's acting without bond, the Court will likely require a bond. It is, therefore, always advisable to determine whether the applicant will be able to obtain a bond prior to bringing the application. Where the estate is worth $65,000 or less, trust companies, and surviving spouses are not generally required to post a bond.

TYPED OR HOLOGRAPHIC

In British Columbia, following the formalities with respect to testamentary documents is important. In order to be valid with respect to real estate situate in British Columbia or other assets (wherever situate) of a person domiciled in British Columbia, a Will made in British Columbia must comply with the formalities set out in the *Wills Act*[120] as follows:

1. The Will must be in writing;[121]
2. The Will must be signed at its end by the person making it (the testator); or
    (a) by another person in the name of the testator, in his or her presence and by his or her direction;[122] and
    (b) the signature must be made or acknowledged by the testator in the presence of two or more attesting witnesses present at the same time[123] and the two or more attesting witnesses must subscribe the Will in the presence of the testator;[124]
3. The witnesses to the Will cannot be beneficiaries or spouses of beneficiaries.[125] An affidavit of execution sworn by the witnesses is not required.
4. The testator must be 19 years of age unless he or she is or has been married, or is a member of the Canadian Forces on active service or a mariner or seaman at sea or in the course of a voyage.

Members of the Canadian Forces on active service and mariners or seamen at sea or in the course of a voyage may make a Will in writing provided it is signed at the end or by some other person in the presence of

---

[120] R.S.B.C. 1996, c. 489.
[121] *Ibid.*, s. 3.
[122] *Ibid.*, s. 4(*a*).
[123] *Ibid.*, s. 4(*b*).
[124] *Ibid.*, s. 4(*c*).
[125] *Ibid.*, s. 11(1).

and by the direction of the testator. There is no necessity in that case for witnesses unless the Will is signed by another person, in which case there must be at least one witness.

Holograph Wills have limited validity in British Columbia. If there are assets situate in British Columbia which are not real estate, a holograph Will made outside British Columbia may be valid for the purpose of dealing with these assets if at the time the Will was made, it would have been valid in the place where it was made, or where the testator was domiciled when the Will was made, or where the testator had his or her domicile of origin.[126]

APPOINTMENT OF EXECUTOR

The person appointed to administer an estate under a person's Will in British Columbia is called an executor. There is no requirement that the executor reside in British Columbia, nor is there any requirement for a bond if the executor does not reside in British Columbia. The main concern with having an executor who resides outside of British Columbia is that it is inconvenient.

If an executor renounces his or her appointment, the alternate executor, if there is one named, is next in priority. If there is no alternate executor, or if the alternate executor renounces, then an administrator must be appointed. The administrator will apply for a Grant of Administration with Will Annexed. Again, the consents of all persons with a greater or equal right to apply will be required.

DOCUMENTATION

In British Columbia, there are a number of other types of applications for probate and administration. They include:

- Where an executor dies or wishes to be discharged or is unable or unwilling to continue to act, a "second grant" to an alternate executor may need to be obtained.
- Where more than one executor is appointed, it is possible for one executor to apply for a grant reserving the right of the other executor named in the Will to apply at a later date. The executor to whom power is reserved may at any time after the initial grant, but before

---

[126] *Ibid.*, s. 40.

administration of the estate has been completed, prove the Will by applying for a second grant. It will only apply to the unadministered portion of the estate. The second grant is called "double probate" and it runs concurrently with the first grant.
- A grant made by a Court in the Commonwealth outside of British Columbia may be resealed in British Columbia.[127]
- An ancillary grant may be given where the original grant was made by a non-Commonwealth Court.[128]
- It is possible to get a grant for a special purpose or in respect of a specific portion of the estate. This is called a grant "save and except" or *caeterorum*.
- Where there is a delay in the appointment of an administrator of an estate and it is necessary to appoint someone to collect the assets and protect the estate, a grant of administration *ad colligenda bona* may be obtained.
- Where it is not clear whether a Will is valid and there may be an action with respect to the Will's validity, it is possible to get a grant of administration *pendente lite*. The administrator with such a grant has the right and power of a general administrator but he or she cannot distribute the estate.[129]
- Where an administrator or executor dies leaving part of the estate unadministered, a grant in respect of the unadministered estate will be issued to a new administrator and this grant is called an administration *de bonis non*.

PROBATE

In British Columbia, an executor "applies for probate". When the application is approved by the Court, the Court will issue a Grant of Letters Probate. By issuing the Grant of Letters Probate, the Court authenticates the executor's appointment and confirms that the executor has the authority to represent the estate.

Rule 61 of the *Supreme Court Rules* sets out the procedure for obtaining a Grant of Letters Probate and other Court grants. Under Rule 61(3), the applicant must deposit with the Probate Registrar "the original will, if any", and any Codicils and "file a praecipe and an affidavit of

---

[127] See the *Probate Recognition Act*, R.S.B.C. 1996, c. 376, and British Columbia *Supreme Court Rules*, B.C. Reg. 221/90, Rules 50-57.
[128] See Rule 61(48)(b) of the *Supreme Court Rules*.
[129] *Estate Administration Act*, s. 8.

executor or administrator in Form 69, 70 or 71" of the Rules. There are certain other documents which must accompany the application such as:

- a statement of assets, liabilities and distribution (commonly referred to as the disclosure document) which must be exhibited to the affidavit of the applicant;[130]
- a renunciation by every living person named in a Will or Codicil as an executor who has decided not to act;
- if the applicant is not named as executor in a Will or Codicil, the consents to his or her appointment by all those persons who have an equal or greater right to apply must be provided;[131]
- a Certificate of Search of Wills Notices from the Director of Vital Statistics — such a search will disclose and attach copies of all Wills notices, if any, that have been filed with Vital Statistics in the name of the deceased person indicating that a Will has been made, its date and where it is kept;[132]
- an affidavit with respect to the persons entitled to receive notice under section 112 of the *Estate Administration Act* of the application for the grant. The persons who are entitled to receive a section 112 notice are:
  - all beneficiaries named in the Will;
  - all persons who would be entitled on an intestacy or partial intestacy if there was no Will;
  - all persons entitled to apply under the *Wills Variation Act*[133] (namely spouses and children);
  - all common-law spouses; and
  - separated spouses.
- where a person entitled to a notice is a minor, the minor's parent or guardian and the Public Guardian and Trustee must receive a notice. If the person is mentally disordered, that person's representative or committee must receive a notice as should the Public Guardian and Trustee. If there are unborn or unascertained contingent beneficiaries, practice requires that notices be sent to the Public Guardian and Trustee and to the parent or guardian of the possible unborn and unascertained contingent beneficiary;

---

[130] See the *Supreme Court Rules*, Forms 69, 70 and 71.
[131] Supreme Court Rule 61(20).
[132] Supreme Court Rules 61(31) and (32).
[133] R.S.B.C. 1996, c. 490.

- an Affidavit that the section 112 notice has been provided (together with a copy of the Will, if any) to all persons entitled to a notice;
- a cheque for the payment of probate fees payable to the Minister of Finance.

All beneficiaries named in the Will including any charities must be provided with a full copy of the Will.

British Columbia also has probate fees. If the gross value of an estate in British Columbia exceeds $10,000, the fee is $208 to commence the application for the grant, plus $6 for each $1,000 or part thereof in excess of $25,000 up to $50,000 plus $14 for each $1,000 or part thereof in excess of $50,000. As an example, the fees on an estate valued at $230,000 for probate purposes would be calculated as follows:

first $50,000	$ 358
remaining $180,000	$2,520 ($14 x $180,000/$1,000)
Total fees	$2,878

The application for probate or administration can be filed anywhere in the province.

CHARITABLE BENEFICIARY

Typically, in British Columbia, a charity receives notification of its interest under a Will when it is served with a Section 112 notice and a copy of the Will.

Upon receipt of the section 112 notice and Will, a charitable beneficiary should take the steps recommended previously in this chapter.[134]

In British Columbia, the directors of a charity have fiduciary obligations to use the charity's property for the charity's purposes. The supervisory role with respect to a charity established as a trust falls on the Attorney General for the province. If a charity is established as a society, investigation of the charity is allowed under section 84 of the *Society Act*[135] where the society is acting "contrary to the public interest". A member of the public can bring information forward to the Registrar of Companies, who would, in turn, report it to the Minister who then appoints an investigator. A director, manager, officer or agent of the

---

[134] See the section entitled "The Charitable Beneficiary".
[135] R.S.B.C. 1996, c. 433.

charity may then be examined under oath and be required to produce documents.

Chapter 3

LEGAL FEES, COMPENSATION, TAXES, RELEASES AND COSTS

ONTARIO

At an appropriate time, an estate trustee will attend to providing an accounting of his or her activities to the residuary beneficiaries. The presentation of the accounts provides the beneficiary with the chance to review the activities of the estate trustee and audit the administration of the estate.

As stated in Chapters 2 and 4, a beneficiary who has received a legacy does not receive the estate accounts for review and hence does not have to be concerned with the discussion in this chapter.

As previously indicated, in Ontario, at the end of an administration, an estate trustee may volunteer or may be compelled to "pass" his or her accounts. If there are no objections to the accounts, the matter proceeds without a hearing.[1]

It is important to remember that, in Ontario, a beneficiary who retains counsel to assist in reviewing the accounts on a formal passing is entitled — even if the passing is uncontested — to costs from the estate. These costs are not allowed unless a solicitor is retained. Solicitors' costs allowed on an uncontested passing of accounts range from $800 to $5,000 in accordance with Tariff "C".[2] Accordingly, it is prudent, if in doubt, to forward the accounts for review by a solicitor — just make sure enough time is provided, because there are time limitations.

Entries of particular importance for a charitable beneficiary are those that relate to legal fees, compensation and taxes. After the account review process, a beneficiary should then turn his or her mind to the overall

---

[1] For more discussion, see Chapter 4.
[2] For a review of Tariff "C", see Chapter 4.

outcome of the review process and review the release. This chapter deals with these particular areas of the account review process.

LEGAL AND PROFESSIONAL FEES

One of the more important entries for a residuary beneficiary to review (along with compensation and taxes) consists of the legal and professional fees incurred by the estate trustee. This section discusses the quantification and frequency of these fees.

An estate trustee is entitled to retain the services of professional advisors. Although these professional advisors are retained to act for the estate trustee (and not the estate *per se*), the cost of these retainers is normally borne by the estate, depending on the type of work undertaken. If the estate trustee shows that the charges were proper and not work that he or she should have been able to do personally, they can be charged against the estate. Where the charges are found to be excessive, only the amount reasonable in the circumstances should be borne by the estate.

The usual professional fees are those paid to accountants to prepare returns, to investment advisors and to solicitors. Where the estate trustee is justified in retaining investment counsel or an accountant, the amounts paid will be allowed and not necessarily deducted from the estate trustee's compensation.[3]

Usually, estate trustees are lay individuals who require the services of a solicitor to advise them on various aspects of administering an estate. Although professional estate trustees, such as trust companies, are more sophisticated and experienced in administering estates, legal issues may still arise and legal paperwork still needs to be prepared, requiring them also to retain legal counsel. Accordingly, some payment to a solicitor should be expected except in the rare case where an estate trustee is a solicitor who waives his or her entitlement to fees.

There is no regulated tariff with respect to legal fees rendered in the administration of an estate.[4] The general rule is that the estate will be liable for reasonable legal fees where it is shown that the services related to the estate.

Generally, the fees normally charged for services rendered by a solicitor are based on the time spent. Normally a solicitor charges his or her time at

---

[3] *Re Miller Estate* (1987), 26 E.T.R. 188 (Ont. Surr. Ct.); *Re Goldlust Estate* (1991), 44 E.T.R. 97 (Ont. Gen. Div.).
[4] In Ontario, in 1999 the Metropolitan Toronto Lawyers Association prepared a "suggested" fee schedule (with the emphasis on "suggested").

an hourly rate that is usually fixed (although subject to review and change with notice) on an annual basis. It is rare for a solicitor to charge a fixed fee for administering an estate or a fee based on the value of the estate.

A residuary beneficiary is entitled to ask the estate trustee to provide a copy of the solicitor's invoice(s) or account(s) for review. The accounts should be rendered in sufficient detail to provide a description of the tasks performed and the time spent on each task on a daily basis. Ideally, they should provide such details as the work performed, who performed the work and whether that person is a clerk or a lawyer, the hourly rate of each timekeeper, and how long it took to perform the task. The accounts should be more than a "catch-all" description of services rendered followed by a "total fee" amount. After the fee section, the account will indicate the disbursements incurred and the Goods and Services Tax (G.S.T.) incurred and chargeable.

If the accounts lack this detail, a beneficiary is entitled to request the backup documentation or "dockets". Most solicitors record on a daily basis the details of the task performed and the amount of time spent as the work is done; this is recorded on docket sheets. The information from the docket sheets then provides the basis for preparing and rendering the accounts.

As well as insisting that the solicitor provide all the detail required if it is not set out in first instance, a residuary beneficiary can challenge the amount of legal fees charged, even if the account has been paid. Typically, by the time the estate accounts are presented for review, at least 9 to 12 months have passed since the date of death. A solicitor does not need to wait (in contrast with estate trustee compensation) for beneficiary approval before the estate trustee pays his or her account. However, the solicitor and the estate trustee should be aware that a beneficiary can challenge the quantum of the fees charged and paid. A solicitor and estate trustee should be prepared to answer questions and attempt to resolve differences over the accounts. If those differences cannot be resolved then a beneficiary can ask for the accounts to be assessed or taxed. This is because the amount paid affects the amount of the residue.[5] The costs of an assessment are considered part of the administration expenses of the estate and are a first charge on the estate. At this stage, if there is concern over the extent of the legal fees, a beneficiary should consult with its own legal counsel for further advice.

---

[5] *Hardy v. Rubin* (1998), 23 E.T.R. (2d) 113 (Ont. Gen. Div.).

SOLICITOR ACTING AS ESTATE TRUSTEE

Caution should be exercised when reviewing accounts where the estate trustee is a practising lawyer. An estate trustee is entitled to employ a solicitor and be reimbursed for those fees properly incurred, but not where the estate trustee should have or might have done the work him or herself.

Whenever a solicitor is acting as estate trustee (whether by default or by appointment), a beneficiary should insist that separate accounts be provided for the time expended as solicitor as compared to the time spent as estate trustee in order to ensure that the time expended in the role of estate trustee is not billed twice ("double dipping").

This "double dipping" may also occur where a solicitor assisting an inexperienced estate trustee ends up by default or otherwise doing those things that the estate trustee should be doing.

The general rule (subject to exceptions) at common law was that a solicitor acting as estate trustee was not entitled to charge the estate for professional services as this violated the rule that the estate trustee was not to place him or herself in a position of conflict. In some provinces such as Ontario (but not British Columbia and Alberta), this common law rule has been (since 1903) overruled by statute. The Ontario *Trustee Act*[6] allows for payment of an "allowance" (*i.e.*, compensation) to a solicitor acting as an estate trustee for his or her care, pains, trouble and time expended in administering the estate.

Acting as an estate trustee is distinct from acting as a solicitor.[7] Often the two roles have no relation to each other, especially when compensation is being quantified. Usually, the solicitor charges his or her time as in the normal course (*i.e.* the time spent multiplied by the hourly rate) when performing estate trustee duties, and this may not result in appropriate compensation. Rather, a solicitor should open one matter to record his or her time as solicitor and another matter to record his or her activities as estate trustee. Other personnel in the office performing work for the estate should similarly docket or record their time to the relevant matter.[8] The failure to properly distinguish between estate trustee and solicitor's work and account separately for it, can result in the solicitor being unable to collect compensation as estate trustee.

---

[6] R.S.O. 1990, c. T.23, s. 61(4).
[7] For a list of duties typically performed by an estate trustee (as compared to a solicitor) see Chapter 2.
[8] *Kimberley & Naylor v. Prior* (1974), 5 O.R. (2d) 593 (S.C. Taxing Officer); *Re Goldlust Estate* (1991), 44 E.T.R. 97 (Ont. Gen. Div.); *Eisenstat Estate v. O'Hara* (1995), 7 E.T.R. (2d) 187 (Ont. Gen. Div.).

The solicitor's time performing trustee duties should not be paid from the estate if the estate trustee is claiming full compensation, as this results in the estate paying twice for the same service. Rather, there is one charge for compensation. This usually means that the solicitor's time is paid out of the compensation claimed by the estate trustee, resulting in a sharing of the compensation. Often this can be a delicate issue, as the solicitor may not have explained this consequence to his or her client, the estate trustee. The client is expecting full compensation because he or she has been told that as estate trustee he or she is entitled to "compensation based on 5% of the value of the estate". If this has occurred then the solicitor is in an awkward (but self-imposed) situation where he or she now has to tell the client that he or she is not entitled to "full compensation" but rather that it is to be shared with the solicitor. Often this is the dynamic behind the resistance that a beneficiary may face from the estate trustee or solicitor when this issue is raised.

If it is anticipated by the circumstances (for example, a co-estate trustee situation where the deceased names his solicitor and his widow but the widow is elderly and not inclined to deal with the details of administering an estate) that this may occur, then a beneficiary should consider confirming (by letter) at the outset with the solicitor and estate trustee that it expects that the solicitor will keep records of any work done as solicitor separate from records of work done as estate trustee, and that compensation will be dealt with separately from legal fees and on a global basis as between the co-estate trustees.

Sometimes, a solicitor acting as estate trustee will not charge compensation *per se*, but rather will take the position that he or she as estate trustee has "delegated" those functions to him or herself as solicitor, and will charge his or her time in the normal course as a solicitor. The solicitor then takes the further position that he or she is not "claiming" compensation. Leaving aside whether an estate trustee can "delegate" his or her duties, in such a case, a beneficiary should still review the amount taken (usually described as legal fees) as it would any other claim for compensation. The same factors and considerations apply to determine whether the amount taken is "fair and reasonable" in the circumstances.

Finally, it should be noted that the Will may address the situation where a solicitor is named an estate trustee. A clause may be included in the Will that allows the estate trustee to charge for his professional services. These clauses tend to be strictly construed. Even so, a beneficiary still retains the right to challenge, and the Court retains the inherent jurisdiction to review, the charges.[9]

COMPENSATION

At common law, before statutory enactment, an estate trustee was not allowed to "profit" from his or her position. This meant that an estate trustee could not charge for his or her services.[10]

By statute this general rule was overturned. Accordingly, an estate trustee is now entitled, but not required, to receive compensation for his or her work as estate trustee. This remuneration for his or her services is a primary charge against the estate and ranks before the payment of most debts and before the payment of bequests.

In Ontario, these principles are set out in section 61 of the *Trustee Act*. This section provides for a "fair and reasonable allowance" for the estate trustee's "care, pains and trouble, and the time expended in and about the estate" unless the allowance is "fixed" by the Will. The amount of the compensation can be settled even if the estate is not before the court, and a judge at a passing of accounts may "from time to time" allow this allowance. Accordingly, it is at the stage of presenting the accounts that an estate trustee can claim and receive compensation.

The claim by an estate trustee for compensation is a source of frequent carelessness and unintentional abuse. It is one item that should always be reviewed.

The accounts should include a Statement of Compensation. This statement shows the amount of compensation claimed by the estate trustee. It should be in sufficient detail to allow the beneficiary to know the basis for the calculation.

Trustee compensation is a matter of provincial jurisdiction and thus the rules differ across the country. Many corporate trustees administer estates pursuant to fee or compensation agreements signed by the testator when the will was executed. This agreement governs if it was in place at the time of execution and is usually referred to in the Will. These

---

[9] *Walker v. Bostwick* (1986), 26 E.T.R. 52 (B.C.C.A.).

[10] It should be pointed out that other personal representatives, such as guardians appointed for mentally incapable persons, are also entitled to compensation in the same way as estate trustees. In Ontario, the rate of compensation for guardians or attorneys for property (which is higher than the usual percentage basis set for estate trustees) is set out by regulation to the *Substitute Decisions Act, 1992*, S.O. 1992, c. 30. In British Columbia, the rate of compensation is similar to that of estate trustees and is fixed on the passing of accounts before the Public Guardian and Trustee. See *Patients Property Act*, R.S.B.C. 1996, c. 349, s. 14.

agreements are recognized by section 61(5) of the *Trustee Act* and are generally accepted by the Courts. The terms of these agreements can vary and tend to allow greater compensation than the "customary" rate. If such an agreement is signed, there is not much a beneficiary can do about the compensation claimed and taken — it was the deceased who entered into the agreement and agreed to pay that rate of compensation.

If there is more than one estate trustee the compensation is divided among them. The estate trustees, reach an agreement among themselves, usually based on the amount of work each performed. Where one of the estate trustees is a corporate trustee there may be an agreement among the estate trustees that governs this issue. This is not a matter that typically concerns a beneficiary, who is generally concerned with the global amount claimed — how that amount is divided is an issue for the estate trustees.

The calculation of compensation is not as simple as it may appear or as the estate solicitor may like you to believe.

In Ontario, there is no statutory rate for estate trustees.[11] The starting point in Ontario is the mathematical calculation or "customary" rate, calculated as 2.5 per cent of receipts (*i.e.*, what comes into the estate as shown in the capital receipts and revenue receipts statements) and 2.5 per cent of disbursements (*i.e.*, what goes out of the estate as shown in the capital disbursements and revenue disbursements statements). The calculation is on the whole amount distributed even if it includes a legacy or residual distribution to the estate trustee.[12] For example, where an estate trustee sells a car, the compensation would be calculated as 2.5 per cent of the proceeds from selling the car and 2.5 per cent of the amount distributed to the beneficiaries. Colloquially, this calculation is sometimes described as 2.5 per cent of the "ins and outs" or, roughly stated, 5 per cent of the value of the estate.

Calculating compensation in this manner is a custom or practice, not a legal entitlement. For example, in one case the solicitor for the estate sent the following letter (reproduced in part) to the beneficiaries:

> ...In accordance with the Estate Department of the Ontario Court the Trustee Act allows the Executors to receive a fee of <u>FIVE PERCENT</u> (5%) of

---

[11] As compared to guardians of property, where, by Regulation under the *Substitute Decisions Act, 1992*, S.O. 1992, c. 30, the rate of compensation is fixed at 3 per cent of estate receipts, 3 per cent of estate disbursements and three-fifths of 1 per cent of the value of the estate as the care and management fee. This may lead some estate trustees to claim the same percentage as compensation. The courts have not yet accepted these higher rates as the starting point in Ontario.

[12] *Re Atwell Estate* (1997), 19 E.T.R. (2d) 234 (Ont. Gen. Div.); *Re Stanley Estate* (1996), 13 E.T.R. (2d) 102 (Ont. Gen. Div.).

the total value of the estate. Accordingly this would equate to the sum of $24,032.81. We have enclosed herewith a consent form which we would ask that you sign and return to our office consenting to the said amount being paid to Stephen Kelly, the Executor of the said estate.

Please be advised that should you not agree to execute the said consent, we will have no other option [but] to apply to the Supreme Court for a ruling on the same thus eliminating any distribution of the said estate until Judgment has been set down.

As well, we wish to advise that our legal fees for the administration of this estate will be THREE AND ONE HALF PERCENT (3-½%) of the total value of the estate plus any applicable taxes and any actual disbursements, i.e. beneficiary registrations, courier charges, etc. incurred by our firm in the settling of the same. We have enclosed herewith a consent form which we would ask that you sign and return to our office consenting to the said amount being paid to our firm.[13]

In reviewing this letter, the court stated that it was greatly concerned with the tenor of the letter and "the misstatement as to the basis for the calculation of compensation".[14] It also stated that the comment that the "Estate Department of the Ontario Court" and the *Trustee Act* allow a fee of 5 per cent was "patently false", and that if consents had been signed relying upon this statement the beneficiaries would not be bound by them.[15] Further, the court repeated that the estate trustee is not allowed to take compensation before it is allowed by the Court.[16]

The customary rate of 2.5 per cent of the receipts and 2.5 per cent of the disbursements is the maximum normally allowed (recognizing that compensation is ultimately a matter of discretion and there is provision for a special fee in the rare case). A special fee over and above the ordinary claim for compensation may be requested and granted in rare instances. The basis for the claim should be very detailed and should include docketed information and affidavit evidence.

An estate trustee is not entitled to compensation on transfers between bank accounts or other adjusting entries, payments on account of compensation, payments for executors' duties performed by someone else,[17]

---

[13] *Cronan Estate v. Hughes* (2000), 37 E.T.R. (2d) 27 (Ont. S.C.J.) at para. 25.
[14] *Ibid.*, at para. 27.
[15] *Ibid.*
[16] *Ibid.*
[17] What constitutes "executors' duties performed by someone else" depends on the circumstances. For example, the preparation of income tax returns, unless extremely complex, should be done by the estate trustee and, if not, the charges incurred by having a professional do them are generally set off from the compensation claim: *Re Clowater Estate* (1993), 49 E.T.R. 184 (N.B.

capital losses, and refunds of payments made previously by the trustees such as income tax refunds.

In certain circumstances, compensation is subject to Goods and Services Tax, depending on whether the estate trustee carries out his or her duties as part of his or her normal course of business. Typically, corporate trustees and solicitors who hold themselves out as being in the business of acting as estate trustees will charge G.S.T.

Where the estate is ongoing (*i.e.*, a life interest exists), the estate trustee is entitled to a care and management fee calculated annually on the average value of estate assets at the rate of two-fifths of 1 per cent. Estate trustees must indicate in their Statement of Compensation how the average value of the trust assets has been determined. The charge for the care and management fee is normally allocated one-third to revenue and two-thirds to capital. An estate trustee is not entitled to a care and management fee if the estate is distributable outright, but it has taken the estate trustee time (over a year) to administer. Although it is rare for a Court to refuse a management fee, the Courts do not consider the concept of such a fee an absolute entitlement, but rather one that must be justified in each case.[18]

It is now common for trust companies to charge care and management fees based on the average annual *market value* of an estate rather than the original date of death value or investment costs. It is also common for trust companies to charge the care and management fee at the rate of three-fifths of 1 per cent.[19]

Although these rates are the "custom" (and have been in Ontario since 1975), they are not an automatic entitlement. The application of "customary" compensation percentages in a large but relatively simple estate could result in a significant claim that might not be justifiable.

Prob. Ct.); *Re Campin Estate* (1992), 49 E.T.R. 197 (Ont. Gen. Div.). Investment counsel fees are somewhat different. In Ontario, it is usually considered reasonable and prudent to retain the assistance of professional advisors if the size or complexity of the fund under administration warrants it. In such cases (and subject to the Will), these fees can be allowed in addition to the compensation taken: *Re Miller Estate* (1987), 26 E.T.R. 188 (Ont. Surr. Ct.); *Re Holt Estate* (1994), 2 E.T.R. (2d) 163 (Ont. Gen. Div.).

[18] *Re Jeffery Estate* (1990), 39 E.T.R. 173 (Ont. Surr. Ct.).

[19] With the coming into force of new investment provisions in the *Trustee Act* in Ontario, it is quite common for estate trustees to retain the services of investment advisors. If it is considered prudent in the circumstances for the estate trustee to have retained such advisors and where the estate has paid an advisor fee, a Court may allow these fees (if reasonable) in addition to the compensation received by the estate trustee: *Re Miller Estate* (1987), 26 E.T.R. 188 (Ont. H.C.); *Re Holt Estate* (1994), 2 E.T.R. (2d) 163 (Ont. Gen. Div.). Note, in contrast, accounting fees paid by the estate are normally not in addition to the compensation received, but rather are usually deducted from the compensation claim: *Re Clowater Estate* (1993), 49 E.T.R. 184 (N.B. Prob. Ct.); *Re Campin Estate* (1992), 49 E.T.R. 197 (Ont. Gen. Div.).

Conversely, "customary" percentages in a smaller but extremely complex estate may not adequately reimburse the trustees for their "care, pains and trouble, and the time expended in and about the estate".[20]

Therefore, the mathematical calculation is subject to various factors. Each claim for compensation must be looked at on its own merits each and every time. Hence, this is one item that must be looked at carefully in each set of accounts. The courts will consider various other factors besides the mathematically calculated result.

One factor is what the testator may state in his or her Will. The testator may have stated that the estate trustee was to receive $10,000 on account of compensation. If the compensation is fixed by the Will the court will not reduce the amount. The amount stated is what the estate trustee should get (although this does not necessarily deter some estate trustees from trying to get more).

Alternatively, the testator by Will may leave the estate trustee a legacy (instead of or in addition to a share of the residue). In this case there is a presumption that the legacy was intended as compensation. This presumption may be rebutted by showing that the legacy was intended to be in addition to any compensation. This may be done by referring to the language of the legacy or from the Will as a whole. If the Will is silent, an argument can be made that the legacy is in substitution of (or in addition to) any compensation. The onus is on the estate trustee to rebut the presumption. Today, it is fairly easy to do so.

Another factor may be the compensation agreement. In Ontario, the *Trustee Act*[21] specifies that an agreement between the estate trustee and the testator overrides the entitlement to claim compensation on the basis of the care, time, pain and trouble expended. The agreement must be in writing.[22]

Accordingly, the compensation payable may be fixed by agreement prior to death. In such cases it will be the agreement that governs the amount of compensation. Typically, professional trustees (*i.e.*, trust companies) commonly administer estates pursuant to a fee agreement signed by the testator and corporation when the will was executed. Where a corporate trustee is in place, you should inquire whether there is a fee agreement in place and ask for a copy of the agreement at the beginning. In Ontario, in order to be effective, the compensation agreement must have been signed at the same time as the Will and should be incorporated by

---

[20] *Trustee Act*, R.S.O. 1990, c. T.23, s. 61(1).
[21] *Ibid.*, s. 61(5).
[22] *Re Budd Estate* (1994), 149 N.B.R. (2d) 266 (Prob. Ct.).

reference in the Will. When reviewing the compensation, compare the amount claimed with the terms of the agreement to ensure compliance with the agreement.

Finally, the mathematical calculation may also be modified by the "five factors" as developed in the case law.[23] The five factors that should be considered in determining appropriate compensation include the size of the estate, the care and responsibility involved, the time spent performing the duties, the skill and abilities shown, and the results obtained or degree of success in the administration.

For example, an estate trustee administering an outright distributable estate that contained only cash in a bank account, left there during the course of administration, would likely not be entitled to the "customary rate". The courts would likely adjust the mathematical value downwards. A downward adjustment could also be appropriate in very large estates or large transactions.[24] A 5 per cent fee may, in the circumstances, be considered inappropriate.

As another example, where the estate trustee acted negligently or fraudulently in administrating the estate, his or her compensation may be reduced or even eliminated.[25]

In Ontario, therefore, as the *Trustee Act* was not particularly helpful, a three-step process[26] has developed to determine an appropriate amount of compensation.

First, the "customary rate" without regard to a care and management fee is calculated. Second, that result is compared with the five factors set out in the case law in order to assess whether the customary rate is reasonable in the circumstances. This requires an overall review of the administration of the estate as well as the particular calculation of compensation on specific assets. For example, no compensation should be taken merely for taking over assets, and no compensation should be taken for assets passing outside the estate either by way of joint tenancy or by way of beneficiary designation. Although compensation may be allowed on the income from these assets, no other compensation is taken until the assets

---

[23] *Toronto General Trusts Corp. v. Central Ontario Railway Co.* (1905), 6 O.W.R. 350 (H.C.); *Re Atkinson Estate*, [1952] O.R. 685 at 695 (C.A.), aff'd. [1953] 2 S.C.R. 41.
[24] *Re Jeffery Estate* (1990), 39 E.T.R. 173 (Ont. Surr. Ct.); *Forrest Estate v. O'Donohue* (1991), 44 E.T.R 171 (Ont. Gen. Div.).
[25] *Re Wood Estate*, [1977] 2 W.W.R. 538 (Sask. Surr. Ct.); *Ontario (Public Trustee) v. Mortimer* (1985), 18 E.T.R. 219 (Ont. H.C.J.).
[26] *Re Laing Estate* (1996), 11 E.T.R. (2d) 268, 89 O.A.C. 321 (Div. Ct.), aff'd. (1998), 113 O.A.C. 335, 25 E.T.R. (2d) 139, 41 O.R. (3d) 571 (C.A.); *Re Jeffery Estate* (1990), 39 E.T.R. 173 (Ont. Surr. Ct.); *Re Wright Estate* (1990), 43 E.T.R. 82 (Ont. Gen. Div.).

are converted or distributed. On capital receipts (*i.e.*, the proceeds paid into the capital account as original assets are sold for the purposes of paying debts, paying legacies or making distributions), compensation is allowed on the total but may be reduced for large receipts. Capital disbursements made in investing and liquidating capital funds do not attract loose compensation. Compensation on capital disbursements cannot be claimed until the asset is distributed.

There are certain other exclusions from the percentages calculations. Cross entries or book entries (*i.e.*, showing a loss in the realization of investments), although they must show in the accounts, are not subject to compensation. The payment of income tax and receipt of income tax refunds are also excluded, as is the write-off of bad debts.

Then, if applicable, a care and management fee will also be imposed. If exceptional circumstances exist, the question of whether a special fee is justified in the circumstances needs to be considered.

The bottom line is that the percentage basis for awarding compensation, although a short cut, should only be considered a rough guide.

PRE-TAKING COMPENSATION

It is not appropriate for an estate trustee to take compensation without either the prior approval of the beneficiaries, where they are competent adults or charitable beneficiaries, or the approval of the Court on a passing of accounts, subject to an express provision to the contrary in the Will.[27] The taking of compensation without either approval is called "pre-taking" compensation. In Ontario, the courts have recently taken a hard line on pre-taking compensation.[28]

However, the bar on pre-taking compensation is not as absolute as it once was and pre-taking an amount (*i.e.*, less than the Courts would allow in the circumstances) is not unheard of. For ongoing trusts an estate trustee (usually a trust company) has in some cases[29] been allowed to "pre-take" compensation if the fees are reasonable and within the range of fees normally allowed by the Court. However, there remains the risk of the beneficiaries objecting and the Court imposing a sanction for pre-taking. Where an estate trustee pre-takes compensation in excess of that

---

[27] *Re Knoch* (1982), 12 E.T.R. 162 (Ont. Surr. Ct.).
[28] *Re Pilo Estate*, [1998] O.J. No. 4521 (Ont. Gen. Div.) (QL); *Andrachuk Estate v. Van Beurden*, (2000), 32 E.T.R. (2d) 1 (Ont. S.C.J.); *Re Flaska Estate*, [2001] O.J. No. 2176 (Ont. S.C.J.) (QL).
[29] *Re King Trust* (1994), 2 E.T.R. (2d) 123 (Ont. Gen. Div.); *Re Wright Estate* (1990), 43 E.T.R. 82 (Ont. Gen. Div.), additional reasons at (1990), 43 E.T.R. 69 (Ont. Gen. Div.).

ultimately allowed or consented to, the estate trustee must repay the difference to the estate with interest. For example, in *Re Goldlust Estate*[30] the court awarded over $153,000 in compensation. However, as the estate trustee had pre-taken $75,000, the court imposed a sanction on the estate trustee equivalent to the lost interest on the $75,000.

Despite this case law, it remains a prudent course of action for an estate trustee, especially on an outright distributable estate, to wait for beneficiary or court approval before taking compensation.

On a final note, the compensation taken is usually payable on the aggregate of the estate. Compensation is allocated between capital and income in their respective amounts. When a care and management fee is taken, it is usually allocated two-thirds to capital and one-third to income. In this way an even-handed treatment between income and capital beneficiaries is attempted.

A careful review of the compensation claimed should always be conducted. Whether compensation has been pre-taken is another area to examine when reviewing accounts. One develops a "feel" for what is appropriate in the circumstances. Certainly the accounts themselves, especially the Statement of Original Assets, the transactions carried out, and a review of the Will will tell you about the size and complexity of the estate, and anticipated difficulties in administering the estate. It is strongly recommended that charitable organizations that regularly receive bequests should assign the same person to be responsible for reviewing the estate accounts — this will ensure experience, consistency and confidence.

INCOME TAXES

As the saying goes, nothing in life is certain except death and taxes. The greatest liability of an estate is most often outstanding income taxes. This liability can represent a significant debt to the estate, especially where there are no charitable beneficiaries.

The estate trustee is responsible for ensuring all payment of the income taxes owing by the deceased and his or her estate (because the taxes are a debt of the deceased and the estate). Also, section 159 of the *Income Tax Act*[31] provides that the estate trustee is jointly and severally liable with the estate for the tax and may become personally liable for outstanding taxes in certain circumstances. If the deceased or the estate has an outstanding

---

[30] (1991), 44 E.T.R. 97 (Ont. Gen. Div.); see also *Sinclair-Cockburn Insurance Brokers v. Richards* (2002), 61 O.R. (3d) 105 (C.A.), application for leave to appeal dismissed [2002] S.C.C.A. No. 450 (QL).
[31] R.S.C. 1985, c. 1 (5th Supp.).

income tax liability, the Canada Customs and Revenue Agency (CCRA) will look to the estate trustee, as agent of the deceased or the estate, to discharge the amount outstanding. The extent of the estate trustee's obligation is limited to the property of the deceased or the estate in the possession or control of the estate trustee.

The *Income Tax Act* also provides that an estate trustee should, before distributing estate assets to beneficiaries, obtain a Clearance Certificate.[32] This Clearance Certificate certifies that all income taxes owing by the deceased or the estate have been paid, and provides the estate trustee with the comfort that he or she will not be held personally liable for outstanding taxes that may arise later.

There are various returns that must or can be filed. First, the estate trustee must determine the income (from employment, investments, *etc.*) of the deceased from January 1 of the year of death to the deceased's date of death and file a T1 or terminal return for this time period. The deceased is considered to have sold or redeemed all investments on his or her date of death and the estate therefore must also report the resulting capital gains and losses in the terminal return. This return must be filed by the later of April 30 of the following year or within six months from the date of death.

Second, if the deceased has any unfiled tax returns, they must be filed as soon as possible after the death and certainly within six months from the date of death, as interest (and penalties) will be accruing.

Third, an estate trustee has the option to file more than one income tax return for the terminal period depending on estate circumstances. For example, the following types of returns may also be filed:

(a) "Rights or Things" return reporting declared but unpaid dividends, unpaid salaries, commissions or vacation pay under certain conditions, and other forms of unpaid income specifically detailed by the *Income Tax Act*.
(b) "Partner or Proprietor" return reporting partnership or proprietor income earned by the deceased from businesses with a fiscal year-end other than December 31.
(c) "Trust Stub" return reporting income earned by the deceased from his or her life interest in a trust with a fiscal period ending other than the end of the calendar year and prior to the deceased's death. For example, if the deceased had a life interest in his or her sister's estate with a fiscal year-end of June 30 and the deceased died on September 1, the income allocated to the deceased by the trust created by the sister's

---

[32] Section 159.

estate from July 1 of the previous year to June 30 of the year of death would be reported in the deceased's terminal income tax return. The income earned by the trust from July 1 of the year of death to September 1 would be reported in the elective trust stub return.

An advantage of filing these elective returns is that the estate trustee has the opportunity to split the deceased's terminal income among two or more income tax returns. Each return allows the deceased taxpayer to claim the full basic exemptions to which he or she would otherwise be entitled, resulting in the taxation of some of the terminal income at a lower marginal rate. There are specified filing deadlines for each type of elective return.

Fourth, as the estate is considered to be a separate legal person, the estate must also file tax returns until it is wound up. The Trust Income Tax and Information Return (T3 Return) must be filed 90 days after the estate's year-end. The estate trustee can choose any year-end, within certain parameters, after the date of death, but the year-end must be no later than the first anniversary of the date of death. It could be for any shorter period (such as a calendar year) selected by the estate trustee. There may be advantages associated with selecting the estate year-end.

In some situations a deceased taxpayer may be required to report significant capital gains in his or her terminal income tax return as of the date of death. In falling markets, it is possible that the value of these assets may drop following the date of death, resulting in capital losses in the estate itself. To the extent that these estate capital losses incurred (and crystallized) in the first estate year exceed the capital gains reported in the terminal income tax return, the estate trustee can elect to carry back the capital losses incurred by the estate to the terminal return. The circumstances in which an estate trustee is entitled to request this loss carry-back are set out in the *Income Tax Act*. If necessary, the guidance of a professional should be sought.

If a significant portion of the residue of the estate is to be donated outright to charities, the estate trustee should file a terminal tax return including the donation credit in order to minimize the tax payable. Further, where some or all of the estate is immediately distributable to charities, the estate trustee may be able to file T3 returns allocating some or all of the estate income to the beneficiary charities in order to minimize the tax payable. In estates with a life tenant preceding the interest of residual charitable beneficiaries, the taxable income is usually allocated to the life tenant, resulting in no tax payable by the estate (the life tenant pays the tax). If income tax is paid in the estate, the estate trustee should allocate the taxes against the income to which the life tenant is entitled.

In some cases, estate income taxes may be charged to the capital of the estate. This is usually the case if, for example, the sale of an asset or trustee investment has resulted in a capital gain. Unless the life tenant has a right to encroach on the capital, he or she does not benefit from the actual capital gain itself, only from the income earned on the reinvestment of the gain. The ultimate capital beneficiaries are not entitled to receive the capital during the life tenancy. Therefore, the taxes generated by the capital gains will be the only ones paid from the estate capital.

Due to the advantages (tax and otherwise) of having charitable beneficiaries, it is crucial for a charitable beneficiary to review this issue during the course of the estate's administration. At every opportunity — in correspondence, in reviewing the estate accounts, at the deadline for filing returns — a charity should be aware of this issue. The responsibility for filing returns on time and accurately rests absolutely on the estate trustee (and estate solicitor). While it is not the beneficiary's role to notify the estate trustee of the deadlines for filing, for example, it is incumbent on a charitable beneficiary to know the deadlines and to confirm that they have been met. If a deadline is not met, the CCRA can impose interest and penalties on any amount owing. Any payments made beyond the actual tax due should not be an expense of the estate. These expenses (*i.e.*, interest, penalties, and arguably the costs of correcting the situation) should be borne by the estate trustee personally. One way to do this is by a set-off of such amounts against any compensation claimed (in addition to taking issue with the amount of compensation taken).

Similarly, a charity should examine closely any taxes being paid by the estate. Frequently, gifts to charities result in no or relatively little tax payable, depending on the size of the gift. In some estates, the payment of taxes may not be avoidable. However, this is an area where too often taxes are paid because the estate trustee lacked sophistication or access to knowledgeable advisors to ensure that, whenever possible, the income tax returns take advantage of the existence of charitable beneficiaries.

Charitable beneficiaries are obligated to protect the charitable status of their interest in the estate by evaluating the gift, properly valuing the gift and issuing proper receipts. A receipt cannot be issued until the gift is actually received. Typically, a copy of the Will is filed with the income tax returns that support the filing showing the existence of charitable beneficiaries. Sometimes this is not enough and a charity will be asked to provide further proof. As a receipt cannot be issued in advance of actual receipt of the gift, a charity may be asked by the estate trustee (through the estate solicitor) or the charity itself may suggest that instead it will issue a Letter of Undertaking. By this letter the charity indicates its acceptance of the gift and undertakes to issue a receipt. A charity should be careful in this situation and should, to the extent possible, place its reliance on a third party, such as the estate solicitor or estate accountant, for the valuation estimate. It may be that at the time of receipting the gift the value is less (or more) than the value expected. It is not within the charity's ability to "opine" on the expected value until the gift is actually received.

A sample letter (using the example of a gift of shares of a private company) follows.

(CHARITY LETTERHEAD)
(Date)
(Name)
(Address)
RE: Estate of (name)
Dear * :
We acknowledge that under the terms of the Will of the late (name of deceased) we are to receive (quantity and class) of the shares of (name of company). The (transfer of the shares) is to be completed by (date) at which time an official tax receipt will be issued by (name of charity) to the Estate.

The (accountants for the Company) estimate that the (name of charity) will receive a donation of shares valued at approximately $(amount).

Yours truly,

(Signature of Authorized Signing Person)

RELEASES AND INDEMNITY

Release

At some stage during the administration of an estate, a residuary beneficiary will receive a set of accounts to review. There are many reasons for delivering accounts, including to exonerate the estate trustee, to appease demanding beneficiaries, and to obtain approval of the compensation claim. At times, interim accounts with interim distributions are presented for approval as soon as appropriate during the administration.

The delivery of accounts is usually accompanied by a covering letter indicating that the accounts are enclosed for review along with a release. The covering letter may go on and request that the beneficiary sign the release and that upon its return the cheque for the beneficiary's share of the residue will be sent. Often, the covering letter also suggests that the funds will not be distributed until all the releases have been received from all of the beneficiaries.

What is a release? A release is requested in order to protect the estate trustee. The release binds the beneficiary's acceptance of the estate trustee's administration (absent fraud) of the estate. The estate trustee wants a release from the beneficiaries so that he or she can rest assured that the beneficiaries take no issue with his or her actions as estate trustee. By signing a release, the charity is confirming to the estate trustee that his or her actions have been reviewed and there are no questions or concerns (for the period) about the administration of the estate. A release with an indemnity goes further and requests that the charity indemnity or compensate the estate trustee if a beneficiary or third party challenges the actions of the estate trustee. Fraud by the estate trustee subsequently discovered is an exception to the strict effect of a release.

An estate trustee can request this sign-off at any stage and for any part of the administration of the estate. In practice, this request occurs when a set of accounts is delivered as it is the accounts that provide the information regarding the administration.

In order to better understand the release, a sample with commentary is reproduced. A release normally includes certain parts. The first part will read something like this:

> I, [signing officer who is authorized to bind the organization according to the by-laws] of the WBI Benevolent Foundation ("Foundation") hereby acknowledge that the Foundation has received the sum of Twenty-Five Thousand Dollars ($25,000) from Pamela Lyons, Estate Trustee of the Estate of Mary Young.

This is also called an acknowledgment. In this section the charity is "acknowledging" that it received a certain sum from the estate. The second part refers to the charity's agreement as to what the acceptance of that sum of money means to the charity now and in the future. It often reads something like this:

> The Foundation agrees that it has received these funds in full satisfaction and payment of such sum as given and bequeathed to the Foundation under the Will of Mary Young. The Foundation further agrees that the provisions of this release shall be binding on its successors and assigns.

The form of release that a charity often receives has been used by the solicitor to obtain individual beneficiary releases — only the name and the amount is changed. Be careful with the wording of the last sentence in the extract above. If the release is taken from an individual sample, the wording will read, "shall be binding on my respective heirs, executors, administrators and assigns". These additional words should be deleted because a charity, as a corporate entity, does not and will not have "heirs, executors, or administrators", only successors and assigns.

The next section is typically in the form of a release and will read something like this:

> And therefore the Foundation by its presents remise, release, quit claim, and forever discharge the said Pamela Lyons, her heirs and estate trustees of and from any and all actions, claims, accounts and demands whatsoever which it now or ever had against the said Pamela Lyons and the Estate of Mary Young in respect of or in connection with the Estate of Mary Young.

This is the section by which the charity releases the estate trustee from any known wrongdoing (absent fraud) of the administration of the estate. Note that the extract above (and the others) speaks in the language of a final release. If it is not a final distribution situation then, at a minimum, check to ensure that the release speaks in terms of an interim or partial distribution limited to the amount received and the appropriate time period.

The final section of the release is the actual signing off and will read something like this:

> In witness thereof I have hereunder set my hand and seal of the Foundation this ...... day of ...., 2003.
>
> WBI Benevolent Foundation
>
> Per: ....

Sometimes the signature section will include the request for a seal and a witness signature. If the charity is a corporation the seal should be sufficient without the need for a witness as well. (Historically, the seal served that purpose.) If no seal is presented, a witness is required.

If there are any doubts, the release should not be signed. Although an argument can be made later that the charity signed without really understanding what the release meant or without the assistance of legal counsel (*i.e.*, independent legal advice), it may not necessarily be successful where a charity subsequently realizes that it should not have signed the release. In case of doubt, questions should be asked or the release modified.

There is no standard legal form of the release (although certain similar language is common). A release can contain whatever the drafter, who is usually the solicitor for the estate trustee, wants to cover off. Accordingly, the release may include an indemnity (see below) or a long list of other acknowledgments, such as one relating to liability for outstanding income taxes, the waiving of a passing of accounts, and the future distribution of the holdback. Each acknowledgment should be reviewed very carefully.

Further, it should be remembered that as there is no standard form release, it is possible for a charity to modify the release to include language that better suits its purposes or the particular circumstances. This is just another legal document containing language that the parties can argue over and negotiate to everyone's satisfaction. Any changes should be initialled.

A release (subject to limited extenuating circumstances) usually means that the activities of the estate trustee during that particular period cannot be revisited. It is, therefore, extremely important to read the document each and every time and if in doubt, to obtain professional advice. In Ontario, a tariff provides that where legal advice is sought, some if not all of the costs of obtaining that advice (as determined by the tariff) are payable by the estate.

In some cases, a charity may wish to consider drafting its own form of release with the assistance of counsel and attempt to use this "standard form" release (modified to the particular estate) instead of the release presented for signature. This may minimize the time spent reviewing and modifying the releases each and every time. Further, a charity that wants to be proactive could present this "standard form" of release to the solicitor for the estate at the beginning of the administration of the estate indicating that this is the form of release that is acceptable to the charity and that it will sign at the appropriate time after reviewing the accounts, assuming the matter is uncontested. Being proactive allows the parties to resolve the language of the release early — not when the pressure is on to receive the distribution — and it also allows the charity to indicate to the estate trustee that the signing of the release is independent of the issuing of the distribution cheque.

As residuary beneficiaries constitute the only class of beneficiary concerned with the administration of the estate, only they should be requested to review the accounts and sign a release. Legatee beneficiaries may be asked to sign a receipt (and not a release) upon receiving their legacy. Sometimes there is confusion over this and a legatee will be asked to sign a release. Legatees should resist this request (although there may not be any practical objections to signing a release that limits the acknowledgment to the amount received once the legacy is received) and instead offer to sign a receipt.[33]

---

[33] See sample in Appendix 2.

The request to sign a release is an indulgence. The estate trustee is asking the charity to put its name on the "bottom line" — a function that was done by the judge in the past. Quite often, the covering letter requesting the "sign-off" also states that the beneficiary will not receive or is not entitled to receive the distribution until the release is signed. Sometimes, the release must also be signed by all the beneficiaries. A charity should not be pressured into signing the release. The role of reviewing the release and signing-off must be taken seriously. There is a Board of Directors who is ultimately responsible. A charity should not feel pressured to sign. After any holdback for contingencies, there is normally no reason why the estate trustee cannot distribute a significant amount of the residue. The release relates to the administration of the estate by the estate trustee and bears no relationship to beneficiaries' direct entitlement to its gift. If there are concerns about the accounts, a suggested response could be, "I would be pleased to issue a charitable receipt for [the amount to be distributed] when it is received and look forward to issuing that receipt as soon as possible, but I still have some questions regarding the administration which I believe I should address before the release is signed." If there is still doubt, then it is recommended that professional advice be obtained, for which, in Ontario, the costs may be recovered by tariff.

In Ontario, Courts have recognized this distinction. In *Brighter v. Brighter Estate*[34] an argument was made that the executrix in that case was justified in requiring a signed release as a precondition of final distribution to the beneficiary. The executrix also argued that if the beneficiary had been willing to sign a receipt, a partial or interim distribution would have been made. The Court severely criticized this position:

> ...Even accepting the [assertion of a receipt for a partial distribution], which somewhat strains credibility in the circumstances, there is no validity to either proposition. An executor's duty is to carry out the instructions contained in the will, which in this case was to distribute the residue equally among the three children of the testatrix. The executor has no right to hold any portion of the distributable assets hostage in order to exhort from a beneficiary approval or release of the executor's performance of duties as trustee, or the executor's compensation or fee. It is quite proper for an executor (or trustee, to use the current expression) to accompany payment with a release which the beneficiary is requested to

---

[34] [1998] O.J. No. 3144 (Ont. Gen. Div.) (QL).

execute. But it is quite another matter for the trustee to require execution before making payment; that is manifestly improper.[35]

Likewise, the court would have had equally strong language for the suggestion that no distributions will be forthcoming until all beneficiaries sign the release. Further, a beneficiary is not a "supplicant" required to ask an estate trustee to deliver the gifts that the Will provides, and should not be required to obtain the assistance of the Court to obtain payment of the gifts; the estate trustee should be forthcoming with the gifts. If not, then the estate trustee runs the risk of having to indemnify the beneficiary and the estate for the legal costs necessarily incurred to obtain the order for payment of his or her share of the estate. This indemnification is personal as it was the estate trustee's failure to perform his or her duty that caused the costs to be incurred.[36]

A proper response in situations where there are questions regarding the administration is to say that you would be pleased to issue a charitable tax receipt for the amount to be distributed when it is received, and that you look forward to issuing that receipt as soon as possible, but that in the meantime you have some questions regarding the administration that need to be addressed before the release can be signed.

Indemnity

A release may also include a request for an indemnity for the estate trustee. This is a contentious area and not always easy to resolve. Typically, it is understood that an estate trustee's personal liability is limited to the value of the assets, translated to mean that the estate trustee will be liable only to the extent that the trustee is entitled to be indemnified or exonerated out of the assets. Despite this understanding, estate trustees seek the comfort of a written indemnity (that may or may not be expressly limited to the share received from the assets of the estate).

The indemnity usually provides that the charity agrees that if, in the future, the estate trustee determines that there are further estate liabilities and no estate assets left to discharge them, then the charity will, in effect, reimburse the estate trustee for that liability. By the charity agreeing, in effect, to pay the liability, the estate trustee is relieved of any personal liability for these debts.

Historically, there was no need for an indemnity (or a release for that matter) as the Courts reviewed the administration and the estate trustee

---

[35] *Ibid.*, at para. 9.
[36] *Ibid.*, at para. 13.

could rely on the judgment obtained (again assuming no fraud). Further, at common law an estate trustee was entitled to an indemnity for liabilities properly incurred in carrying out the trust and that right was enforceable in equity against a beneficiary based on the principle that the beneficiary who gets the benefit of the trust should also bear its burdens. However, as formal passings of accounts are not always the norm today, the request for an indemnity is becoming more common.

Typical indemnity language will read like this:

> The Foundation on behalf of its successors and assigns does further undertake to indemnify and reimburse Pamela Lyons, in her capacity as estate trustee of the Estate of Mary Young, with respect to any claims which may be made against the Estate of Mary Young and for which the said Pamela Lyons may be found liable.

Ideally, the charity should not be asked to sign an indemnity. It is the estate trustee's responsibility to ensure that all the debts of the deceased have been paid before making any distribution. Sometimes this section is simply included because it is in the precedent. A charity should consider deleting this section before signing.

A charity could also make inquiries of the estate trustee as to what in particular he or she is concerned about. Is there a debt or pending action against the estate that may result in a further liability? Some comfort may be taken in the estate trustee's representation that he or she is not aware of any potential need for indemnification.

Income taxes are a joint liability of the estate trustee and the estate because of section 159 of the *Income Tax Act*. It may be because of this section that estate trustees are requesting an indemnity. If that is the case (*i.e.*, it is this particular liability that is of concern), then a charity should request that the holdback be made larger or that the indemnity reflect this particular liability, using language such as:

> The Foundation on behalf of its successors and assigns does further undertake to indemnify and reimburse Pamela Lyons, in her capacity as estate trustee of the Estate of Mary Young, for the payment of all income taxes which might be levied or assessed against the Estate (in excess of the holdback held in the Estate account, and) to the extent of the amount received from the Estate.

If there is any possibility that there are significant or potential liabilities, then an alternative course of action is to either delay the distribution or increase the holdback in order to cover the potential contingency.

Finally, a charity should consider whether its charter permits it to give an indemnity. In effect, giving an indemnity is like incurring a potential liability of an unknown amount. It could potentially put all of the charity's assets at risk. These assets are funds raised for its charitable purposes. Consider the following situation. The charity signs an unlimited indemnity upon receiving $1,000 from the Estate. Five years later the estate trustee advises the charity that the estate is facing a liability of $20,000 and asks the charity, as the sole beneficiary, to pay the liability. If the indemnity is upheld, where are the funds to pay this liability going to come from? Further, the charity could be faced with legal costs in dealing with the situation.

Hence, one practical compromise that many charities follow is, at a minimum, to limit the quantum of the indemnity to the amount received from the estate. Although this does put a figure on the amount at risk, it does not answer the question — where the funds will come from. Again, the complexity and risk of these indemnities speak to a practice of suggesting a form of release at the beginning of the administration and making inquiries as to the need for an indemnity before signing the document.

COSTS IN ESTATE PROCEEDINGS[37]

The costs involved in estate litigation can be just as onerous as the costs of civil litigation. There can be so many parties to the litigation that the logistics alone create an expensive administrative nightmare. Quite often the assumption is made that the estate will bear the costs of the litigation. Again, this is not a universal outcome. The nature and circumstances of the litigation will dictate who bears the costs.

Where the matter is one of Will interpretation, the courts have traditionally viewed this type of proceeding as being the "fault" of the deceased and so the estate should bear those costs. Note that more frequently the solicitor who drafted the Will is being joined into the proceedings (as it was really the solicitor who prepared the Will, not the deceased). In some cases, it may be the solicitor, as the losing party, who may bear the costs.

Where the matter is one of a Will challenge, the costs follow the typical route in litigation matters, *i.e.*, the costs follow the outcome. For example, if the challenger is unsuccessful and it was unreasonable for him or her to start and continue with the litigation, then it is possible that the challenger will be responsible not only for his or her own costs but also for those of the estate. Again, it depends on the circumstances. The important

---

[37] For more discussion, see Chapter 6.

thing to remember about costs is that they are ultimately a matter of the discretion of the court.

The scale of costs is also something to consider. In Ontario, it used to be that the discussion of costs was ordered in terms of party and party or solicitor and client scales. Typically, the estate trustee was entitled to his or her solicitor and client costs, which was interpreted to mean full recovery. A new cost grid was introduced in Ontario in January 2002 that uses the terms "partial indemnity" and "substantial indemnity", with the former relating to the old party and party scale and the latter to the solicitor and client scale. These scales have been converted into tariff-like rates that set maximum hourly rates depending on the scale.

For estate matters, an argument has been made that the substantial indemnity rate does not mean full indemnity, such that the costs of the estate trustee that were normally fully recoverable now are not. As a result, estate practitioners seek costs on a complete or full indemnity basis even though that scale is not part of the language of the new grid. The courts recognize this issue and, in the right circumstances continue to allow costs to be recovered on a complete indemnity basis.

ALBERTA

The comments stated earlier with respect to compensation, legal fees and costs apply in Alberta except as noted in this section.

PERSONAL REPRESENTATIVE'S COMPENSATION

Entitlement to Compensation

As stated earlier, the common law does not provide for payment of compensation to personal representatives. However, section 61 of the *Administration of Estates Act*[38] gives a personal representative the right to seek such compensation. Section 61 provides:

> 61(1) A judge may at any time by an order fix and give directions respecting the remuneration and compensation to be granted to a legal representative.
>
> (2) This section does not apply if the remuneration or compensation of a legal representative is fixed by the will.

---

[38] R.S.A. 2000, c. A-2.

The Surrogate Rules state[39] that if the Will sets out the amount of the personal representative's compensation, the personal representative must accept that amount of compensation or seek all of the beneficiaries' consent to vary the amount of compensation.[40]

If a gift (other than a residuary bequest) is contained in a Will in favour of a personal representative, there is a presumption in law that the gift was intended to be in lieu of compensation. The presumption may be rebutted by very slight evidence of contrary intention shown in the Will and by extrinsic evidence.[41] For example, the presumption may be rebutted where two out of three legal personal representatives are left benefits under a Will.[42]

Where the entitlement of a personal representative to compensation has been fixed by a provision in the Will, and the personal representative was one of the two witnesses to the Will, the gift is void by operation of section 13(1) of the *Wills Act*.[43] However, the personal representatives may still make an application to the court pursuant to section 61 of the *Administration of Estates Act* for compensation.

Where a deceased wishes the personal representative to receive compensation in addition to a gift under the Will, it is advisable to state this in the Will.

The entitlement of a personal representative to compensation may also be fixed by:

(a) an agreement (contract) in writing between the deceased and the personal representative (such contracts are often incorporated by reference into the Will); or
(b) an agreement between the personal representative and the beneficiaries.[44]

Amount of Compensation

If the amount of compensation is not fixed by the Will, by the contract, or by an agreement, the Surrogate Rules set out the general principles to be

---

[39] AR 130/95, Surrogate Rule 4, Schedule 1, Part 1.
[40] *Re Holmes Estate* (1959), 29 W.W.R. 238 (B.C.S.C.); *Williams v. Roy* (1885), 9 O.R. 534 (H.C.).
[41] *Canada Permanent Trust Co. v. Guinn* (1981), 10 E.T.R. 256 (B.C.S.C.).
[42] *Re Ross*, [1976] 3 W.W.R. 465 (B.C.S.C.).
[43] R.S.A. 2000, c. W-12.
[44] *French v. Toronto General Trusts Corp.*, [1924] 1 D.L.R. 288 (Ont. S.C.).

used when determining the personal representative's compensation.[45] The Rules do not give any percentages or dollar amounts for compensation:[46]

> Personal representatives may receive fair and reasonable compensation for their responsibility in administering an estate by performing the personal representatives' duties.

In this regard, the administration of the estate includes both the distribution of the estate and the conclusion of any trusts.

The Surrogate Rules provide the relevant factors that ought to be considered when setting the amount of compensation to be requested by the personal representative.[47] These factors are:

(a) the gross value of the estate;

(b) the amount of revenue receipts and disbursements;

(c) the complexity of the work involved and whether any difficult or unusual questions were raised;

(d) the amount of skill, labour, responsibility, technological support, and specialized knowledge required;

(e) the time expended;

(f) the number and complexity of tasks delegated to others;

(g) the number of personal representatives appointed in the will, if any.[48]

No precise rule can be laid down as to the amount of compensation a personal representative is entitled to ask for. Each case must be dealt with on its own merits.[49] A large estate may not necessarily mean a large compensation fee.[50]

If a lawyer performs some of the duties of the personal representative, the amount payable to the personal representative must be reduced accordingly.[51]

The Alberta Surrogate Court Committee, when re-drafting the Surrogate Rules in 1995, established a "Suggested Fee Guideline" for personal representatives. This Guideline sets fees based on percentages of the value of capital receipts and revenue receipts, and has often been used

---

[45] See Schedule 1, Part 1.
[46] Surrogate Rule 1(1), Schedule 1, Part 1.
[47] Surrogate Rule 2, Schedule 1, Part 1.
[48] See *Toronto General Trusts Corp. v. Central Ontario Railway Co.* (1905), 6 O.W.R. 350 (H.C.) for an elaboration of the above factors.
[49] *Re MacDonald Estate*, [1933] 1 W.W.R. 421 (Sask. C.A.).
[50] *Sproule v. Montreal Trust Co.*, [1979] 2 W.W.R. 289 (Alta. C.A.).
[51] Surrogate Rule 7, Schedule 1, Part 1.

by the courts as a convenient starting point to fix the personal representative's compensation. The Guidelines are as follows:[52]

Capital

On the first $250,000 of capital	3%-5%
On the next $250,000 of capital	2%-4%
On the balance	½ of 1% -3%

Revenue

On revenue receipts	4%-6%

Care and management

On the first $250,000 of capital	3/10-6/10 of 1%
On the next $250,000 of capital	2/10-5/10 of 1%
On the balance	1/10-4/10 of 1%

These percentages should only be used as a guideline, as stated by Haddad J.A. in *Sproule v. Montreal Trust Co.*:

> It would seem to me that the purpose of guidelines to a Surrogate Court should be to provide a means of checking compensation allowed in any given estate to ensure a measure of consistency within its territorial jurisdiction with other estates of comparable value where there is a similarity in the responsibilities discharged by the executors of such estates.

Additional compensation is also permitted:[53]

> Additional compensation may be allowed when personal representatives
> (a) are called upon to perform additional roles in order to administer the estate, such as exercising the powers of a manager or director of a company or business,
> (b) encounter unusual difficulties or situations, or
> (c) must instruct on litigation.

A personal representative may therefore be entitled to charge special fees for special services that are outside the realm of an ordinary administration. For example, a personal representative may be entitled to a special fee for preparing income tax returns, or for winding up a business. The amount of the special fee is dependent on the qualifications and expertise of the personal representative, and on the special service rendered to the estate by the personal representative.

---

[52] The Suggested Fee Guidelines can be found in the Legal Society of Alberta (LESA) Alberta Estate Administration Practice Manual Series.
[53] Surrogate Rule 3, Schedule 1, Part 1.

Keep in mind that the personal representative may receive compensation for care and management of estate property only if there is no outright distribution of the property at the date of death, and the trust is not varied by agreement among the affected beneficiaries or by the Court.[54]

There are some services, however, that the personal representative cannot charge against the estate. For example, the personal representative may not charge solicitors' fees for researching the law to find out what the personal representative may charge the estate for his or her compensation. Such services are for the personal benefit of the personal representative and not for the estate.[55]

If all of the affected beneficiaries of the estate agree with the personal representative's proposed compensation and expenses, the personal representative may pay themselves the compensation, whether it be on an interim or final basis. However, the personal representative must first give the beneficiaries a proposed compensation which will form part of the financial statements.[56] The approval of the proposed interim of final distribution may form part of the release which is signed by the beneficiaries. The personal representative may rely on releases signed by the beneficiaries for confirmation that the beneficiaries have approved the compensation schedule as set out in the financial statements.[57]

If it is not possible to obtain the approval of all the beneficiaries, the compensation must be determined by the Court during a passing of accounts.[58] Such an application is also appropriate where the beneficiaries approve the accounts and only take issue with the proposed compensation.

The compensation of a personal representative and his or her solicitor is treated by the Court as a lien or charge upon the estate. In the case of an insolvent estate, personal representative compensation and legal fees have priority after reasonable funeral and other testamentary expenses.

Where there are two or more personal representatives, the total compensation is determined in the same manner as if there had been one personal representative. Surrogate Rule 5 provides that:

> The compensation once determined must be shared among the personal representatives in proportions agreed to among the personal representatives or as ordered by the court.

---

[54] Surrogate Rule 1(3), Schedule 1, Part 1.
[55] *Re Preboy Estate* (1989), 72 Sask. R. 33 (Surr. Ct.), aff'd (1989), 74 Sask. R. 223 (C.A.).
[56] Surrogate Rule 98(1)(i).
[57] Surrogate Rule 101(b).
[58] Surrogate Rule 113(2)(c).

There is no reason why the compensation of two or more personal representatives could not be unequal having regard to the number and value of the services rendered by each.[59]

OUT-OF-POCKET EXPENSES

In addition to compensation, a personal representative is entitled to recover out-of-pocket expenses that he or she has properly and reasonably incurred during the administration, and in carrying out his or her duties, including:

> ...fees or commissions to agents, including lawyers, accountants, real estate agents, securities brokers, investment advisors, appraisers, auctioneers and other professionals, engaged to perform estate administration services or to buy or sell estate property.[60]

Any compensation received by the personal representative is taxable in his or her hands as income earned and must be declared in his or her tax return. However, the reimbursement of out-of-pocket expenses is not taxable in the hands of the personal representative. The personal representative should be advised to keep detailed records of invoices for the time expended on the administration of the estate, and to keep receipts for all out-of-pocket expenses (such as long-distance charges, mileage, postage and parking costs).

PRE-TAKING COMPENSATION AND OUT-OF-POCKET EXPENSES

Personal representatives, in anticipation of the compensation ultimately to be awarded by the Court or approved by the beneficiaries, commonly and from time to time pay themselves compensation. This is particularly true where there is no other compelling reason to pass accounts, and is especially routine as it relates to compensation on income. There is, however, no statutory authority in Alberta to permit such pre-taking of compensation without prior authority from either the Court or the beneficiaries. Therefore, personal representatives should not pre-take compensation unless the Will allows it, or the Court or all of the beneficiaries have consented to the amount of compensation or have authorized the

---

[59] *Re Macdonald Estate*, [1926] 1 W.W.R. 556 (Alta. C.A.); *Montreal Trust Co. v. Sproule* (1979), 5 E.T.R. 153 (Q.B.), [1979] 4 W.W.R. 670 (Alta. C.A.).
[60] Surrogate Rule 9, in Schedule 1, Part 1.

pre-taking.[61] A personal representative may ask the beneficiaries to allow him or her to pre-take compensation on the basis of an agreement. Such requests should be considered very carefully, and, generally, should be time limited (*i.e.*, for the next two years). When acting for a beneficiary it is not generally recommended that such agreements be entered into.

There is statutory authority to require the executor to reimburse the estate for any excess compensation pre-taken. The Surrogate Rules further provide:

> If all or any part of the amount of compensation paid to a personal representative under subrule (1) is later reduced by the Court, the personal representative must repay the disallowed amount immediately to the estate with interest at a rate and for a period set by the Court.[62]

In contrast, pre-taking reimbursements for proper out-of-pocket expenses without authorization is allowed.

LEGAL FEES

Estate Administration

If the administration of an estate is uncontested, the "estate lawyer" is the solicitor for the personal representative and not for the estate. The distinction is that the personal representative is a legal entity and an estate is not. Therefore, the personal representative has to take into account the interests of all of the beneficiaries, the claims of all creditors and claimants, the intention of the testator and his or her own compensation.

Sometimes there is a suggestion in the Will as to whom the testator would like to act as solicitor for his or her estate (usually the solicitor who drafted the Will). This suggestion is not binding on the personal representative.

> A personal representative named in a Will is entitled to choose which solicitor they will retain for the purposes of assisting in the administration of the estate. The testator's direction in his Will appointing a person as a solicitor for the estate is of no consequence.[63]

---

[61] Surrogate Rule 6(1), Schedule 1, Part 1.
[62] Surrogate Rule 6(2), Schedule 1, Part 1.
[63] *Foster v. Elsley* (1881), 19 Ch. D. 518.

Under the Surrogate Rules, a solicitor is entitled to remuneration for the services rendered to the personal representative of an estate.[64] The Surrogate Rules provide that the lawyer may charge fees for "core legal services" and "non-core legal services" in the administration of an estate.[65] Furthermore, reasonable costs incurred by a lawyer as disbursements and other charges related to performing services in either of these categories are allowed in addition to any legal fees charged.[66]

The Surrogate Rules also set out some guidelines for lawyer's compensation.[67] The personal representative of the estate and the lawyer should discuss the terms of the retention before the lawyer is retained and should agree to the categories of services that the lawyer will perform and to an arrangement of fees for each of those categories.[68]

The Surrogate Rules divide lawyer's fees into "core legal services" and non-core legal services.[69] Core legal services are defined as the legal services normally rendered by a lawyer for a personal representative in connection with the administration of an estate. Non-core legal services are defined as legal services rendered by a lawyer for a personal representative that are in addition to the core legal services required in the administration of an Estate. The Surrogate Rules state:[70]

Table 1

(a) Core Legal Services

1   Receiving instructions from the personal representatives.
2   Giving the personal representatives information and advice on all matters in connection with the administration of the estate, including the following:
    (a) the basis for the lawyer's fees for the different categories of legal services;
    (b) the basis for the personal representatives' compensation and preparation of the proposed compensation schedule;
    (c) providing a copy of this Schedule to the personal representatives.
3   Reviewing the will or the provisions of the Intestate Succession Act with the personal representative.
4   Receiving information from personal representatives about the following:
    (a) the deceased;
    (b) the beneficiaries;

---

[64] See Schedule 1, Part 2.
[65] Surrogate Rule 1, Schedule 1, Part 2.
[66] Surrogate Rule 6, Schedule 1, Part 2.
[67] See Schedule 1, Part 2.
[68] Surrogate Rule 3, Schedule 1, Part 2.
[69] Surrogate Rule 1, Schedule 1, Part 2.
[70] Ibid.

Chapter 3: Legal Fees, Compensation, Taxes, Releases and Costs 101

   (c) the estate property;
   (d) the deceased's debts;
   (e) minors.
5   Obtaining details of all the property and debts of the deceased for the purposes of an application to the court, including the following:
   (a) the full nature and value of the property of the deceased as at the date of death including the value of all land and buildings and a summary of outstanding mortgages, leases and any other encumbrances;
   (b) any pensions, annuities, death benefits and any other benefits;
   (c) any debts owed by the deceased as at the date of death;
   (d) preparing all required documents for grant applications;
   (e) preparing notices to all beneficiaries;
   (f) arranging for surviving spouse to receive notices under the Family Relief Act and Matrimonial Property Act, if necessary;
   (g) arranging for dependants to receive notices under the Family Relief Act, if necessary;
   (h) attending on signing of application for grant, filing with the court, payment of fees and dealing with the clerk;
   (i) advising the Public Trustee, if necessary;
   (j) receiving the grant.
6   Preparing documents to advertise for claimants, arranging for advertising and obtaining affidavit of publication.
7   Preparing declarations of transmission and powers of attorney for stocks and bonds transferrable under the Alberta grant.
8   Preparing transmission and transfer documents for land transferrable under the Alberta grant.
9   Preparing all other documents required to transmit and transfer property transferrable under the Alberta grant.
10 Advising the personal representatives on any trusts required by the will.
11 Advising the personal representatives to prepare and file tax returns.
12 Confirming receipt of clearance certificates from Revenue Canada.
13 Submitting personal representatives' financial statements for approval to the beneficiaries on an informal basis.
14 Preparing releases and obtaining and filing them with the court if so instructed by the personal representatives.
15 Generally advising the personal representatives on all matters referred to in this Table.

Table 2
Non-Core Legal Services

1   Acting as conveyancing lawyer on any sale of land.
2   Acting as lawyer on the sale of other property or businesses.
3   Preparing personal representatives' financial statements for submission to residuary beneficiaries.

4 Preparing all documents and acting for the personal representatives in any court proceedings involving the estate, including but not limited to the following:
   (a) formal proof of a will;
   (b) formal passing of accounts;
   (c) all other contentious matters.
5 Negotiating with any taxing authorities in Alberta or elsewhere with respect to the assessment and payment of any taxes or duties levied against the deceased, the estate or the beneficiaries and preparing all documents in connection with the negotiations.
6 Arranging to obtain a resealed or ancillary grant in another jurisdiction.
7 Preparing all documents and obtaining a resealed or ancillary grant in Alberta.
8 Preparing all documents and obtaining a grant of double probate.
9 Preparing all documents and obtaining a grant of trusteeship of minors' estates.
10 Dealing with any claims by claimants.
11 Setting up any trusts required by the will and arranging for the reimbursement of the trustees for services rendered to the trusts.
12 Identifying property not forming part of the estate but passing by survivorship or passing directly to a named beneficiary outside the will, including
   (a) preparing documentation to transfer land and other property held in joint tenancy to the surviving tenants;
   (b) preparing documentation to pass property to designated beneficiaries outside the will.
13 Arranging for any other legal services not included in Table 1.
14 Generally advising the personal representative on all matters referred to in this Table.

Although the Surrogate Rules do not provide specific fees that may be charged for the two categories of legal services, they do provide a list of factors that are relevant when determining the fees charged by a solicitor:[71]

(a) the complexity of the work involved and whether any difficult or novel questions were raised;

(b) the amount of skill, labour, responsibility and specialized knowledge required;

(c) the lawyer's experience in estate administration;

(d) the number and importance of documents prepared or perused;

(e) whether the lawyer performed services away from the lawyer's usual place of business or in unusual circumstances;

(f) the value of the estate;

(g) the amount of work performed in connection with jointly held or designated assets;

---

[71] Surrogate Rule 5, Schedule 1, Part 2.

(h) the results obtained;
(i) the time expended;
(j) whether or not the lawyer and the personal representative concluded an agreement and whether the agreement is reasonable in all the circumstances.

The fee guideline suggests that if the solicitor performs only the normal core legal services, the fees that can be charged consist of a base fee of $2,250 and an estate value component, being a percentage fee of .05 per cent of the gross value of the estate for estates up to $150,000, or 1 per cent of the gross value of the estate for estates over $150,000. It is important to note that there is no split on the percentage. What this means is that if an estate is valued at $200,000, the 1 per cent would be applied to the whole gross value of the estate, not just to the amount (in this case, $50,000) in excess of $150,000.

It is important to know that lawyers are not bound by these fee guidelines. The guidelines are merely a starting point to calculate fees for the services provided.

The reason that the fee guidelines are divided between base fee and estate value component is that the estate value component is designed to increase at a point where the size of the estate is likely to introduce more complexity in its administration. When calculating the gross value of the estate, the value of the following property ought not to be included:

(a) all property held in joint tenancy by the deceased and another person;
(b) all property passing directly to a named beneficiary outside of the Will;
(c) Canada Pension Plan payments to a spouse or child of the deceased; and
(d) property that has not passed through the hands of the personal representative.

If the estate contains property outside Alberta, then consideration ought to be given for the fees to be charged for the services provided in respect to dealing with such property. Property outside Alberta may still be the responsibility of the personal representative, and therefore the solicitor may need to make an application in another jurisdiction for an ancillary grant or for resealing the Alberta grant. It is important to remember that property located in another jurisdiction will not be listed in the Alberta Application for Probate or Administration. Such property will not form part of the aggregate value of the estate used to calculate the fees. That is why it is important to set the fees for such additional services at the same time as the fees for the two categories already discussed are set.

The guidelines suggest that the fees for non-core legal services are to be set on a *quantum meruit* basis.

Solicitors are also entitled to charge fees for any personal representative's duties they are required to perform.[72] If the solicitor was instructed to perform duties that the personal representative was to have performed, the personal representative's compensation should be decreased proportionately.[73] The personal representative should be clearly advised of this fact in the retainer letter. Personal representative's duties are defined in the Surrogate Rules as a list of tasks that a personal representative normally performs.[74]

When a solicitor is appointed as the personal representative under a Grant, that solicitor will be entitled to receive compensation for acting as the personal representative. As well, he or she may charge additional fees for the core and non-core legal services performed for the estate.[75]

Form of Solicitor's Account

When a solicitor renders an account to the personal representative, the solicitor is required to provide a written statement of fees, disbursements, G.S.T. and other charges. The account should also show the details of the services performed, together with a copy of Schedule 1, Part 2 of the Surrogate Rules.[76]

The personal representative is liable to pay the solicitor's account, but he or she may be reimbursed by the estate, provided the costs are reasonably and properly incurred.

Assessing the Solicitor's Account

The personal representatives, and not the beneficiaries, may "tax" or "assess" the lawyer's fees in the normal manner under Rules 627 to 658 of the Alberta Rules of Court.[77] The taxing officer may increase or decrease

---

[72] Surrogate Rule 2, Schedule 1, Part 2.
[73] Surrogate Rule 7, Schedule 1, Part 2.
[74] See the table at the end of Schedule 1, Part 1, "Personal Representative's Duties". See also Chapter 2, "Estate Administration", Alberta Section.
[75] Surrogate Rule 4, Schedule 1, Part 2.
[76] Surrogate Rule 7(1), Schedule 1, Part 2.
[77] AR 390/68.

fees, disbursements or other charges.[78] The statement of account must be brought before the taxing officer by the solicitor or the personal representative prior to the taxation in a document called an Appointment for Taxation. If a beneficiary disputes the solicitor's account, the beneficiary can raise it at the passing of accounts but not at the Taxation.[79]

An account must be taxed within the limitation period, unless the court orders otherwise. Rule 647 of the Alberta Rules of Court provides:

> Unless the Court otherwise orders no bill of costs is subject to taxation
>
> (a) after judgment has been obtained in respect thereof, or,
>
> (b) if it is unpaid after one year from the date of delivery thereof, or
>
> (c) if it was fully paid before the completion of the services for which it was rendered, after six months from the date of completion or the delivery of the bill, whichever is later, or,
>
> (d) if it was fully paid following the completion of the services, after six months from delivery.

The limitation period does not apply to the passing of accounts where a beneficiary disputes the legal fees incurred by the personal representative.

COSTS IN ESTATE LITIGATION

Common examples of estate litigation are formal proof of a Will, contested motions for advice and directions and *Dependants Relief Act*[80] applications. All matters relating to estates must be dealt with by the Court of Queen's Bench (Surrogate Matter).[81] Contentious matters are dealt with in Part 2 of the Surrogate Rules. Part 34 of the Alberta Rules of Court deals expressly with estate administration matters. Alberta Rules of Court 417(2) and 601 are the general costs provisions that give the Court complete discretion in the matter of awarding costs. There are also a number of Surrogate Rules that deal specifically with costs.

---

[78] Surrogate Rule 8, Schedule 1, Part 2.
[79] *Re Bullock Estate* (1954), 12 W.W.R. (N.S.) 551 (B.C.S.C.).
[80] The title and chapter number of the *Family Relief Act*, R.S.A. 2000, c. F-5 was amended by the *Adult Interdependent Relationships Act*, S.A. 2002, c. A-4.5, s. 35 to the *Dependants Relief Act*, S.A. 2002, c. D-10.2. The *Adult Interdependent Relationships Act* came into force on June 1, 2003, except for s. 17 which came into force on January 1, 2003 and except for sections 26, 52, 60 and 71 which are not yet in force as of June 2003.
[81] S.A. 2000, c. 20.

1. Rule 62(3) provides that the costs of a lawyer appointed to represent a class of parties under Rule 62(2) may be paid from the estate only if specifically ordered by the Court.

2. Rule 69 (Division 1, General) allows the court to order security for costs to be posted by any party at any stage of proceedings under Division 1.

3. Rule 74(2) allows costs to be ordered against a caveator if the caveat is frivolous or vexatious.

4. Rule 89 entitles a witness to an appearance fee and allows for a preparation fee.

5. Rule 90(h) allows costs to be ordered against a person who requires formal proof of a Will if the application is frivolous or vexatious or causes undue delay.

6. Rule 113(2)(k) allows the Court to direct payment of costs on a passing of accounts.

The court, in determining whether to award costs to a certain party, will consider all of the circumstances of the dispute, including:

1. the source of the dispute;
2. the conduct of each of the parties;
3. whether each party had a personal interest in the outcome, or was disinterestedly performing a duty; and
4. whether it was reasonable to commence or continue litigation.

If the reason for the litigation is the testator or the residuary beneficiaries, the costs may properly be paid out of the estate. If there are sufficient and reasonable grounds to question, for example, either the signing of the Will or the capacity of the testator, a party, even though unsuccessful, may properly be relieved from the costs.[82] However, if undue influence or fraud is alleged, and the allegations are not substantiated, costs will be awarded against the alleger of the undue influence or fraud.

---

[82] *Mitchell v. Gard* (1863), 164 E.R. 1280.

Costs could even be assessed against a solicitor personally if he or she takes a case to Court without proof of the alleged fraud or undue influence.[83]

A personal representative is entitled to be indemnified from the estate for all costs that have been reasonably incurred, including an application to the court for advice and direction regarding the administration of the estate, and for the costs of an action reasonably defended.[84]

Because costs are always in the discretion of the Court, the personal representative may not always be entitled to be indemnified for his or her costs from the estate.[85] For example, where a personal representative sued on behalf of an insolvent estate and failed, he was held personally liable for the costs of the action.[86] When a personal representative is bringing or defending an action on behalf of the estate, the personal representative would be well advised to obtain the consent of the beneficiaries to proceed with the matter and obtain an indemnity in case the action is unsuccessful, or to obtain the direction of the Court before bringing or defending the action in order to ensure that he or she will be fully indemnified from the estate for the costs incurred.

There is an increasing tendency for the Courts to apply the same rules to estate litigation as to general civil litigation, with the result that the losing party bears his or her own costs, and pays the costs of the unsuccessful party as well.

It is not uncommon, however, for the court to award costs on a solicitor-client basis from the estate to all parties in a family relief action.[87]

BRITISH COLUMBIA

The comments in this chapter with respect to legal and professional fees, taxes and releases also apply in British Columbia. However, where you have a British Columbia estate, the statutory compensation available to executors, administrators and trustees (who for consistency in language are referred to in this part as estate trustees) is different. As well, while the

---

[83] *Re Bisyk* (1980), 32 O.R. (2d) 281 (H.C.), aff'd. (1981), 32 O.R. (2d) 281n (C.A.); *Orleski v. Reid*, [1985] 3 W.W.R. 560 (Sask. Q.B.), affd. [1989] 3 W.W.R. 186 (Sask. C.A.).
[84] *Thompson v. Lamport*, [1945] 2 D.L.R. 545 (S.C.C.); *Goodman Estate v. Geffen*, [1991] No. 14, W.A.C. No. 81 (S.C.C.) at 321.
[85] *Scott v. Cresswell*, [1976] 3 W.W.R. 382 at 384 (Alta. S.C. App. Div.).
[86] *Shafer v. Jones (No. 2)*, [1950] 2 W.W.R. 625 (Alta. S.C.).
[87] *Stone Estate (Public Trustee of) v. Stone Estate* (1994), 154 A.R. 307 at 315 (Q.B.), var'd (1997), 54 Alta. L.R. (3d) 225 (C.A.); *Raniseth (Public Trustee of) v. Raniseth Estate* (1990), 80 Alta. L.R. (2d) 274 (Q.B.); and *Webb v. Webb Estate* (1995), 28 Alta. L.R. (3d) 110 (Q.B.).

principles of costs in estate proceedings are similar, the terminology with respect to costs is different.

COMPENSATION

In British Columbia, the principles governing compensation for estate trustees derived from statute are set out in section 88 of the *Trustee Act*.[88] Section 88 provides that an estate trustee is entitled to a "fair and reasonable allowance, not exceeding 5% on the gross aggregate value, including capital and income, of all the assets of the estate" for his or her "care, pains and trouble and his or her time spent in and about" the estate. The amount may be set by the Court (or Registrar of the Court if so directed by the Court) at a passing of accounts from "time to time". As in Ontario, it is at the stage of presenting the accounts that an estate trustee can claim and receive compensation.

He or she can also claim an annual two-fifths of 1 per cent care and management fee on the average market value of the assets.[89] The comments earlier in this chapter with respect to care and management fees also apply in British Columbia.

Section 88 does not govern the remuneration of an administrator *pendente lite*[90] or an administrator *ad colligenda bona*.[91]

Section 88 is also not applicable when the compensation has been fixed by the instrument creating the trust.[92] Therefore, if the testator has fixed the compensation in the Will, the amount stated is what the estate trustee will get (unless the beneficiaries agree otherwise).

Section 88 will also not apply where an agreement has been made between the testator and estate trustee, or where an agreement has been made between the estate trustee and beneficiaries after the testator's death. Where there is a corporate trustee, it is common for the corporate trustee to try to get the testator to sign a fee or compensation agreement at the time the Will is executed, which agreement is usually referred to in the Will. While there is no statutory recognition of these agreements in British

---

[88] R.S.B.C. 1996, c. 464.
[89] *Ibid.*, s. 88(3).
[90] *Wright v. Canada Trust Co.* (1984), 55 B.C.L.R. 349 (S.C.), affd. (1985), 21 E.T.R. 80 (B.C.C.A.), which held that an administrator *pendente lite* is entitled to such reasonable remuneration as the Court thinks fit under s. 10 of the *Estate Administration Act*, R.S.B.C. 1996, c. 122.
[91] *Re Shalapay Estate* (1995), 3 B.C.L.R. (3d) 217 (S.C.), which held that an administrator *ad colligenda bona* is entitled to reasonable remuneration rather than a percentage of the estate.
[92] *Trustee Act*, R.S.B.C. 1996, c. 464, s. 90.

Columbia, they are generally accepted by the courts. These agreements do tend to allow greater compensation than the section 88 rates.

The value of the estate for the purposes of calculating remuneration on capital under section 88 is the realized value of the original assets of the estate. This value means the gross proceeds of sale of the assets if they have been sold or, if an asset has been distributed *in specie* to a beneficiary, its value at the date of distribution.[93]

If there are unrealized original assets when remuneration is being sought, the assets can be valued at the time of passing and interim remuneration awarded on that value. If the value is different when the asset is ultimately realized or distributed, then there has to be an adjustment.

While it is common for an estate trustee to receive 5 per cent of income receipts as remuneration, it is not common for a full 5 per cent capital fee to be approved. The five factors previously referred to in this chapter will be considered in determining the capital fee, namely, the size of the estate, the care and responsibility involved, the time spent performing the duties, the skill and ability shown and the results obtained or degree of success in the administration.

Where there are two or more estate trustees, the total remuneration is determined in the same manner as if there had been one, and usually they agree as to how the total remuneration is to be shared. The Registrar, on the passing of accounts, can also be asked to make a recommendation in this regard.[94]

Maximum remuneration will never be awarded before the completion of an administration because it leaves no allowance for a succeeding estate trustee and because it cannot take into account subsequent performance.

COSTS IN ESTATE PROCEEDINGS

In British Columbia, "special costs" take the place of solicitor and client costs. An award of "special costs" means the person awarded costs will get all or almost all of his or her actual legal costs. Under the *Supreme Court Rules*, however, it is provided that costs payable out of a fund in which others are interested are payable as party and party costs unless the Court

---

[93] *Re Laing* (1997), 3 B.C.L.R. 105 (S.C).
[94] If there is to be no passing of accounts, it could also be settled by the Court on an application under s. 89 of the *Trustee Act*, R.S.B.C. 1996, c. 464, or by an application under Rule 10 of the *Supreme Court Rules*, B.C. Reg. 221/90.

otherwise orders.[95] Therefore, a specific Court Order is required. The only exception is where costs are payable for non-contentious business under Rule 61, in which case they must be assessed as special costs.[96]

In practice, however, estate practitioners seek special costs on a full indemnity basis even though that is not the language of the Rules, and in the right circumstances, Courts do allow costs to be recovered on a full indemnity basis.

---

[95] *Supreme Court Rules*, B.C. Reg. 221/90, Rule 57(1)(b) and (c).
[96] *Ibid.*, Rules 57(5), 61.

Chapter 4

ESTATE ACCOUNTING

ONTARIO

At an appropriate time (which varies depending on the nature of the estate), an estate trustee will provide an accounting of his or her activities to the beneficiaries.

It is the fundamental obligation of an estate trustee to maintain proper accounts. This is a common law obligation been codified in the Ontario *Rules of Civil Procedure*,[1] which states that an estate trustee must "keep accurate records of the assets and transactions in the estate".[2]

The maintenance of accounts is an absolute duty owed to the beneficiaries. It can be satisfied by maintaining proper accounts separate and apart from any other accounts the estate trustee may have, preserving receipts or vouchers to support the transactions, making the vouchers available for inspection, and delivering the accounting at appropriate and regular intervals. However, this obligation is to maintain accounts, not to submit them to the Court for approval (unless requested by a beneficiary or court ordered). The estate trustee should also produce the accounting and provide accurate information on a regular basis[3] when reasonably requested by the beneficiaries. If the estate trustee acts in breach of this duty, then they risk being removed as estate trustee and being personally held liable for any wrongdoing.

Correspondingly, a beneficiary has the right to inspect and investigate the accounts, including an examination of the vouchers or back-up documentation. At any time during the administration, a beneficiary is entitled to complete and accurate information and an answer to any reasonable question. This right exists clear of any solicitor-client privilege

---

[1] R.R.O. 1990, Reg. 194.
[2] *Ibid.*, Rule 74.17.
[3] *Barkin v. Royal Trust Co.* (2002), 45 E.T.R. (2d) 1 (Ont. S.C.J.); *Re Ballard Estate* (1994), 20 O.R. (3d) 350 (Gen. Div.).

claim that documents containing professional advice taken by the estate trustees as trustees are producible because the documents contain advice taken by the trustee for the beneficiaries.[4] A personal representative should inform the beneficiaries of this right and voluntarily disclose any breaches of trust. With accurate accounts, the beneficiaries can determine the status of the administration of the estate at any time.

Where all residual beneficiaries are competent adults, they, as beneficiaries, can approve the accounts or waive the requirement for an accounting. Where there are incapable or minor beneficiaries or beneficiaries who do not wish to consent, the estate trustee will have no choice but to go to court to have his or her accounts approved by the Court. This presentment of the accounts to Court is called the "passing of accounts".

The "passing" or "audit" of accounts refers to the presentation of formal accounts in proper form to the beneficiaries and Court, which are either approved (*i.e.*, passed) in the form presented; amended by Court Order and passed in revised form; or not passed. An estate trustee may voluntarily "pass accounts" or may be compelled to do so. Although the estate trustee's obligation is not to pass accounts, but rather to maintain them, this obligation is not discharged until the accounts are approved.

The passing of accounts process can be initiated by the estate trustee or by a beneficiary. A beneficiary is also entitled to retain counsel to assist them in this process. Where counsel is retained, part of the costs (based on whether the matter is contentious or not, as discussed later in this chapter), are automatically recoverable from the estate.

In complicated estates, it is always prudent for the estate trustee to pass accounts. The accounting process provides the opportunity for beneficiaries to gain knowledge and review the transactional details of the estate's administration. Such detail is only relevant to those entitled to the residue, as the residue is the "net" amount remaining after the realization of assets and the payment of liabilities. It is those transactions that need to be reviewed in order to ensure satisfaction with the calculation of the "net" amount. Therefore, a beneficiary who is entitled to a fixed amount, such as a legacy, or gift *in specie*, and has received their entitlement, will not be concerned with the other transactions of the estate and the accounts. Once the legacy or *in specie* gift is received, the beneficiary has no further interest in the estate, has no right or need to review the accounts, and will not receive them for review.

---

[4] *O'Rourke v. Darbishire*, [1920] A.C. 581 (H.L.), quoted with approval in *Barkin v. Royal Trust Co.* (2002), 45 E.T.R. (2d) 1 (Ont. S.C.J.).

PURPOSE

Incorporated into the Ontario Application for a Certificate of Appointment of Estate Trustee is an oath which is sworn by each estate trustee that he or she will "...administer the deceased person's property according to law and render a complete and true account of my administration when lawfully required". Hence, accounts are normally voluntarily produced to provide beneficiaries with the details of the administration of the estate, to exonerate the trustees from liability and to request the beneficiaries' approval of the compensation claimed.

The purpose of preparing and passing accounts is to provide the beneficiaries with an accounting of all of the transactions that occurred during the administration of the estate. Once approved, the estate trustee can be assured that his or her actions for that period have been accepted by the beneficiaries. Thus, the beneficiaries can take no issue with the steps taken in administering the estate up to that point, and the opportunity to criticize or ask questions ends, unless fraud is subsequently discovered. A beneficiary may be able to argue that they were not fully informed or unable to have the benefit of legal advice at the time, but once that release is signed, this is a difficult argument to make. The success of these arguments depends on the circumstances of the administration, the nature of the subsequently determined facts and the experience level of the staff person involved at the organization.

The presentment of accounts also allows an estate trustee to claim and receive compensation. A detailed discussion of compensation is found in Chapter 3.

TIMING

Accounts are usually passed towards the end of an uncomplicated outright distribution type of estate. In an estate with an outright distribution, there is usually at least one accounting before a major distribution to the beneficiaries is made. If funds have been retained for outstanding issues or a final Tax Clearance Certificate, a further and final accounting will be provided when the conditions that necessitated the holdback have been resolved and the funds can be released.

On longer administrations, or where trusts are involved, accounts are passed periodically. In estates where there is an ongoing trust, accounts should be rendered on a regular basis once the initial work connected with the administration of the estate has been completed by the estate trustees and the investment plans are in place. Subsequent accounts are usually provided periodically thereafter, depending on the individual trust circumstances. A time frame of three to five years for each passing of accounts is fairly common. These accounts are called "interim" accounts and are specific to a particular period of time.

COMPELLING A PASSING OF ACCOUNTS

At any time into the administration of the estate (at least six months after death), a beneficiary may request an accounting from the estate trustee. This request may be by letter to the estate trustee, or if the communications have been with the solicitor for the estate, to the solicitor. The response should be a letter advising when the accounts will be delivered.

In Ontario, it is a good idea at this stage to request that the accounts, if possible, be provided in "court-format". Asking for them in "court-format" means asking for them to be presented in the format required by the *Rules of Civil Procedure* (discussed below). This allows for a standardized review process and avoids the need to convert the accounts into this format if it turns out that the estate trustee must pass the accounts in court. A Court will only accept accounts for passing in the format set out in the *Rules of Civil Procedure*.

It is possible that an estate trustee may balk at providing the accounts in "court-format". At this stage, if the estate appears uncomplicated, then a beneficiary may not need to pursue that request. However, the estate trustee should be advised that if a formal passing is required, then they will be required to put the accounts in proper form and that the cost of doing so is their "cost", *i.e.*, it is not a cost borne directly by the estate, but rather is paid from the compensation received as estate trustee.

Quite often, a beneficiary is advised that the estate trustee would be happy to convert the accounts into "court-format", but that the costs of doing so will be borne by the beneficiary making the request directly or by the estate. This is not an accurate statement — an estate trustee should not be suggesting to a beneficiary that the costs of putting accounts in proper form is a cost that is anyone else's responsibility but the estate trustee's. If requested, a beneficiary is entitled to get the accounts in proper "court-format" and is not required to pay for it directly (*i.e.*, as a credit against the beneficiary's share of the residue or as a direct invoice) or indirectly as an additional charge to the estate.

If he or she meets with resistance, a beneficiary may consider retaining counsel to assist in obtaining the accounts. At times, a letter from the beneficiary's counsel carries more weight. Discussions counsel-to-counsel can produce results short of having to rely on the more formal avenues available to compel the production of accounts.

In Ontario, if the accounts are not provided when reasonably requested by the beneficiaries, the trustees can be compelled by the court to produce their accounts for formal audit. Rule 74.15(1)(h) of the *Rules of Civil Procedure* provides that any person having a financial interest in the estate may request a Court Order requiring or citing an estate trustee to pass his or her accounts. This procedure is one of the Orders for Assistance provided in Rule 74 of the *Rules of Civil Procedure*. It is a straightforward process and should be able to be completed at a reasonable cost.

A beneficiary normally retains the assistance of counsel to prepare the materials and obtain the Order. The Order is obtained by way of motion to the Court and is usually made without notice to the estate trustee. The materials that need to be prepared consist of a Notice of Motion (which sets out the relief sought from the Court and the grounds for such relief) and an affidavit filed in support of the motion. This affidavit should be from the "client" or beneficiary and should set out the facts behind the request for an order compelling the accounts to be produced. The affidavit will set out the attempts of the beneficiary (and solicitor, if relevant) to obtain the accounts. It is, therefore, extremely important to keep a record of all attempts, whether by telephone, e-mail or letter, to obtain the accounts and the response (or lack of response) received. As well, a system should be in place to ensure that the follow-up requests are made on a timely basis (*i.e.*, every 30 days at first and then with more frequency if no response is being received). The file should be well maintained — the more detailed information that can be put in the affidavit, the more persuasive the motion material and the more likely the Court will grant the Order.

A typical Order requires that the estate trustee, within a certain time period (*i.e.*, 30 to 60 days), deliver accounts for the period set out in the Order and it may also require the estate trustee to file an Application to Pass Accounts within a certain period of time.

If made without notice, the motion (upon payment of a filing fee) is filed with the Court with a draft order without having to give the estate trustee notice that the Order is being sought. The motion proceeds without a formal hearing or over-the-counter. If the judge who reviews the material is satisfied, he or she will sign the draft order. That Order is then "issued and entered" with the Court and can be "served" (sent) to the estate trustee. Upon receipt, the estate trustee must comply with the terms of the Order.

If the estate trustee ignores the Order, a beneficiary may seek an Order that finds the estate trustee in contempt of a Court Order and/or removes them as estate trustee. That Order is also sought by way of motion or application, but would (unless the circumstances are so egregious) be made on notice to the estate trustee.

Compelling an estate trustee to pass accounts also provides a forum for the suspected and real concerns about the administration of the issue to be resolved by a Court, if the parties are unable to resolve them informally. The ability, therefore, to obtain this Order, cannot be underestimated and is a standard tool for any practitioner working in this area.

FORMAT

Estate accounts provide detailed information with respect to the assets held in the estate for a particular period of time. The accounts are prepared on a cash basis. There is no "balance sheet" of assets and liabilities, or "income statement" of income and disbursements.[5]

The accounts simply provide, at any given time, what assets remain unrealized and what has been done with the assets that have been realized. The entries consist of a detailed listing of every transaction in that period, including the realization of original assets, payment of debts and investments made by estate trustees, in chronological order. Although difficult at times to distinguish, the receipts and expenses of an estate are divided between capital and income (revenue). Speaking generally, capital is considered to be the original assets of the deceased and income is the asset generated by the capital.

Difficulties can arise when it comes to allocated expenses, such as, for example, repairs to maintain a property. Typically, ongoing maintenance expenses (*i.e.*, lawn cutting or snow removal) are charged to income and the long-term capital expenses (*i.e.*, repairs to roof or furnace) to capital. This distinction is more important when one beneficiary has a life interest in a property and another has the capital interest.

Estate accounts are considerably different from the common accounting format provided by accounting professionals, which are typically in the form of a summary at one given point in time. Common reports included in accountants' financial statements include the Balance Sheet, Income Statement and Statement of Retained Earnings. Accountants' financial statements commonly also include asset depreciation and income accrual.

---

[5] For an example, see the "corrected version" of the accounts provided with the case study in Chapter 5.

While there is no fixed rule that determines the presentation of accounts (unless a formal passing of accounts is being contemplated), they can be loosely classed into three categories:

- "Court Passing": This format follows the format required by the *Rules of Civil Procedure*. It segregates the receipts and disbursements and includes a separate investment account.
- "Trust Company": This format provides the list of transactions where income, capital and investment receipts and disbursements are reported on the same page.
- "Hybrid": This format represents all other types of accounts typically presented by the lay estate trustee who has provided the accounts without professional assistance. This format is frequently the most creative and confusing produced.

As noted above, beneficiaries are entitled to have the accounts put in a proper "court-format" at the "cost" of the estate trustee. This means the cost of putting the accounts into proper form is borne by the estate trustee out of the compensation even if the accounts are put in proper form by a third party. Properly prepared accounts should be insisted upon (if a reasonable request in the circumstances).

A passing of the accounts, in effect, ends the estate trustee's accountability (for the particular period of time). However, there is no statutory or judicial finding confirming this. A court will presume that the issues resolved at the passing of accounts, as well as those which could have or should have been resolved, will not be reconsidered at a later time. Those matters that were not known or could not have expected to be known are not normally "caught" by this presumption and can be raised later.[6]

PROCEDURE

In Ontario, the *Rules of Civil Procedure* are enacted by legislation which governs procedural matters before the Superior Court of Justice and the Court of Appeal. Rule 74 is the rule governing non-contentious estate matters, while Rule 75 governs contentious matters. There are other rules that also affect estate matters.

---

[6] *Barkin v. Royal Trust* Co. (2002), 45 E.T.R. (2d) 1 (Ont. S.C.J.).

One matter that Rule 74 provides for is the procedure for passing accounts as well as the expected "court" or formal form of the accounts. Rule 74.17 details the information that an estate trustee is required to provide when preparing accounts in court passing format. That Rule requires the accounts to be organized in the following chronological sections:

- Statement of Original Assets
- Statement of Capital Receipts
- Statement of Capital Disbursements
- Statement of Revenue Receipts
- Statement of Revenue Disbursements
- Statement of Investment Account
- Statement of Unrealized Original Assets
- Cash Summary
- Statement of Trustee's Investments
- Statement of Liabilities
- Statement of Estate Trustee's Compensation

The transactions are recorded chronologically within each section. Each transaction should be placed in the proper section — not always an easy undertaking. Although the backup documentation to each transaction does not form part of the accounts themselves, the estate trustee should keep them accessible (and organized) and make them available for review as requested by a beneficiary. This backup documentation or vouchers will contain invoices, receipts, and investment statements, *etc.*, and should be cross-referenced with the account entries. A common request by a beneficiary is to either ask for further information about a transaction or for a copy of the voucher and an estate trustee should be able to respond to such a request within a reasonable time.

If such requests are not responded to in a diligent manner, a beneficiary can request that the estate trustee bring an Application to Pass Accounts (if this was not done at the time that the accounts were delivered). If an Application has been served and the estate trustee has either not dealt with a beneficiary's inquiries or has not dealt with those inquiries in a satisfactory manner, then the matter may be raised in court by counsel for the beneficiary at the passing of accounts.

A description of each section of a proper "court-format" account in Ontario follows.

Statement of Original Assets

The Statement of Original Assets lists the deceased's assets (*i.e.*, inventory) at the time of death. Original assets do not include assets jointly held with another individual or which have an individual named as beneficiary (*i.e.*, insurance policies, RRSP/RRIFs). The Statement lists the assets as well as the value as of the date of death.

Original assets may include:

ASSET CLASS	INFORMATION WHICH SHOULD BE INCLUDED IN ACCOUNTS
Cash/Bank Accounts	Cash on hand, name and address of institution, account numbers, account interest (if any), balance at date of death.
Investment accounts	Name of brokerage firm; detailed list of assets held.
GICs	Issuer, face value, interest rate, payment frequency, accrued interest, maturity date, certificate number.
Bonds, Debentures	Issuer, face value, maturity date, value at date of death, interest rate, payment frequency, accrued interest, certificate number.
Stocks	Number of shares, value at date of death, certificate number (includes ex-dividends).
Insurance & Annuities	Included only if the estate is the beneficiary.
Mutual Funds	Name of fund, number of units held, unit value at date of death.
Real Estate (Only asset where debts are deducted for probate purposes)	Appraised value, outstanding mortgage balance, interest rate, payments, maturity date.
Foreign Assets	Value converted to Canadian funds using date of death exchange rate.

ASSET CLASS	INFORMATION WHICH SHOULD BE INCLUDED IN ACCOUNTS
Mortgage Investments	Property secured, outstanding principal, interest rate, payment amount, payment frequency, accrued interest and maturity date.
Private Corporations	Number and class of shares (may also include shareholders' loan account).
Chattel Mortgages, Promissory Notes, *etc.*	All other amounts due to deceased with payment dates, interest rates, maturity dates.
Other Assets	Personal property, partnership interests, estate or trust interests, accrued salary payable, pension benefits payable, government benefits payable.

The estate trustee may seek the assistance of a professional advisor to assist in determining the value of an asset. For example, a real estate agent may need to be retained to provide a value of the real property. If, for example, the value of a property "appears" undervalued, then it is reasonable to request a copy of any appraisals obtained or to suggest that appraisals be obtained.

When determining the value of the estate's assets, it is the "gross" value — there is no provision for the deduction of any costs or liabilities, including tax liabilities, with one exception. In the case of real estate, any mortgages against the property can be deducted from the fair market value of the property, such that it is the value of the "net" amount that is included.

The Statement of Original Assets is very important. The total value of the assets listed is the value the estate trustee uses to calculate the estate administration tax or probate fee. Each beneficiary can draw certain conclusions from the list of assets — *i.e.*, are the assets straightforward? Are the assets mostly cash on hand? Is the estate comprised of mostly offshore property holdings that will need to be sold? This Statement (along with the testamentary documents) will guide the expectations of a beneficiary regarding the complexity of the administration of the estate and the time it will take to administer.

Statement of Capital Receipts

The Capital Receipts section shows all Original Assets as they are realized. The Statement records the transactions related to assets owned by or debts due the deceased at death. With the exception of capital gains on the sale of trust investments and minor refunds, all transactions recorded in this section should be cross-referenced to the applicable asset in the Statement of Original Assets.

Entries would include such things as the proceeds of sale or redemption of assets; accrued interest and ex-dividends due to the deceased but not received as of the date of death; miscellaneous subscription refunds; insurance premium refunds; income tax refunds; insurance policy proceeds payable to the estate; and the Canada Pension Plan death benefit.

The Statement of Capital Receipts also records the distribution of estate assets "*in specie*". *In specie* distributions are distributions of the actual asset in its existence form — *i.e.*, the stock certificate instead of the cash value of the shares after liquidation. Such a record would show the transfer of the asset directly to the ultimate beneficiaries by re-registering the actual asset into the beneficiary's name rather than selling or otherwise realizing the asset.

Statement of Capital Disbursements

The transactions recorded in the Capital Disbursements section generally represent the payment of debts owed by the deceased at death. Transactions included in this statement are related to such items as:

- funeral expenses and marker engraving;
- estate administration tax (probate fees);
- outstanding personal debts (household expenses, credit cards, *etc.*);
- income tax payable to date of death together with any arrears and penalties;
- costs of appraisals;
- "*in specie*" distributions;
- legacies;
- distributions to beneficiaries; and
- legal fees.

Capital Disbursements may also include encroachments on capital on behalf of a life tenant (if permitted by the testamentary documents), any losses incurred on the realization of trustee investments, and the capital portion of estate trustee's compensation charged against the estate.

Legal fees incurred during the course of administration are also included in this section. This is one item that should always be reviewed.

A detailed discussion of compensation and legal fees is found in Chapter 3.

Statement of Revenue Receipts

All income items such as interest income from bonds, debentures, and estate bank accounts; dividend income; rental income; and other investment income are recorded in the Statement of Revenue Receipts.

Statement of Revenue Disbursements

The Statement of Revenue Disbursements records all payments out of the revenue account. These payments include income payments made to life tenants or residual beneficiaries; expenses related to the operation of rental property; mortgage interest payable; brokerage or management account fees; and estate income tax payable. Unless otherwise directed by the testamentary documents, insurance premiums and property taxes payable on real property owned by the estate may be allocated between the Capital Disbursements and Revenue Disbursements accounts at the trustees' discretion, especially where there are income and capital beneficiaries.

Statement of Investment Account

The Investment Account records the investment of the capital of the estate by the estate trustee pending its ultimate distribution. When an asset is sold and the proceeds reinvested elsewhere than in the estate bank account, the purchase of the investment will be recorded in this account.

Estate trustees are frequently given considerable discretion in the investments they make on behalf of the estate. It is not uncommon for estate investments to include mortgages on real property and mutual funds in addition to stocks, bonds, and other forms of investment certificates.

A trustee's investment power is contained in the testamentary documents and in the Ontario *Trustee Act*.[7] The powers contained in the *Trustee Act* were significantly amended as of July 1, 1999. A higher standard

---

[7] R.S.O. 1990, c. T.23, ss. 26-35.

of care is now required when dealing with investments. The standard of care is now of a "prudent investor"; meaning that when reviewing the investment activities of an estate trustee, the court will consider those activities against an objective standard of whether a prudent investor investing his or her own funds would have, in the circumstances, acted as did the estate trustee.

An Ontario estate trustee is mandated to consider (initially and at regular intervals), certain enumerated criteria before and while the investments are held, such as general economic conditions; the possible effect of inflation or deflation; the expected tax consequences of investment decisions or strategies; the role that each investment or course of action plays within the overall trust portfolio; the expected total return from income and the appreciation of capital; the need for liquidity, regularity of income and preservation or appreciation of capital; and an asset's special relationship or special value, if any, to the purposes of the trust or to one or more of the beneficiaries. Diversification is mandated, and mutual fund investments are now expressly allowed.

In Ontario, an estate trustee may retain the services of a professional investment advisor, however, the advisor and the estate trustee on behalf of the estate must enter into a written agreement. The estate trustee must develop an investment policy and review that policy on a regular basis. It is recommended that this review take place on a quarterly basis unless circumstances dictate otherwise.

This is an area that is closely monitored by beneficiaries, especially if a trust has been created whereby one beneficiary, usually the surviving spouse, is entitled to the income from the trust for their lifetime, and another beneficiary, usually charitable, are entitled to the capital upon the death of the spouse (also known as the life tenant). Both beneficiaries may take issue with the investment activities — for different and potentially opposite reasons. An estate trustee should, therefore, document all investment activities, including the creation of an investment plan, obtaining investment advice, and the recording of minutes of meetings, all with a view of being able to show that a prudent investor would have taken the same action in similar circumstances. That documentation would form part of the vouchers available for disclosure upon request by a beneficiary.

A beneficiary has the right to examine and question the investments selected by trustees, especially where it appears that competing interests have not been addressed or where original assets retained (such as a significant holding in private corporate shares with a limited market) could result in a significant loss of value to the estate.

One area of potential conflict between beneficiaries is where a trust has been created. The estate trustee is expected to maintain an "even hand" between classes of potentially adverse beneficiaries, such as the life tenant and the capital beneficiaries. This means that the trust's investments must attempt to maximize the income produced from the capital (the life tenant's interest) with preserving the capital of the trust (the capital beneficiary's interest). This becomes difficult with falling market situations where the life tenant also has the right to encroach on the capital if the estate trustee deems it necessary within the exercise of his or her discretion.

If a charity is a capital beneficiary (which is frequently the case when there is a life tenant), it is particularly important to review the investment portfolio as a whole to see whether that balance is being maintained between these two competing interests. Particulars of all capital encroachments should be given. If this detail is lacking, further information should be requested even if the right to encroach exists in the Will.

Cash Summary

This Statement lists all cash from any source on hand at the end of the accounting period.

Investments are listed at their original cost to the estate so that the amount under investment in the Cash Summary must equal the amount under investment in the Investment Account and the total set out in the Statement of Trustee Investments. The cash on hand at the end of the period should also equal the total of all uninvested funds in the estate bank account(s). The amount of uninvested funds should be a minimum amount. If upon review, a large amount remains in the solicitor's trust account or the estate's bank account, the reason for this should be queried. An estate trustee has an obligation to preserve and maximize the return on assets, which traditionally means investing surplus funds — even if in a rolling 30 day GIC.

Statement of Unrealized Original Assets

The Statement of Unrealized Original Assets represents the summary of any original assets that were not realized by the estate trustee during the accounting period.

This Statement lists these assets at the *date of death* value rather than the market value at the end of the accounting period. If the estate holds corporate shares or mutual funds, especially when the trust will continue for a number of years, the current market value will be different. In order to understand the present value of these assets, a beneficiary should ask the estate trustees for that information. It may be that upon receipt of this information, further questions are raised, for example, where an original asset has depreciated in value, why has it been or why is it being retained (*i.e.*, because the asset is subject to a specific *in specie* distribution).

Statement of Trustees' Investment

The Statement of Trustees' Investments lists the investments made by the estate trustee at their original investment cost rather than ending market value and does not provide any information with respect to potential capital gains or losses or current value.

Statement of Outstanding Liabilities

The Statement of Outstanding Liabilities lists all outstanding or contingent liabilities to be paid by the estate at the end of the accounting period. There is no definition of what constitutes a contingent liability, but to the extent known or anticipated, these liabilities should be disclosed.

These liabilities can include income taxes assessed but not yet paid, legal fees, accounting fees, and mortgage principal payments to be made during the period. More uncertain liabilities, such as capital gains tax payable when an estate asset is finally sold or any unresolved spousal equalization or dependant support claims against the estate should be recorded, although the estate trustee may not (yet) be able to quantify such liabilities accurately. In these instances, this Statement should outline the nature of the potential liability and, if possible, estimate an amount.

Statement Of Estate Trustee's Compensation

An estate trustee is entitled to (but not required to) receive compensation for his or her work. The claim by an estate trustee for compensation is normally a source of frequent carelessness and unintentional abuse, and is an item that should always be reviewed.

The Statement of Compensation shows the amount of compensation claimed by the estate trustee. It must be in sufficient detail to allow the beneficiary to know the basis for the calculation.

A detailed discussion of estate trustee compensation is found in Chapter 3.

RELEASE AND INDEMNITY

As accounts are usually passed with the intent to exonerate the estate trustee, to appease demanding beneficiaries, and to obtain approval of the compensation claim, interim distributions are often made at the same time that the accounts are presented for approval. With this "package" will often be the request that the beneficiary sign the release or release and indemnity provided. It is always prudent to read the document through before deciding whether or not to sign off.

A detailed discussion of releases is found in Chapter 3.

FORMAL PASSING OF ACCOUNTS

As previously indicated, at the end of an administration, an estate trustee may volunteer or may be compelled to "pass his accounts". An estate trustee is entitled to have his accounts taken to court and approved or passed. Approval from the beneficiaries if *sui juris*[8] may suffice; if not, a court application is required.

In Ontario, the *Trustee Act*[9] provides the basis for a voluntary passing of accounts. Rule 74.15 of the *Rules of Civil Procedure*, provides that a person who appears to have a financial interest in an estate may compel a passing of accounts.[10]

"OVER THE COUNTER"

In Ontario, on a passing without a hearing, there is a tariff which sets the costs of the passing, and, in keeping with the approach taken in other aspects of estate matters, is based on the amount of receipts. Where the estate trustee has acted with gross negligence, he may be ordered to pay, or may be disallowed, costs.

The process to formally pass accounts begins when the accounts verified by affidavits completed by the trustees together with the requisite supporting documentation are delivered to the court offices and an appointment is made to have the accounts audited. The completed Notice of Application to Pass Accounts, a draft Notice of Objection to Accounts,

---

[8] In other words, the beneficiary is not under a legal disability.
[9] Section 23.
[10] This summary procedure is not available in other fiduciary situations such as *inter vivos* ("living") trusts, guardianship of a minor, committees or guardians of estates of mentally incapable individuals. In those cases, an application under Rule 14.05(3)(a) or (b) of the Ontario *Rules of Civil Procedure* must be made or an Order compelling a formal passing must be sought.

and a copy of the draft Judgment are served on each person who has a contingent or vested interest in the estate by regular mail. In the event any person served is resident outside Ontario, the documents must be served at least 60 days before the hearing date of the application. If all interested persons reside in Ontario, the documents must be served at least 45 days before the hearing date.

In the event no objections are raised by any party at least 20 days before the date fixed for the hearing, the passing proceeds "over the counter". Once the additional supporting documentation with respect to service and claims has been filed, the material is forwarded to a judge. The judge, if satisfied, will sign the Judgment in chambers (*i.e.*, in his or her office) without a court appearance.

In Ontario, solicitors' costs are allowed on passing of accounts that proceeds "over the counter" without a hearing. The costs are fixed depending on the amount of receipts and the party in accordance with Tariff "C":

Tariff C – Solicitors' Costs Allowed on Passing of Accounts Without a Hearing

(1) ESTATE TRUSTEE

Amount of costs	Amount of receipts
Less than $100,000	$ 800
$100,000 or more, but less than $ 300,000	1,750
$300,000 or more, but less than $500,000	2,000
$500,000 or more, but less than $1,000,000	2,500
$1,000,000 or more, but less than $1,500,000	3,000
$1,500,000 or more, but less than $3,000,000	4,000
$3,000,000 or more	5,000

(2) PERSON WITH FINANCIAL INTEREST IN ESTATE

If a person with a financial interest in an estate retains a solicitor to review the accounts, makes no objection to the accounts (or makes an objection and later withdraws it) and serves and files a request for costs, the person is entitled to one-half of the amount payable to the estate trustee.

(3) CHILDREN'S LAWYER OR PUBLIC GUARDIAN AND TRUSTEE

If the Children's Lawyer or the Public Guardian and Trustee makes no objection to the accounts (or makes an objection and later withdraws it) and serves and files a request for costs, he or she is entitled to three-quarters of the amount payable to the estate trustee.

Note: If two or more persons are represented by the same solicitor, they are entitled to receive only one person's costs.

Note: A person entitled to costs under this tariff is also entitled to the amount of G.S.T. on those costs.

Accordingly, a person with a financial interest in the estate who retains a solicitor to review the accounts and makes no objection is entitled to one-half the amount payable to the estate trustee, and the Children's Lawyer or the Public Guardian and Trustee is entitled to three-quarters the amount. If the same solicitor represents two or more persons, they are entitled to receive only one set of costs. G.S.T. is in addition. In order to obtain such costs, a Request for Costs must be served and filed and the Judgment will reflect the payment of these costs. Therefore, it is prudent, if in doubt about the accounts, to forward them to a solicitor for review — just make sure enough lead time is provided as there are time frames which must be followed.

In the event a beneficiary wishes to claim costs over those awarded by Tariff "C" (*i.e.*, "increased costs"), in which case a Request for Increased Costs must be made or in the event objections are raised which cannot be resolved, the parties appear in court on the appointed date. At that time, consideration will be given as to whether the outstanding issues can or should be resolved by way of mandatory mediation or a full trial.

CHARITIES' PERSPECTIVE

There is a positive obligation or duty on a charity to scrutinize the accounting. In the past, Ontario charities could rely upon the Public Guardian and Trustee to act as a "watchdog". Times have changed. The role of the Public Guardian and Trustee is reduced, namely because of reduced funding and because charities are considered to be *sui juris*.[11]

The Public Guardian and Trustee used to send a letter (when he or she was required to be notified of an Application for a Certificate whenever a charitable interest was mentioned in a Will) in response to the notification that contained the following:

> Please be advised that we will not be participating in this Application since the charitable interests in this estate are apparently *sui juris* organizations that are legally competent to protect the charitable interests in the estate, have a fiduciary[12] responsibility for protecting the charitable interests in the estate, are accountable for protecting the charitable interests in the estate and which, together with the person responsible for administering and operating the charitable organization, may be held liable for failure to protect the charitable interests in the estate.

Although the letter is no longer sent (because the notification requirements have changed), the principle remains. The responsibility rests with the charity to satisfy itself that everything has been done properly, that the assets have been accounted for, that the liabilities have been properly discharged and that the compensation claimed is appropriate.

If there is one problem with the administration of the estate, then there are probably others. These problems usually flow from the fact that the estate trustee did not understand that they and the charitable beneficiaries are in a fiduciary position.

Estates typically fall into four categories. First, there are those estates where everything "passes". There are no questions, no complaints, and no issue about compensation or legal fees. Second, come the estates where there are a few questions that need clarification or where the legal fees seem high. An appropriate response would be to send a letter asking those questions, but in a gentle manner. At this stage, one is simply requesting more information and advising that a response will be available upon consideration of the additional information.

The third category are those estates where there are various issues. An appropriate response should go beyond asking questions. One could also quote the paragraph from the Public Guardian and Trustee's letter (see above). Sometimes, it is just a matter of educating the estate solicitor that

---

[11] In this context, *sui juris* means that the charity possesses all social and civil rights, is able to protect itself and is not under any legal disability.

[12] The term "fiduciary" is derived from Roman law. A fiduciary is a person acting in the character of a trustee who must act beyond reproach, in good faith and in the best interests of the beneficiary.

the estate trustee has fiduciary responsibilities and that it is entitled to ask questions and demand satisfactory answers.

The fourth category are those estates where there are too many issues and, accordingly, there is little choice but to appear before a Judge on a formal passing of accounts. Even with these estates, it is worthwhile to begin the dialogue to see whether some of the issues can be resolved, if not all. Sometimes you may be surprised. It will depend not only on the issues involved, but also the personality type of the executor and/or solicitor. An example of an estate falling into this category would be where the executor does not understand his role and obligations to such an extent that at the hearing, the beneficiary will be asking the Judge to remove the estate trustee in order to remove him from a control position. The estates falling into this category are rare.

AUDITING ESTATE ACCOUNTS

The review process can be tedious and a step-by-step process works best. Go through each section of the accounts looking for any unusual items. Some things to look for include the length of time it took to administer in the circumstances. For example, where it is an immediately distributable estate (*i.e.*, it has not been held up during a lifetime of someone), an "executor year" should be sufficient unless it is a substantial estate or contains assets like real property or a business; or the assets of the estate should attract tax, yet there have been no payments to the Canada Custom and Revenue Agency or to an accountant.

A form of audit checklist is found in Appendix 3.

While each estate is unique, most have certain classes of assets in common which usually require similar administrative procedures. The detailed process of auditing estate accounts typically follows the steps outlined in the sections below.

REVIEWING TESTAMENTARY DOCUMENTS

It is important to have all of the testamentary documents. An easy way to ensure this is to ask for a copy of the complete Certificate of Appointment (which also attaches the testamentary documents) when the first response letter upon being notified is sent to the solicitor.

Questions to ask while reviewing the testamentary documents include:

- Is the estate an outright distribution?
- Are one or more trusts created? If so, note terms and beneficiaries.

- Are there restrictions with respect to trustee investments, capital encroachments for the benefit of life tenant(s) or compensation?
- Does the Will include other special instructions (such as permitting the estate trustee to purchase estate assets)?

Questions to ask while reviewing the Statement of Original Assets include:

- Do any of the assets include commercial or business real property?
- Are any of the assets located outside Ontario?
- Are the assets cross-referenced with related entries in the Capital Receipts?
- Are any assets which do not appear to have a cross-reference listed in the Statement of Unrealized Original Assets at the end of the accounting period?
- Do the estate assets include mutual funds? (These are significantly more time-consuming to administer from an accounting standpoint.)

The following should also be confirmed:

- Foreign assets should be reported in Canadian dollars using the exchange rate as of the date of death.
- Guaranteed Investment Certificate, bond and debenture information should include the name of the issuer, maturity date, interest rate and amount of accrued interest calculated from last interest payment to date of death.
- Details with respect to equity holdings should include name of corporation, number and class of shares and value at date of death.
- Check mathematics.

The following should be done in a review of Capital Receipts:

- Check entries against cross-references in Statement of Original Assets.
- Compare proceeds received on disposition of asset with value of asset at date of death (to determine whether assets realized a gain or loss on disposition).
- Check number of mutual fund units or shares sold to determine:
  - if the transaction is only a partial realization of the asset; and

- if only a partial realization of the asset, are the remaining units or shares listed in the Statement of Unrealized Original Assets.
- Check mathematics.

Questions to ask while reviewing the Capital Disbursements include:

- Are capital payments made to income beneficiaries? If so, why?
- Have legacy payments and specific bequests of assets *in specie* been made?
- Are details provided with respect to estate trustee's out-of-pocket expenses?
- Is the estate trustee also the solicitor for the estate? Do payments to solicitor or solicitor's firm detail whether the services were provided as solicitors or in the solicitor's capacity as estate trustee? Request and review legal accounts.
- Do other capital payments appear to be reasonable?
- Check mathematics.

Questions to ask while reviewing Revenue Receipts and Revenue Disbursements include:

- If there are ongoing investments paying semi-annual or annual income, do all payments appear to have been received?
- Do the securities pay dividend income regularly?
- Does the estate hold a "wasting asset" (such as a cottage property which does not generate income but has ongoing expenses)? How are these disbursements allocated?
- Check mathematics.

Questions to ask while reviewing the Investment Account include:

- Has the estate trustee appeared to maintain an "even hand" when selecting investments?
- Are investments earning income?
- Is a list of trustee's investments at the end of the accounting period included with the accounts?
- Does the investment total in the list of investments agree with the amount under investment in the Cash Summary?
- Check mathematics.

Questions to ask while reviewing the Compensation Calculations include:

- What percentage was used to calculate the compensation and is it appropriate?
- Has the compensation calculation been adjusted for capital losses, transfers between accounts, adjusting entries, refunds and solicitor or other professional accounts?
- Has compensation been reduced by interim payments made to estate trustee on account of compensation?
- Check mathematics.

GENERAL REVIEW

There should also be a general review that includes:

- Checking totals reported in Cash Summary against actual totals for that particular section of the accounts (*i.e.*, compare total Capital Receipts in accounts with amount of Capital Receipts set out in Cash Summary).
- An adequate explanation of unusual circumstances.
- "Spot checks" to see if information appears to be reported correctly. If there are inconsistencies, a closer review may be required.
- If an interim distribution, the extent of the holdback.

RESPONSE TO THE ACCOUNT REVIEW

Once the accounts have been reviewed, the charity should decide (ideally, right after completing the review) on a course of action and write that response to the estate trustee. If undecided, or if there are some issues that merit further discussion, then the charity should consider consulting with the other beneficiaries in the same class and/or their solicitor.

AUDITING TRUST COMPANY ACCOUNTS

Frequently, beneficiaries receive trust company statements for review. These statements list the estate transactions chronologically, however, all receipts, disbursements and investments are typically visible at the same time. The process of reviewing these statements is basically the same as any other account format.

A review in this case should include:

- A review of the Statement of Original Assets and a check of cross-references.
- If a continuing statement of accounts, a comparison of the list of assets/investments at end of previous period with the list of assets/investments at end of current period noting additions, deletions or missing assets and changes in quantity.
- A review of the investment and capital accounts to determine when changes occurred.
- A check for capital gains/losses.
- A comparison of the revenue receipts with the previous accounting period for increase/decrease in routine revenue.
- If only a portion of a security is sold, to note remaining number of shares and new adjusted cost base.
- A check for account adjustments (transfers between capital and revenue, asset set up entries, adjusting entries, *etc.*)
- Highlight and total trust company fees (excluding G.S.T.).
- Calculate compensation and adjust for fees pretaken by trust company. Compare with amount allowed by the compensation agreement, if any.
- Review the summary detailing the estate assets and note the difference between the "original/invested value" of the assets/investments (being the value at the date of death value or the actual cost to purchase the investment) and the "market value" (which is the value of the estate assets as of statement date). Overall, have the assets increased or decreased in value and is difference significant?

Remember, a charitable beneficiary should not "cross the line" when it comes to making decisions or considering consenting to a request for a course of action proposed by the executor. It is the estate trustee's responsibility to make those prudent decisions and it is at the passing of accounts that the beneficiary reviews those decisions. A charity's duty is to be a conscientious and diligent beneficiary.

ALBERTA

Most of the earlier comments apply equally to Alberta.

REQUIREMENT TO ACCOUNT

The general rule is that the personal representative has a duty, both at common law[13] and statute law[14] to account to the beneficiaries of the estate. To account properly means the personal representative should maintain an accurate record of the steps taken during the administration of the estate and show that the administration has been prudent and honest.

The statutory requirement for estate accounting is contained in the *Administration of Estates Act*:[15]

> 45(1) The legal representative shall make an accounting before the court of the legal representative's administration of the estate whenever the legal representative is ordered to do so by the court, either at the instance of the court or on the application of a person interested in the estate, a creditor or a surety for the due administration of the estate.
>
> (2) A legal representative may at any time apply to the court to make an accounting of the legal representative's administration of the estate before the court.
>
> 46. An executor who is also a trustee under the will may be required to account for the executor's trusteeship in the same manner as the executor is required to account in respect of the executor's executorship.

A personal representative's duty to account is owed to the following individuals:[16]

1. All residuary beneficiaries of a Will.[17]
2. A person interested in the estate[18] who applies to the Court of Queen's Bench of Alberta (Surrogate Matter) (hereinafter referred to as "the Court") and obtains an order requiring the personal representative to give an accounting of the administration of the estate. These "interested persons" include the personal representative of a residuary beneficiary, the next-of-kin of the deceased entitled in distribution, persons who appear to be interested, creditors of the deceased, or a surety who has posted a bond for the administration of the estate.

---

[13] *Freeman v. Fairlie* (1817), 3 Mer. 24 at 42; *Re Ross*, [1946] O.W.N. 767 (H.C.); *Re Lutz*, [1928] 1 D.L.R. 72 (C.A.).
[14] *Administration of Estates Act*, R.S.A. 2000, c. A-2.
[15] See ss. 45-49.
[16] The requirements for estate accounting are set out in Part 3 of the Surrogate Rules, AR 130/95, and specifically Surrogate Rules 97, 98 and 99.
[17] Surrogate Rule 97(1)(a).
[18] Surrogate Rule 97(2). Persons interested in the estate are a broad class described in Surrogate Rule 57.

3. The beneficiary of a specific gift under a Will.[19] A specific bequest beneficiary is entitled only to an accounting in respect of that specific gift and not entitled to apply to the Court for any further accounting once the gift has been received.[20]

The personal representative, when making an application for a Grant of Probate or a Grant of Administration, must take an oath[21] that they will render an accurate accounting of the estate and their administration whenever required by law to do so. Pursuant to Surrogate Rule 97(2), a personal representative is required to give an accounting at regular intervals. At the very least, an accounting of the administration of the estate should take place every two years. The time period may be altered by the Court on application to either extend or shorten the time period.

Generally, a personal representative need not be compelled to account. Most personal representatives voluntarily render an accurate accounting of the estate and their administration by making an application to the Court to pass the accounts.

PREPARATION OF ACCOUNTS

Personal representatives should remember that it is crucial to maintain the estate's accounts in the proper format. Surrogate Rules 98 and 99 set out the format's guidelines.

> 98(1) The financial statements respecting an estate must include the following:
>
> (a) an inventory of property and debts at the beginning and end of the accounting period;
>
> (b) a statement of all property and money received during the accounting period showing whether it is capital or income;
>
> (c) a statement of all property distributed and money paid out during the accounting period showing whether it is capital or income;
>
> (d) a statement of all changes to property made and all debts of the estate paid or incurred by the personal representative during the accounting period;
>
> (e) a statement of all expenses incurred or paid during the accounting period;

---

[19] Surrogate Rule 97(4)(*a*).
[20] Surrogate Rule 97(4)(*b*).
[21] Surrogate Form NC 2.

(f) in the case of a final passing of accounts, a statement of anticipated receipts and disbursements;

(g) a reconciliation, where necessary, showing the items required to balance the opening net value of the estate with the closing net value of the estate;

(h) a distribution schedule, including interim distributions and the proposed final distribution, if appropriate;

(i) a proposed compensation schedule for the personal representative showing the basis on which it is calculated and its allocation to income or capital.

(2) The financial statements may be separate or combined as long as they can be followed clearly.

(3) The financial statements may be in any format, but each entry must be numbered consecutively.

(4) If the will or other trust instrument specifies separate capital and income interest, the financial statements must distinguish entries respecting capital from entries respecting income.

(5) The court, at any time, may require further financial statements or more particulars with respect to the financial statements presented.

99. The following documentation is sufficient to confirm ownership by the estate of the property referred to:

(a) in the case of publicly traded securities and commercial paper,

(i) a certificate, or

(ii) a letter from a dealer registered under the Securities Act, a bank or a trust corporation, whether registered under the Loan and Trust Corporations Act or not, carrying on business in any jurisdiction in Canada stating that the dealer, bank or trust corporation is holding securities for the estate, either by having them in its possession, through a securities depository or by some other means that is in accordance with current practice in the industry;

(b) in the case of private company shares,

(i) a certificate, or

(ii) a letter from a duly authorized officer of the company or from the company's lawyer confirming the holding;

(c) in the case of bank balances, cash, term deposits, treasury bills, annuities, pensions, retirement plans, royalty trust, and similar property,

(i) a certificate or statement of account, or

(ii) a letter from a financial institution stating that the financial institution is holding property for the estate, either by having it in its possession, through a securities depository, or by some other means that is in accordance with current practice in the industry;

(d) in the case of household goods and personal effects,

  (i) a letter or bill of lading from any depository where the goods or effects are stored, or

  (ii) an inventory, the accuracy of which is attested to by the personal representative, indicating possession of the goods or effects on behalf of the estate;

(e) in the case of real property, a current copy of the certificate of title.

When preparing accounts, it is usually not sufficient to use only the inventory contained in either the Application for a Grant of Probate or Grant of Administration.[22] Such an inventory might be used as an opening balance for the accounting, but all additional assets and/or debts should be included. This shows each item of the deceased's property that has entered into or has been paid by the estate after the Grant Application was made whether or not it actually came into the hands of the personal representative. Although there is no prescribed order for the listing of the assets, they are generally listed in order of liquidity. For example, cash and bank accounts, bonds, stocks, mortgages, real estate, book debts, business interests, household goods, chattels, items of personality and other assets.

Since accounting for all monies received and disbursed need to be shown, the accounts should be divided into capital (principal) and revenue (income) accounts[23] to facilitate allocation of income and expenditures for taxation purposes.

When listing the assets of the estate, each asset should be clearly described, showing its value at the date of death, and also showing how the asset was disposed of. This may be accomplished by referencing the item in the Application for a Grant of Probate or Grant of Administration to the same item in the accounts and showing its disposition by receipt or disbursement. It is better to give more information than not being detailed enough when describing the asset and its disposition.

It is also advisable to keep an invoice file for all of the estate's disbursements. This type of record keeping can easily be done if an estate bank account is established that allows all cheques written by the personal representative to be recorded on the account's bank statement. The bank statement is then returned by the bank, and retained by the personal representative. It should also be noted that there is no longer a

---

[22] See inventory in Surrogate Form NC 7.
[23] See Surrogate Rule 98(1).

requirement that the accounts be approved by the Clerk of the Court, unless so ordered by the Court.

After the estate property has been accounted for, and the receipts and disbursements of monies and other assets have been listed subsequent to the date of death, the accounts must show all property remaining in the personal representative's hands.

Finally, a reconciliation summary should be prepared[24] showing the items required to balance the opening net value of the estate with the closing net value.

Accounts which are kept in the proper form and contain all relevant information will facilitate a smooth and orderly passing of accounts and will also assist the personal representative in his or her application for compensation.

PROCEDURES FOR PASSING ACCOUNTS

A personal representative has three options for passing their accounts. The three procedures are:

- Informal Accounting and Release
- Court Application Dispensing with a Formal Passing of Accounts
- Court Application for a Formal Passing of Accounts

Informal Accounting and Releases

This is the usual procedure a personal representative uses to pass his or her accounts. In this case, the personal representative obtains signed releases from all the beneficiaries. In signing the releases, the beneficiaries acknowledge that they have received, reviewed and accept the accounting provided by the personal representative. The beneficiaries also acknowledge that they have no issue with the compensation requested by the personal representative (which ought to be set out in the accounts). Under this procedure, a Court review (referred to as formal passing of accounts) is not necessary.

The Surrogate Rules provide as follows:[25]

---

[24] Surrogate Rule 98(1)(g) does not make it mandatory to prepare such a summary.
[25] Part 3, Division 2, see Rules 100(1)-102.

100(1) A personal representative may, on the presentation of accounts to the residuary beneficiaries, obtain releases in Form ACC 12 from the residuary beneficiaries.

(2) The releases obtained under subrule (1) need not be filed.

101. A personal representative may rely on a release for confirmation that, in the opinion of the residuary beneficiary giving the release,

(a) the accounting in respect of the estate presented to the beneficiary is satisfactory;

(b) the personal representative may be compensated as set out in the statement of compensation included in the financial statements;

(c) the personal representative may distribute the estate in accordance with the statement of distribution included in the financial statements.

102. Releases obtained under rule 100 do not constitute the cancellation of a bond.

Releases do not need to be filed with the Court,[26] although this is highly recommended so that there is a permanent record available should the beneficiaries forget that they had given such a release.

If all the residuary beneficiaries are competent adults, have signed releases, and are satisfied with the accounting provided by the personal representative as well as the compensation requested by the personal representative,[27] the personal representative may choose to distribute the estate without having the estate accounts passed by the Court.

Court Application Dispensing with a Formal Passing of Accounts

This application is necessary if a personal representative requires a Court Order to discharge a bond; to set the personal representative's compensation; or in a situation where although not all the beneficiaries have signed releases, they have not provided an actual objection to the accounting. In such situations, a personal representative may apply to the Court to dispense with a formal passing of accounts and request a less onerous form of review. A personal representative may also choose to make this application even if all of the beneficiaries have provided signed releases, if

---

[26] See Surrogate Rule 100(2).
[27] See Chapter 3 for a detailed discussion of personal representatives compensation.

he or she believes there are any uncertainties or liability issues with the estate.

The personal representative may choose to apply to the Court for an order dispensing with formal passing of accounts and seek to have the accounts passed informally. A personal representative could choose this option where one or more of the residuary beneficiaries have failed to sign and return their release, but the personal representative does not believe that there are any substantial matters in dispute with respect to the accounting.

The relevant Surrogate Rules for informal passing of accounts are set out in Surrogate Rules 103-106:

103(1) A personal representative may apply for an order dispensing with the formal passing of accounts and passing the accounts informally by filing the following and serving copies on the persons interested in the estate who have not given releases:

(a) Form ACC 10;

(b) Form ACC 11;

(c) the financial statements;

(d) all signed releases in Form ACC 12.

(2) A personal representative need not serve a beneficiary from whom the personal representative has received a signed release under rule 100.

104. If no notice of objection is filed by a person interested in the estate or if all residuary beneficiaries have signed releases, an application under rule 103 may proceed without notice to any other person.

105. Even if all the residuary beneficiaries have signed releases, the Court

(a) must be satisfied with all the required documentation respecting the estate whether or not all the residuary beneficiaries have signed releases;

(b) may make the order applied for;

(c) may do anything it may do under rule 113.

106.(1) If any person interested in the estate objects to an application under this Division 3, that person must file and serve a notice of objection in Form ACC 3 in accordance with rule 114.

(2) If a notice of objection is filed, the Court must hold a hearing under Division 4 on the matter.

If the Court is satisfied that the accounting is in order, and no interested person objects to the application dispensing with a formal passing of accounts, then pursuant to Surrogate Rule 113(1)(d), the Court may "dispense with the formal passing and pass the accounts on an informal basis".

Court Application for a Formal Passing of Accounts

In the absence of releases being voluntarily provided by the beneficiaries, a personal representative would initiate a formal passing of accounts application. A person interested in the estate may also make an application to the Court requesting the Court to compel the personal representative to fully and properly account. The Court may also, on its own initiative, order a formal passing of accounts.

The process of the formal passing of accounts is set out in Surrogate Rules 107 through 117. The beneficiaries are provided with an accounting in advance of the date set for the Court application. The accounting will include any proposed compensation for the personal representative and the basis upon which that compensation is calculated. Beneficiaries who object to anything contained in the accounting or the supporting documentation are required to indicate exactly what matters are in dispute and to provide reasons to the Court for such objections by preparing Surrogate Form ACC 3.

Where a dispute arises over one or more entries in the financial statements provided by the personal representative, the personal representative can be ordered to be examined by an accountant pursuant to Surrogate Rule 115. Under the formal passing of accounts process, the Court will determine the nature, scope and extent of the accountant's examination, and provide a form of appointment for the accountant.[28]

The personal representative is required under Surrogate Rule 116 to fully co-operate with the accountant appointed, which includes making available all records and documents to the appointed accountant. Ultimately, the appointed accountant must file a report in the specified Surrogate Court form[29] and serve a copy of that report by ordinary mail on both the personal representative and all persons interested in the estate. In the event further Court hearings are required to pass the accounts formally, the accountant may be required to attend the hearing.

The fees incurred for this process are payable out of the residue of the estate, or otherwise as directed by the Court, however, the Court may be guided by common law principles of costs and the applicable Alberta Rules of Court. For example, if an objection against a personal representative was

---

[28] See Surrogate Form ACC 4.
[29] Surrogate Forms ACC 5.1 and 5.2.

found to be frivolous, the costs of the application could be ordered against the party making the allegations.

Subject to Surrogate Rule 97(2), the personal representative, having an obligation to account on a regular basis, is usually not compelled at any specific time to pass their accounts, unless ordered to do so by the Court pursuant to section 47 of the *Administration of Estates Act*. However, it is a common practice to pass the accounts of the estate from time to time, for three reasons.

Firstly, the claim for compensation for the personal representative is made at the same time as the passing of accounts, and in an ongoing estate, the personal representative should be compensated for their services on a periodic basis. Secondly, it is more convenient to prepare and pass the accounts on a periodic basis, rather than to wait until the estate administration has run its course and face the onerous task of preparing and passing accounts for the entire period. And, thirdly, passing the accounts on a periodic basis keeps persons interested in the estate informed and can obviate unnecessary disputes due to lack of information on the part of these persons.

How often a personal representative should pass the accounts in an estate depends on factors such as the size of the estate, the activity in the estate, the number of interim distributions to be made, and upon other events such as the date of appointment of a trustee for a dependent adult beneficiary or on an infant attaining majority.

While Part 3 of the Surrogate Rules deals with the formal passing of accounts, Surrogate Rule 107 sets forth the documents required when an application is made by a personal representative for an order formally passing the accounts:

> 107(1) A personal representative may apply for an order formally passing accounts by filing the following and serving copies on the person interested in the estate who have not given releases.
>
> (a) Form ACC 1;
>
> (b) Form ACC 2;
>
> (c) the financial statements;
>
> (d) all signed releases in Form ACC 12;
>
> (e) any notice of objection in Form ACC 3.
>
> (2) The personal representative must serve the notice of hearing attached to Form ACC 1 not less than 30 days before the hearing.

The Surrogate Rules also provide that a person interested in an estate may also apply to the Court for an Order requiring the personal representative to have their accounts formally passed. The procedures setting out this process are contained in Surrogate Rules 108-111.

The Court, when ordering and passing the accounts of the personal representative, has the powers set out in section 47 of the *Administration of Estates Act*:

> 47(1) The court, on passing the accounts of the legal representative of an estate, may
>
> > (a) enter into and make full inquiry and accounting of and concerning the whole property that the deceased or minor was or is possessed of or entitled to, and the administration and disbursement of that property, including the calling in of creditors and adjudicating on their claims, and for that purpose may take evidence and decide all disputed matters arising in the accounting, and
> >
> > (b) inquire into and adjudicate on a complaint or claim by a person interested in the taking of the accounts of misconduct, neglect or default on the part of the legal representative, and the court, on proof of the claim, may order that the legal representative be charged with any sum by way of damages or otherwise as it considers just, in the same manner as if the legal representative had received the sum.
>
> (2) The court may order the trial of an issue of a complaint or claim under subsection (1)(b), and may make all necessary directions for that trial.
>
> (3) If accounts submitted to the court are intricate or complicated and, in the opinion of the court, require expert investigation, the court may appoint an accountant or other skilled person to investigate and to assist it in auditing the accounts, and the costs thereof shall be borne by the estate or by the person that the court directs.[30]

Once the accounts of a personal representative have been passed formally in the Courts, and the Court has determined that no further accounting or disclosure is required, the Court will order the discharge of the personal representative.

An order discharging a personal representative has the effect of releasing the personal representative in respect of all claims that could be made against him or her relating to the administration of the estate.

The effect of a Court Order passing the personal representative's account is to confirm the status of the assets shown on the accounts at the end of the accounting period, and to approve the personal representative's administration of the estate during the period under review. An Order passing the accounts is conclusive, following the expiration of the appeal

---

[30] See also Surrogate Rule 113 which sets out further powers the Court has when hearing a formal application for the passing of accounts.

period, against all persons having notice of the passing of accounts application. However, it is also open to interested parties to revisit the administration where matters such as fraud, mistake, omission, accident, undue advantage, or undisclosed acts are raised subsequent to the Court releasing the personal representative. The burden of proof rests on the party seeking to impeach the accounts. Even where grounds are proven, the Courts may not set aside a statement or settlement if the grounds do not affect the final balances of the accounting.

The Court Order passing the accounts should approve the accounts for the period under review, set the compensation of the personal representative, allocate the payment of the compensation awarded to the personal representative as between the capital and revenue accounts, award the solicitor's compensation for the application and deal with other ancillary matters before the Court. If necessary, the Court Order should also stipulate that the service effected upon all persons interested in the estate was good and sufficient, especially if persons interested in the estate live outside the province. Surrogate Rule 113(2) sets out what the Court may order.

In the event that questions have arisen during the course of the administration of the estate such that the advice and direction of the Court is necessary, the passing of accounts application may be used as a convenient forum to address these issues, saving the estate the expense of a further attendance in Court for a separate advice and directions application. If necessary, however, a separate application for advice and directions may be commenced under section 60 of the *Administration of Estates Act* by issuing a Notice of Motion in the Court, and can be returnable at the same time as the passing of accounts.

Before the personal representative proceeds to make a final distribution, he or she should ensure that a Clearance Certificate, for distribution purposes, has been obtained from Canada Customs and Revenue. The personal representative should also set aside sufficient funds for the personal representative's compensation, for any future legal and accounting fees, and for representation of the estate, and of any beneficiaries at the final passing of accounts before distributing to the beneficiaries.

BRITISH COLUMBIA

Executors, administrators and trustees in British Columbia (who for consistency in language are referred to in this part as estate trustees) are required in their application for appointment to swear that they will render a just and true account of the estate whenever required by law. Most of the comments in this chapter regarding estate accounting apply equally in British Columbia.

However, there are differences between the procedure to compel a passing of accounts and the procedure for a voluntary passing of accounts. There are also some differences to note in the legislation governing trustee investments and how the unrealized assets of the estate are accounted for in any interim accounts.

COMPELLING A PASSING OF ACCOUNTS

An estate trustee has to be ready at all times to account to the beneficiaries and to creditors. This does not mean that full accounts need be prepared and maintained on a daily basis, but rather that the estate trustee must be in a position to give reasonable information from time to time.

In British Columbia, the estate trustee is required to pass his or her first accounts within two years[31] from the date of Grant of Probate or Letters of Administration and thereafter at such time as the Court directs.

Despite this requirement, a beneficiary can require an estate trustee to pass his or her accounts annually within one month from the anniversary of the grant by giving notice to the estate trustee to do so.[32] If the estate trustee fails to pass his or her accounts within the first two years or fails to comply with a notice to pass accounts,[33] or if the accounts are incomplete or inaccurate, he or she can be required to attend before the Court to explain why the accounts have not been passed.

Usually, it is only when a beneficiary wishes to have accounts passed earlier than two years from the date of the estate trustee's appointment that the beneficiary resorts to the notice procedure. Otherwise, he or she simply proceeds directly to bring on an application to the Court.

Such an application is commenced by Petition with supporting Affidavit and it may be issued out of any Registry.[34] The estate trustee is given time to file an Appearance.[35] If the estate trustee does so, a Notice of Hearing must be served on him or her.

The Petition will ask for an Order that the estate trustee show cause before the Registrar why his or her accounts have not been passed or a

---

[31] *Trustee Act*, R.S.B.C. 1996, c. 464, s. 99(1).
[32] *Ibid.*, s. 99(2).
[33] *Ibid.*, s. 99(3).
[34] *Supreme Court Rules*, B.C. Reg. 221/90, Rule 32(10) and Rule 10.
[35] *Ibid.*, Rule 14(3).

proper proceeding in connection with them taken. If the application is successful, the Court will order that the accounts of the estate trustee be passed before the Registrar at a date to be fixed and will usually order the estate trustee to fix the date within a certain period of time. The Order must be served on the estate trustee. If the estate trustee does not comply with the Order, the beneficiary may seek an Order to find the estate trustee in contempt and/or may seek an order to remove him or her as estate trustee.

If the estate trustee initiates a passing of accounts, he or she can do so without notice by Notice of Motion in the existing probate proceedings. In that case, the Notice of Motion must be issued out of the same Registry that issued the grant.

FORMAT

In British Columbia, no form of account is prescribed; the only rule is that the items in the accounts must be numbered consecutively.[36] However, the governing principle with respect to accounts is that they are for the information of the beneficiaries. Therefore, they must be "as nearly as accounts can ever be, self-explanatory, and simple to follow".[37] While no form is prescribed, the form of "court-format" account described earlier in this chapter is the preferable format and is the format which a Registrar would like to see on a passing of accounts. While the comments with respect to the various Statements in the accounts also apply in British Columbia, the following comments with respect to the Statement of Investment Accounts and the Statement of Unrealized Original Assets should be noted.

Statement of Investment Account

In British Columbia, an estate trustee's investment powers are either contained in the Will and/or Codicils or if those documents are silent, in the British Columbia *Trustee Act*.[38] The powers of investment for trustees contained in the British Columbia *Trustee Act* were significantly amended as of February 28, 2003. The standard of care in British Columbia is now that of a "prudent investor". As in Ontario, this means that when reviewing the investment activities of an estate trustee, the Court will consider those activities against an objective standard of whether a prudent

---

[36] *Ibid.*, Rule 32(13).
[37] *Re Lotzkar Estate*, [1971] 2 W.W.R. 234.
[38] Sections 15.1 to 15.5.

investor investing his or her own funds would have, in the circumstances, acted as did the estate trustee.

In British Columbia, however, estate trustees do not have a statutory mandate to consider enumerated investment criteria nor is diversification mandated. It was thought that some trust funds would be sufficiently small that diversification would hardly be possible. Investment criteria were not included out of concern that such a list would in time become another checklist approach to assessing whether or not prudence took place. Mutual funds investments are now expressly allowed, as are common trust funds. The British Columbia legislation provides that investment in such a fund is not a "delegation of authority" with respect to investments.[39]

An estate trustee may retain the services of a professional investment advisor and delegate to that advisor (called an agent) his or her authority to invest. While a written agreement with the agent is not required, common sense dictates that the agreement be in writing. The Act requires prudence in selecting the agent, establishing his or her terms of authority, advising the agent with respect to the trust's investment objectives and monitoring the agent's performance.

Statement of Unrealized Original Assets

In British Columbia, this statement usually lists these assets at the market value at the end of the accounting period rather than at the date of death value. The market value is estimated and this estimated value is included for the purpose of calculating the estate trustee's remuneration for the accounting period. As previously noted in Chapter 3, if the realized value of the asset or its value at distribution to a beneficiary is different, an adjustment must be made to the estate trustee's compensation.

FORMAL PASSING OF ACCOUNTS

As noted earlier, an estate trustee in British Columbia may volunteer or may be compelled to "pass his (or her) accounts". A passing is not necessary if all of the beneficiaries are *sui juris* (in other words, not under any legal disability) and if all the beneficiaries consent to the accounts.

If one or more of the beneficiaries is a minor or under some other legal disability, the accounts will have to be passed. The estate trustee would make this application without notice by Notice of Motion.[40] In the Notice

---

[39] *Ibid.*, s. 15.1(7).
[40] *Supreme Court Rules*, Rule 61(58).

CHAPTER 4: ESTATE ACCOUNTING 149

of Motion, Orders would be sought from the Court that the estate trustee's accounts be passed before the Registrar and that the Registrar fix the estate trustee's remuneration (if remuneration is being sought). The Court might also be asked to appoint someone to represent persons who are under a disability[41] or for payment into Court of a beneficiary's share[42] and finally, if it is a final passing of accounts, for the discharge of the estate trustee.[43]

While it is common to refer matters of passing of accounts and estate trustee remuneration to the Registrar, the *Supreme Court Rules* do not require this.[44] For example, if the accounts are being passed because a minor is involved, it may be possible to have the accounts and remuneration approved by the Court without reference to the Registrar if all of the adult beneficiaries have approved the accounts and have approved the estate trustee's remuneration (particularly if the minor's guardian has reviewed and approved the accounts and remuneration). While neither a guardian nor the Public Guardian and Trustee have authority to approve accounts on behalf of a minor, such approval may be helpful.

If the Court orders a reference to the Registrar, it may also order that the Registrar's certificate, when filed, will be binding on the parties.[45] Otherwise, the Registrar will state the results of the passing in the form of a report and recommendation to the Court.

To initiate the arrangements for reference to the Registrar, an Appointment[46] needs to be prepared and submitted to the Registrar together with a copy of the Order and the required fee.

All persons to whom a duty to account is owed must be served. These persons include the income and capital beneficiaries, vested or contingent; any unpaid legatees or creditors; any successor trustees; and any other persons who may have an interest in the deceased person's assets. The documents to be served are the following:

- Affidavit in Support of Application to Pass Accounts[47]
- Accounts attached as an exhibit to the Affidavit in Support
- Affidavit (or memorandum attested to by Affidavit) with respect to the work done by the estate trustee

---

[41] *Ibid.*, Rule 6(10).
[42] *Trustee Act*, s. 40.
[43] *Estate Administration Act*, R.S.B.C. 1996, c. 122, s. 27.
[44] *Supreme Court Rules*, Rule 61(59).
[45] *Ibid.*, Rule 32(2).
[46] *Ibid.*, Rule 32(6), Form 24.
[47] *Ibid.*, Rule 61(58), Form 84.

- Solicitor's bill if it is to be assessed at the same time
- The estate trustee's proposal for remuneration, if it is not specifically referred to in the Accounts
- The Appointment to pass the accounts
- Court Order referring the matter to the Registrar

It is possible to send these documents by mail to each person to whom a duty to account is owed asking that the person approve the accounts in writing and consent to the estate trustee's remuneration and any solicitor's bill which is being assessed.

If all persons acknowledge receipt of the documents and so consent, their responses in that regard can be attached to an Affidavit of Service which must be filed.

If there are issues related to the accounts, it is best if the estate trustee tries to address and satisfy those issues prior to the hearing.

On the date set for the hearing, the estate trustee will attend (with or without his or her solicitor) and any persons to whom the duty to account is owed also have the right to attend personally or by their solicitors and to question the estate trustee about the accounts.

If the accounts are in order, the Registrar will sign a report. This report is often prepared in advance and will contain the Registrar's recommendations for remuneration of the estate trustee. If a solicitor's bill is presented for assessment, it may be assessed and a Certificate of Costs signed. If the original Court Order allows a Certficate to be filed rather than referred back to the Court, it will not be necessary to have a report confirmed by the Court.

Otherwise, the Registrar's report must be approved by the Court and Notice of Motion must be filed together with the fee. If an estate trustee wants to make a final distribution immediately after the Court confirmation of the Registrar's report and to be discharged by the Court, his or her application for discharge and application for cancellation of any bond should be made at the same time as the application for confirmation of the Registrar's report.

Copies of the Notice of Motion and the Registrar's report and, in due course, the resulting Order are served on all the persons who were served with the Notice of the Appointment.

In British Columbia, there is no tariff of costs which are allowed to solicitors on a passing of accounts. Normally, the estate trustee in the original Court application would ask for an Order that legal costs with respect to the application and passing be paid out of the estate on an indemnity basis.

The estate trustee, in the original application to the Court, may also ask the Court to make an order appointing someone to represent persons who are not *sui juris*[48] or who are not ascertained (for example, potential unborn beneficiaries).[49] The solicitor for the estate trustee will contact other counsel in advance of the application to ask whether they would be prepared to be appointed by the Court in this regard. If so, at the hearing of the application, the counsel for the estate trustee will put forward the names of such counsel who are prepared to act and the Court will appoint someone. The costs of these counsel are normally paid out of the estate. Sometimes, the Public Guardian and Trustee is prepared to be appointed in this role, assuming that its costs will be paid out of the estate.

A beneficiary is not entitled by statute to any costs relating to a passing of accounts. If a beneficiary wished to seek such costs, either out of the estate or against the estate trustee, he or she would have to make a submission in that regard.

---

[48] *Ibid.*, Rule 6(10).
[49] *Ibid.*, Rule 5(14).

Chapter 5

CASE STUDY

ESTATE OF MARY SOPHIA YOUNG
aka THE GOOD, BAD & THE UGLY

CASE STUDY[1]

ESTATE OF MARY SOPHIA YOUNG
AKA THE GOOD, BAD & THE UGLY

Mary Sophia Young, an elderly widow, died on January 21, Year 0.[2] Her estate is worth over $1 million. Her Will appointed The Trust Company and her solicitor, Pamela Lyons as Estate Trustees. The Certificate of Appointment was granted to Pamela Lyons alone after The Trust Company renounced.

The Will provides as follows:

1. Cash legacies of $5,000 to each grandniece and grandnephew (a total of four individuals).
2. Specific bequests of 1000 Bank of Nova Scotia shares to each of her nephew, William Young and her niece, Lillian Day.
3. After the payment of the bequests, the estate is held in trust during the life of her sister, Martha Young. During her lifetime, Martha Young is entitled to the income generated by the trust, but there is no power to encroach on the capital.
4. Upon Martha Young's death, the residue is distributed to the WBI Benevolent Foundation, a registered charity.

Martha Young died on July 9, Year 1. The Foundation has received a set of estate accounts, release and covering letter from the estate solicitor. The letter indicates that the bulk of the trust will be distributed upon receipt of the signed release. The Foundation's year-end is September 30 and the Foundation has fallen behind in its revenues this year.

The issues:

1. Is the administration of the estate as reflected by the accounts satisfactory?
2. Should the Foundation execute the release?

---

[1] CAUTION: This is a fictitious case study created by Deborah L. Campbell for teaching purposes. Deborah L. Campbell, M. Jasmine Sweatman of Miller Thomson LLP. Copyright 2003.
[2] In this case study, Year 0 refers to the year of death, while Year 1 refers to the next year. For example, if Year 0 means 2003, then Year 1 means 2004.

LAWLESS & LYONS LLP
Barristers and Solicitors
123 Main Street
Anywhere, Ontario L5G 1K1
Telephone: (905) 525-1234
Facsimile: (905) 525-9150

September 7, Year 1

WBI Benevolent Foundation
c/o White & Knight LLP
Barristers and Solicitors
2 Bloor Street West, Suite 2500
Toronto, Ontario M7K 2K2

Dear Sirs:

Re: Estate of Mary Sophia Young

As you are aware, I am the Trustee of the Estate of Mary Sophia Young. The life tenant, Martha Young, died on July 9th and I am now in a position to wind up the administration of this estate.

Enclosed for your information is a copy of the estate accounts for the period from January 21, Year 0 to August 31, Year 1 together with a form of release for your signature. Please review the accounts and sign the enclosed release. Once the release has been received, we will make an interim distribution.

Canada Customs and Revenue Agency (CCRA) has requested documentary evidence of the donation to your Foundation in order to re-assess Mrs. Young's terminal income tax return. To satisfy this request, it is imperative that a tax receipt be issued immediately. CCRA's decision to allow or disallow the requested reassessment will result in the gain or loss of thousands of dollars. You will note that the term deposit in this estate will be maturing on October 26, Year 1. We therefore expect receipt of the tax receipt and release from you as soon as possible.

Yours truly,
LAWLESS & LYONS LLP

Pamela Lyons
Enclosures
1. Will dated September 27, Yr-10
2. Set of Accounts (flawed)
3. Release (flawed)

LAST WILL AND TESTAMENT OF
MARY SOPHIA YOUNG[3]

LAWLESS & LYONS LLP

Barristers & Solicitors
123 Main Street
Anywhere, ON

---

[3] This is a fictitious case study created by Deborah L. Campbell for teaching purposes. Deborah L. Campbell, M. Jasmine Sweatman of Miller Thomson LLP. Copyright 2003.

THIS IS THE LAST WILL AND TESTAMENT of me, MARY SOPHIA YOUNG, of the City of Anywhere, in the Province of Ontario.

I.   I HEREBY REVOKE all Wills and testamentary dispositions of every nature or kind whatsoever previously made by me.

II.   I APPOINT my solicitor, PAMELA LYONS, and THE TRUST COMPANY to be the Executors and Trustees of this my Will.

III.   I GIVE all my property of every nature and kind and wheresoever situate, including any property over which I may have a general power of appointment, to my said Trustees upon the following trusts:

(a) To deliver to my sister, MARTHA YOUNG, all articles of personal, domestic and household use or ornament, including consumable stores, motorized vehicles, boats and accessories thereto owned by me at the date of my death.
(b) Except as hereinbefore provided, to use their discretion in the realization of my estate, with power to my Trustees to sell, call in and convert into money any part of my estate not consisting of money at such time or times, in such manner and upon such terms, and either for cash or credit or for part cash and part credit as my said Trustees may in their discretion decide upon, with power and discretion to postpone such conversion of my estate or any part or parts thereof for such length of time as they may think best, and I hereby declare that my Trustees shall have a separate and substantive power to retain any portion of my estate in the form existing at the date of my death in their discretion without responsibility for loss to the intent that investments so retained shall be deemed to be authorized investments for all purposes of this my Will. No reversionary interest shall be sold unless my Trustees in their discretion sees reason to the contrary but any such interest shall be retained until it falls into possession and no property not in fact producing income shall be treated as producing income.
(c) To pay out of and charge to the capital of my general estate my just debts, funeral and testamentary expenses, income tax and all estate, inheritance and succession duties or taxes whether imposed by or pursuant to the law of this or any other jurisdiction whatsoever that may be payable in connection with any property passing

or disposed of (or deemed so to pass or be disposed of by any governing law) on my death or in connection with any insurance on my life or any gift or benefit given or conferred by me either during my lifetime or by survivorship or by this my Will or any Codicil thereto and whether such duties or taxes be payable in respect of estates or interests which fall into possession at my death or at any subsequent time; and I hereby authorize my Trustees to commute or prepay any such taxes or duties. This direction shall not extend to or include any such duties or taxes that may be payable by a purchaser or transferee in connection with any property transferred to or acquired by such purchaser or transferee upon or after my death pursuant to any agreement with respect to such property.

(d) If my sister, MARTHA YOUNG survives me to hold and keep invested the residue of my estate and to pay the net income derived therefrom solely to or for the benefit of my said sister, during her lifetime to the extent possible in convenient monthly instalments.

(e) Upon the death of my said sister, or if she does not survive me my Trustees shall pay or transfer the residue of my estate to the WBI BENEVOLENT FOUNDATION. The receipt of the person who professes to be the Treasurer or other proper officer of the said organization shall be a sufficient discharge to my Trustees who shall not be bound to see to the application thereof.

IV. IN ADDITION to all the powers conferred by law, I give my Trustee the power to exercise and perform all acts of ownership with respect to the property comprising my estate from time to time to the same extent and with the same effect as if my Trustee were the absolute owner of my estate, without the consent or intervention of any beneficiary or judicial authority, and such powers shall, without limiting the generality of the foregoing, include the following powers which may be exercised from time to time by my Trustees in their absolute discretion:

(a) To make any investments, including investments in mutual funds, common trust funds, unit trusts or similar investments, which my Trustees in their absolute discretion may consider advisable without being limited to investments authorized by law for trustees, to alter or vary such investments from time to time in a similar manner, and to retain such investments for such length of time as my Trustees may consider advisable and my Trustees shall not be liable for any loss that may happen to my estate in connection with any such investment made by them in good faith;

(b) To make, or refrain from making, all elections, allocations, determinations, and designations available or permitted under the provisions of the *Income Tax Act* (Canada) or by any other relevant taxing statute or regulation of any country, province, state or territory from time to time in force, as my Trustees may consider in the best interests of my estate and the beneficiaries whether or not such election, determination or designation would have the effect of conferring an advantage on any one or more of the beneficiaries or could otherwise be considered but for the foregoing as not being an impartial exercise by my Trustees of their duties hereunder or as not being the maintaining of an even hand among the beneficiaries (unless any advantage so conferred is at the expense of any other beneficiary), and all such exercises of her discretion shall be binding upon all of the beneficiaries and shall not be subject to question by any person, official, authority, court or tribunal whatsoever or whomsoever; and

(c) To pay, compromise or settle any liability, direct or indirect that I may be under or that others may be under to me at the date of my death, or arrange for any extension of time for the payment thereof including the making of arrangements for the gradual liquidation of any liabilities owing by me at my death, including, without limiting the generality thereof, claims against my estate arising before or after my death under the *Family Law Act* (Ontario) and to compromise, settle, waive or pay any claims at any time owing to my estate, or which my estate may have against others, for consideration or no consideration, and upon such terms and conditions as my Trustees may deem advisable, and to refer to arbitration all such claims if my Trustees deem advisable, and I hereby specifically exonerate my Trustee in connection with any such settlements if she acts *bona fide*;

V. I EXONERATE my Trustee from any responsibility or liability for loss or damage which may be occasioned to my estate through a *bona fide* exercise by her of any of the powers conferred hereby or by law. Any decision or action whether actually made or taken in writing or implied by my Trustee's acts shall be conclusive and binding upon all persons concerned.

VI. I HEREBY SPECIFICALLY DIRECT that any right, title or interest, whether possessory or proprietary, of any beneficiary under this my Will or any Codicil hereto and all income, accretions and capital gains arising therefrom or accrued or realized thereon, including any property into which such interest, income and capital gains may be traced, shall be the private and separate property of such beneficiary and shall be excluded from and not fall into or form part of any family assets, net family property, community of property or partnership of acquests or be subject to any other matrimonial or conjugal rights of the spouse or consort of such beneficiary and shall not be liable for the satisfaction of the obligations of such beneficiary in respect of any such spouse, consort or community.

IN TESTIMONY WHEREOF I have to this my Last Will and Testament, written upon this and five (5) preceding pages of paper, subscribed my name this 27th day of September Yr. – 10.

SIGNED, PUBLISHED AND)
DECLARED by the said Testatrix,)
MARY SOPHIA YOUNG, as and)
for her last Will and Testament, in)
the presence of us, both present at)
the same time, who, at her request,)
in her presence and in the presence)
of each other, have hereunto)
subscribed our names as witnesses.)
)
)
_____)   _____
Signature of Witness   )   Mary Sophia Young
)
)
_____)
Address   )
_____)
)
)
)
)
)
_____)
Signature of Witness   )
)
_____)
Address   )
_____)

ESTATE OF MARY SOPHIA YOUNG

STATEMENT OF ESTATE ACCOUNTS
For the Period January 21, Year 0 to August 31, Year 1
[FLAWED VERSION OF ACCOUNTS][4]

ESTATE TRUSTEE: Pamela Lyons

DATE OF DEATH: January 21, Year 0

DATE OF APPOINTMENT: May 18, Year 0

LAWLESS & LYONS LLP
Barristers and Solicitors
123 Main Street
Anywhere, Ontario L5G 1K1

---

[4] CAUTION: This is a fictitious case study created by Deborah L. Campbell for teaching purposes. Deborah L. Campbell, M. Jasmine Sweatman of Miller Thomson LLP. Copyright 2003.

ESTATE OF MARY SOPHIA YOUNG
STATEMENT OF ESTATE ACCOUNTS

For the Period January 21, Year 0 to August 31, Year 1

INDEX

	Page Nos.
Statement of Original Assets - January 21, Year 0	1 - 2
Capital Receipts	3 - 5
Capital Disbursements	6 - 10
Revenue Receipts	11 - 14
Revenue Disbursements	15 - 16
Investment Account	17 - 18
Cash Summary	19
Statement of Trustee's Compensation	20
Statement of Unrealized Original Assets - August 31, Year 1	21
Statement of Proposed Distribution	21

ESTATE OF MARY SOPHIA YOUNG
STATEMENT OF ORIGINAL ASSETS
As of January 21, Year 0

Bank Accounts

The Trust Company, Winnipeg, Manitoba
Investment Administration Acct. No. 405-020460-1 - Balance $6,302.30

The Trust Company, Ottawa Main Branch, Ottawa, Ontario
Chequing Acct. No. 354-595415   56.33

Bonds and Debentures

Canada Savings Bonds due Nov. 1, Year 4 - Principal   60,000.00

AGT Ltd. 9.5% Debenture due Aug. 24/Y4
- Principal $25,000.00 @ $1.0490   26,225.00

Ford Credit Canada due April 8/Y0
- Principal $55,000.00 @ $.98938   54,415.90

Stocks

Bank of Nova Scotia - 3000 shares @ $31.85   95,550.00
    Bank of Nova Scotia - ex-dividend   630.00
Royal Bank of Canada - 1200 shares @ $76.20   91,440.00
Enbridge Inc. - 2470 shares @ $69.25   171,047.50
Enermark Income Fund - 2600.00 units @ $2.78   7,228.00
Teck Corporation, Class "B" - 200 shares @ $10.10   2,020.00
BC Gas Inc. New - 1700 shares @ $29.50   50,150.00
BCE Inc. - 2050 shares @ $60.60   124,230.00
TransAlta Corporation - 3500 shares @ $23.00   80,500.00
Exxon Corporation - 1400 shares @ US $71.125   151,055.28
First Australia Prime - 3500 shares @ $10.60   37,100.00
Toronto-Dominion Bank - 500 shares @ $62.25   31,125.00
    Toronto-Dominion Bank - ex-dividend   170.00

Mutual Funds

Templeton Growth Fund - 3463.797 units @ $7.9125   27,407.29

Real Property

22 Sussex Drive, Ottawa   750,000.00

Annuities

Trust Company Fixed Term Annuity   8,724.26

Miscellaneous

CPP - January, Year 0	287.70
OAS - January, Year 0	410.82
Prior Year Income tax refund (estimated)	5,292.39
Globe & Mail - subscription refund	105.43
Continental Insurance Brokers - premium refund	434.16
Jewellery, Furniture, Art and personal effects	10,000.00

TOTAL ORIGINAL ASSETS $1,793,419.03

ESTATE OF MARY SOPHIA YOUNG
<u>CAPITAL RECEIPTS</u>
For the Period January 21, Year 0 to August 31, Year 1

1.	Jan. 21/Y0	The Trust Company Investment Administration Acct. #405-020460-1 - Balance	$6,302.30
2.	Jan. 21/Y0	The Trust Company Chequing Acct. #354-595415 - Balance	56.33
3.	Jan. 27/Y0	Bank of Nova Scotia - ex-dividend	630.00
4.	Jan. 31/Y0	Toronto-Dominion Bank- ex-dividend	170.00
5.	Feb. 1/Y0	Trust Company Fixed Term annuity payment	186.10
6.	Feb. 16/Y0	Globe & Mail - subscription refund	105.43
7.	Mar. 1/Y0	Trust Company Fixed Term annuity payment	186.10
8.	Mar. 7/Y0	Government of Canada - Jan/Y0 CPP payment	287.70
		- Jan/Y0 OAS payment	410.82
9.	Mar. 31/Y0	Trust Company Fixed Term annuity payment	186.10
10.	Apr. 8/Y0	Ford Credit Canada - investment principal	54,316.14
11.	Apr. 8/Y0	Lakeshore Lodge - refund of account overpayment	2,674.92
12.	May 6/Y0	Trust Company Fixed Term annuity payment	186.10
13.	May 31/Y0	Trust Company Fixed Term annuity payment	186.10
14.	June 30/Y0	Trust Company Fixed Term annuity payment	186.10
15.	July 2/Y0	Canada Savings Bonds - redeemed	60,000.00
16.	July 15/Y0	Usually, Always, Wright - proceeds from sale of 22 Sussex Drive	676,287.54

17.	July 28/Y0	Nortel Networks - sold 560 shares	65,349.00
18.	Aug. 6/Y0	Continental Insurance Brokers - insurance premium refund	434.16
19.	Aug. 9/Y0	BC Gas Inc. - sold 1000 shares	48,065.79
20.	Aug. 9/Y0	Enermark Income Fund - sold 2600 units	10,195.99
21	Aug. 9/Y0	First Australia Prime Income Fund - sold 3500 units	33,398.14
22.	Aug. 9/Y0	TransAlta Corp. - sold 3500 shares	72,675.66
23.	Aug. 26/Y0	Trust Company Fixed Term annuity payment	186.10
24.	Aug. 31/Y0	Trust Company Fixed Term annuity payment	186.10
25.	Aug. 31/Y0	Teck Corporation - Class "B" - sold 200 shares	2,265.00
26.	Sept. 14/Y0	Trust Company Fixed Term annuity - balance	7,712.78
27.	Sept. 14/Y0	Government of Canada - prior year income tax refund	5,253.92
28.	July 28/Y1	Bank of Nova Scotia - sold 1000 shares	37,982.50
29.	July 28/Y1	Toronto-Dominion Bank - sold 1000 shares	35,482.50
30.	July 28/Y1	Royal Bank of Canada - sold 1200 shares	97,292.50
31.	July 28/Y1	Nortel Networks - sold 2000 shares	2,765.00
32.	July 28/Y1	Enbridge Inc. - sold 4940 shares	161,517.50
33.	July 28/Y1	BCE Inc. - sold 2050 shares	66,665.00
34.	July 28/Y1	Record gain on sale of CIBC 5.65% Preferred shares	58,370.93
35.	July 28/Y1	Record gain on sale of Westcoast Energy 9.7% Bond	220.00
36.	Aug. 24/Y1	AGT Ltd. Debenture redeemed	25,000.00
37.	Aug. 31/Y1	Adjusting entry	7,653.36

TOTAL CAPITAL RECEIPTS $1,541,029.71

ESTATE OF MARY SOPHIA YOUNG
CAPITAL DISBURSEMENTS
For the Period January 21, Year 0 to August 31, Year 1

1.	Jan. 25/Y0	Lakeshore Lodge - February rent	$3,897.50
2.	Jan. 25/Y0	Central Health Services - paid outstanding account	130.01
3.	Feb. 1/Y0	Tartan Properties - rent	1,000.00
4.	Feb. 28/Y0	Lawless & Lyons - paid account	42,800.00
5.	Mar. 1/Y0	Tartan Properties - rent	1,000.00
6.	Mar. 15/Y0	Bell Canada - paid outstanding account	13.14
7.	Mar. 15/Y0	Lakeshore Nursing Services - paid outstanding account	3,648.21
8.	Mar. 15/Y0	Central Health Services - paid outstanding account	187.79
9.	Mar. 15/Y0	Municipal Hydro - paid account	45.09
10.	Mar. 17/Y0	Minister of Finance - paid probate fees	14,185.00
11.	Mar. 21/Y0	Bell Canada - paid account	23.29
12.	Mar. 23/Y0	Lakeshore Funeral Chapel - paid funeral expenses	3,709.79
13.	Apr. 1/Y0	Martha Young - payment to income beneficiary	3,500.00
14.	Apr. 1/Y0	Tartan Properties - rent	1,000.00
15.	Apr. 21/Y0	Bell Canada - paid account	19.72
16.	Apr 30/Y0	Lawless & Lyons - paid account	4,575.39
17.	May 2/Y0	Lakeshore Pharmacy - paid outstanding account	479.74
18.	May 1/Y0	Martha Young - payment to income beneficiary	3,500.00
19.	May 1/Y0	Tartan Properties - rent	1,000.00
20.	May 17/Y0	Municipal Hydro - paid account	47.39

21	May 21/Y0	Bell Canada - paid account	21.23
22.	June 1/Y0	Martha Young - payment to income beneficiary	3,500.00
23.	June 1/Y0	Tartan Properties - rent	1,000.00
24.	June 21/Y0	Bell Canada - paid account	18.16
25.	July 2/Y0	Martha Young - payment to income beneficiary	3,500.00
26.	July 2/Y0	Tartan Properties - rent	1,000.00
27.	July 15/Y0	Legacy payments to grandnieces and grandnephews as follows:	
		- Robert Day	5,000.00
		- Cheryl Day	5,000.00
		- Bruce Young	5,000.00
		- Janna Young	5,000.00
28.	July 15/Y0	William Young - paid expenses	1,291.06
29.	July 15/Y0	Sunnybrook & Women's College Health Sciences Centre – paid account	170.00
30.	July 15/Y0	Lawless & Lyons – paid account	3,253.76
31.	July 15/Y0	Municipal Hydro – paid account	54.17
32.	July 21/Y0	Bell Canada – paid account	27.10
33.	July 30/Y0	Lawless & Lyons – paid account	7,846.04
34.	Aug. 1/Y0	Martha Young – payment to income beneficiary	3,500.00
35.	Aug. 1/Y0	Tartan Properties – rent	1,000.00
36.	Aug. 21/Y0	Bell Canada – paid account	21.75
37.	Sept. 1/Y0	Martha Young – payment to income beneficiary	3,500.00
38.	Sept. 1/Y0	Tartan Properties – rent	1,000.00
39	Sept. 15/Y0	Lawless & Lyons – paid account	17,925.20
40.	Sept. 15/Y0	Municipal Hydro – paid account	54.47
41.	Sept. 15/Y0	EnRoute/Diners Club – paid outstanding account	67.43
42.	Sept. 21/Y0	Lawless & Lyons – paid account	494.35

43.	Sept. 21/Y0	Bell Canada – paid account	22.50
44.	Oct. 1/Y0	Martha Young – payment to income beneficiary	3,500.00
45.	Oct. 1/Y0	Tartan Properties – rent	1,000.00
46.	Oct. 18/Y0	William Young – reimburse for additional expenses	764.00
47.	Oct. 18/Y0	Lillian Day – reimburse for expenses	440.50
48.	Oct. 21/Y0	Bell Canada – paid account	23.39
49.	Nov. 1/Y0	Martha Young – payment to income beneficiary	3,500.00
50.	Nov. 1/Y0	Tartan Properties – rent	1,000.00
51.	Nov. 4/Y0	Western Cemetery Lettering – paid marker engraving	292.11
52.	Nov. 17/Y0	Municipal Hydro – paid account	56.50
53.	Nov. 21/Y0	Bell Canada – paid account	27.65
54.	Nov. 30/Y0	Lawless & Lyons – paid account	12,442.85
55.	Dec. 1/Y0	Martha Young – payment to income beneficiary	3,500.00
56.	Dec. 1/Y0	Tartan Properties – rent	1,000.00
57.	Dec. 21/Y0	Bell Canada – paid account	21.75
58.	Jan. 4/Y1	Martha Young – payment to income beneficiary	10,000.00
59.	Jan. 4/Y1	Tartan Properties – rent	1,000.00
60.	Jan. 18/Y1	Municipal Hydro – paid account	63.44
61.	Jan. 21/Y1	Bell Canada – paid account	18.15
62.	Jan. 31/Y1	Lawless & Lyons – paid account	10,276.13
63.	Feb. 1/Y1	Martha Young – payment to income beneficiary	3,500.00
64.	Feb. 1/Y1	Tartan Properties – rent	1,000.00
65.	Feb. 1/Y1	Receiver General for Canada – paid estate taxes	2,271.87

Chapter 5: Case Study

66.	Feb. 1/Y1	Receiver General for Canada - terminal T1 taxes	186,355.60
67.	Feb. 21/Y1	Bell Canada - paid account	19.76
68.	Mar. 1/Y1	Martha Young - payment to income beneficiary	3,500.00
69.	Mar. 1/Y1	Tartan Properties - rent	1,000.00
70.	Mar. 15/Y1	Municipal Hydro - paid account	62.74
71.	Mar. 21/Y1	Bell Canada - paid account	27.60
72.	Mar. 31/Y1	Lawless & Lyons - paid account	3,778.06
73.	Apr. 1/Y1	Martha Young - payment to income beneficiary	3,500.00
74.	Apr. 1/Y1	Tartan Properties - rent	1,000.00
75.	Apr. 21/Y1	Bell Canada - paid account	20.45
76.	May 1/Y1	Martha Young - payment to income beneficiary	3,500.00
77.	May 1/Y1	Tartan Properties - rent	1,000.00
78	May 15/Y1	Beancounters - paid preparation terminal tax return	1,605.00
79.	May 19/Y1	Municipal Hydro - paid account	47.54
80.	May 21/Y1	Bell Canada - paid account	22.73
81.	May 31/Y1	Lawless & Lyons - paid account	2,709.84
82.	June 1/Y1	Martha Young - payment to income beneficiary	3,500.00
83.	June 1/Y1	Tartan Properties - rent	1,000.00
84.	June 21/Y1	Bell Canada - paid account	27.42
85.	June 30/Y1	Loss on sale of 1000 shares Laidlaw Inc.	12,580.38
86.	June 30/Y1	Lawless & Lyons - paid account	1,613.91
87.	July 1/Y1	Martha Young - payment to income beneficiary	3,500.00
88.	July 1/Y1	Tartan Properties - rent	1,000.00

89.	July 15/Y1	Municipal Hydro - paid account	71.50
90.	July 21/Y1	Bell Canada - paid account	19.54
91.	July 28/Y1	Loss on sale of 3000 shares NS Power Holdings Inc.	8,746.00
92.	Aug. 30/Y1	Lawless & Lyons - paid account	5,383.11

TOTAL CAPITAL DISBURSEMENTS $455,318.80

ESTATE OF MARY SOPHIA YOUNG
REVENUE RECEIPTS
For the Period January 21, Year 0 to August 31, Year 1

1.	Jan. 31/Y0	The Trust Company Investment Administration Account - interest	$8.80
2.	Feb. 15/Y0	First Australia Prime Income Fund - dividend	280.00
3.	Feb. 22/Y0	Enermark Income Fund - dividend	104.00
4.	Feb. 24/Y0	Royal Bank of Canada - dividend	552.00
5.	Feb. 28/Y0	BC Gas Inc. - dividend	476.00
6.	Feb. 28/Y0	The Trust Company Investment Administration Account - interest	.35
7.	Mar. 1/Y0	Enbridge Inc. - dividend	1,420.25
8.	Mar. 1/Y0	The Trust Company Investment Administration Account - interest	.02
9.	Mar. 7/Y0	The Trust Company- adjustment regarding Jan. 6/Y0 fees	302.34
10.	Mar. 10/Y0	Exxon Corporation - dividend (US $574.00)	828.57
11.	Mar. 15/Y0	First Australia Prime Income Fund - dividend	280.00
12.	Mar. 22/Y0	Enermark Income Fund - dividend	78.00
13.	Mar. 31/Y0	The Trust Company - estate account interest	1.49
14.	Apr. 4/Y0	TransAlta Corporation - dividend	875.00
15.	Apr. 15/Y0	First Australia Prime Income Fund - dividend	280.00
16.	Apr. 20/Y0	Enermark Income Fund - dividend	78.00
17.	Apr. 28/Y0	Bank of Nova Scotia - dividend	630.00
18.	Apr. 30/Y0	Toronto-Dominion Bank - dividend	170.00
19.	Apr. 30/Y0	The Trust Company - estate account interest	36.78
20.	May 16/Y0	First Australia Prime Income Fund - dividend	280.00
21	May 20/Y0	Enermark Income Fund - dividend	130.00
22.	May 24/Y0	Royal Bank of Canada - dividend	552.00

23.	May 31/Y0	BC Gas Inc. - dividend	501.50
24.	May 31/Y0	The Trust Company - estate account interest	48.09
25.	June 1/Y0	Enbridge Inc. - dividend	1,494.35
26.	June 10/Y0	Exxon Corporation - dividend (US $574.00)	798.19
27.	June 14/Y0	The Trust Company - reverse duplicate custodial fee	430.56
28.	June 15/Y0	First Australia Prime Income Fund - dividend	280.00
29.	June 21/Y0	Enermark Income Fund - dividend	78.00
30.	June 30/Y0	Teck Corporation - dividend	20.00
31.	June 30/Y0	The Trust Company - estate account interest	43.82
32.	July 2/Y0	TransAlta Corporation - dividend	875.00
33.	July 16/Y0	First Australia Prime Income Fund - dividend	280.00
34.	July 18/Y0	First Australia Prime Income Fund - dividend	280.00
35.	July 20/Y0	Enermark Income Fund - dividend	78.00
36.	July 28/Y0	Bank of Nova Scotia - dividend	630.00
37.	July 31/Y0	Toronto-Dominion Bank - dividend	170.00
38.	July 31/Y0	The Trust Company - estate account interest	45.40
39	Aug. 13/Y0	First Australia Prime Income Fund - dividend	280.00
40.	Aug. 24/Y0	Royal Bank of Canada - dividend	576.00
41.	Aug. 24/Y0	AGT Ltd. 9.5% Debenture - semi-annual interest	1,187.50
42.	Aug. 31/Y0	The Trust Company - estate account interest	10.18
43.	Sept. 1/Y0	Enbridge Inc. - dividend	1,494.35
44.	Sept. 10/Y0	Exxon Corporation - dividend (US $574.00)	849.80
45.	Sept. 16/Y0	Treasury Bill interest	765.26
46.	Sept. 17/Y0	Scotiabank - term deposit interest	109.48
47.	Sept. 20/Y0	The Trust Company - estate account interest	7.49
48.	Oct. 28/Y0	CIBC 5.65% Preferred - dividend	1,341.85
49.	Oct. 28/Y0	Bank of Nova Scotia - dividend	210.00
50.	Oct. 31/Y0	Toronto-Dominion Bank - dividend	170.00

51.	Nov. 15/Y0	Laidlaw Inc. - dividend	66.55
52.	Nov. 15/Y0	NS Power Holdings Inc. - dividend	622.50
53.	Nov. 15/Y0	Westcoast Energy 9.7% Bond - semi-annual interest	970.00
54.	Nov. 24/Y0	Royal Bank of Canada - dividend	576.00
55.	Nov. 25/Y0	Secure Capital - account interest	13.06
56.	Dec. 1/Y0	Enbridge Inc. - dividend	1,494.35
57.	Dec. 10/Y0	Exxon Corporation - dividend (US $574.00)	833.74
58.	Dec. 25/Y0	Secure Capital - account interest	57.45
59.	Jan. 25/Y1	Secure Capital - account interest	35.70
60.	Jan. 28/Y1	CIBC 5.65% Preferred - dividend	1,342.50
61.	Jan. 28/Y1	Bank of Nova Scotia - dividend	210.00
62.	Jan. 31/Y1	Toronto-Dominion Bank - dividend	170.00
63.	Feb. 15/Y1	Laidlaw Inc. - dividend	66.55
64.	Feb. 15/Y1	NS Power Holdings Inc. - dividend	622.50
65.	Feb. 24/Y1	Royal Bank of Canada - dividend	576.00
66.	Feb. 24/Y1	AGT Ltd. 9.5% Debenture - semi-annual interest	1,187.50
67.	Feb. 25/Y1	Secure Capital - account interest	19.42
68.	Mar. 1/Y1	Enbridge Inc. - dividend	1,494.35
69.	Mar. 10/Y1	Exxon Corporation - dividend (US $574.00)	846.65
70.	Mar. 25/Y1	Secure Capital - account interest	18.53
71.	Apr. 25/Y1	Secure Capital - account interest	12.75
72.	Apr. 28/Y1	CIBC 5.65% Preferred - dividend	1,342.50
73.	Apr. 28/Y1	Bank of Nova Scotia - dividend	210.00
74.	Apr. 30/Y1	Toronto-Dominion Bank - dividend	170.00
75.	May 15/Y1	Laidlaw Inc. - dividend	66.55
76.	May 15/Y1	NS Power Holdings Inc. - dividend	622.50
77.	May 15/Y1	Westcoast Energy 9.7% Bond - semi-annual interest	970.00

78.	May 24/Y1	Royal Bank of Canada - dividend	576.00
79.	May 25/Y1	Secure Capital - account interest	9.34
80.	June 1/Y1	Enbridge Inc. - dividend	1,494.35
81.	June 10/Y1	Exxon Corporation - dividend (US $574.00)	823.69
82.	June 25/Y1	Secure Capital - account interest	7.75
83.	July 15/Y1	Scotiabank - GIC interest	30,150.00
84.	July 25/Y1	Secure Capital - account interest	7.82
85.	July 28/Y1	CIBC 5.65% Preferred - dividend	1,342.50
86.	July 28/Y1	Bank of Nova Scotia - dividend	210.00
87.	July 31/Y1	Toronto-Dominion Bank - dividend	170.00
88.	Aug. 15/Y1	NS Power Holdings Inc. - dividend	622.50
89.	Aug. 24/Y1	AGT Ltd. 9.5% Debenture - semi-annual interest	1,187.50
90.	Aug. 24/Y1	Royal Bank of Canada - dividend	576.00
91.	Aug. 25/Y1	Secure Capital - account interest	8.13

TOTAL REVENUE RECEIPTS $72,221.65

ESTATE OF MARY SOPHIA YOUNG
<u>REVENUE DISBURSEMENTS</u>
For the Period January 21, Year 0 to August 31, Year 1

1.	Mar. 7/Y0	The Trust Company Market Value fee to Jan. 21	$280.60
2.	Mar. 7/Y0	The Trust Company Security Trade fee to Jan. 21	21.74
3.	Mar. 10/Y0	Exxon Corporation - non-resident tax	86.09
4.	Mar. 31/Y0	The Trust Company - estate account overdraft charges	36.38
5.	Apr. 5/Y0	The Trust Company - Fees for executors' work to Apr. 1/Y0	1,070.00
6.	Apr. 6/Y0	The Trust Company - custodial fee - Feb. 20 to Mar. 19/Y0	428.00
7.	Apr. 13/Y0	The Trust Company - custodial fee - Jan. 21 to Feb. 19/Y0	413.02
8.	Apr. 25/Y0	The Trust Company - custodial fee - Feb. 20 to Mar. 19/Y0	430.56
9.	Apr. 30/Y0	The Trust Company - estate account overdraft charges	21.69
10.	June 10/Y0	Exxon Corporation - non-resident tax	86.10
11.	June 14/Y0	The Trust Company - custodial fee - Mar. 20 to Apr. 19/Y0	430.56
12.	June 22/Y0	The Trust Company - Market Value fee	432.89
13.	July 2/Y0	The Trust Company - chequing account service charges	9.20
14.	July 21/Y0	The Trust Company - Market Value fee	133.75
15.	July 25/Y0	First Australia Prime Income Fund - reverse duplicate entry	280.00
16.	Aug. 23/Y0	The Trust Company - Market Value fee	133.75
17.	Sept. 12/Y0	Exxon Corporation - non-resident tax	127.47

18.	Sept. 17/Y0	Westcoast Energy 9.7% Bond - paid accrued interest	664.38
19.	Sept. 20/Y0	The Trust Company - Market Value fee	133.75
20.	Dec. 10/Y0	Exxon Corporation - non-resident tax	125.06
21	Mar. 10/Y1	Exxon Corporation - non-resident tax	130.10
22.	Apr. 15/Y1	Beancounters - paid preparation of T3 return	650.00
23.	June 10/Y1	Exxon Corporation - non-resident tax	127.00

TOTAL REVENUE DISBURSEMENTS $6,522.09

ESTATE OF MARY SOPHIA YOUNG
INVESTMENT ACCOUNT
For the Period January 21, Year 0 to August 31, Year 1

			PURCHASED	REDEEMED
1.	July 15/Y0	Scotiabank purchase GIC for 1 year @ 4.5% due July 15/Y1	670,000.00	
2.	Aug. 9/Y0	Purchase $166,000.00 Treasury Bills @ $.99539 due Sept. 16/Y0	165,234.74	
3.	Aug. 18/Y0	Purchase Scotiabank Term Deposit for 30 days @ 3.0% due Sept. 17/Y0	44,400.95	
4.	Sept. 16/Y0	Treasury Bills matured		$165,234.74
5.	Sept. 17/Y0	Scotiabank term deposit matured		44,400.95
6.	Sept. 17/Y0	CIBC 5.65% Preferred - purchase 3800 shares @ $27.60 plus commission $996.07	105,876.07	
7.	Sept. 17/Y0	Laidlaw Inc. - purchase 1000 shares @ $19.25 plus commission $436.63	19,686.63	
8.	Sept. 17/Y0	NS Power Holdings Inc. - purchase 3000 shares @ $20.00 plus commission $853.75	60,853.75	
9.	Sept. 17/Y0	Westcoast Energy 9.7% Bond due Nov. 15/Y4 - Principal $20,000.00 @ $1.0690	21,380.00	
10.	June 30/Y1	Laidlaw Inc. - sold 1000 shares @ $7.50 less commission $393.75		7,106.25

11.	June 30/Y1	Record loss on sale of Laidlaw shares		12,580.38
12.	July 15/Y1	Scotiabank GIC matured		670,000.00
13.	July 28/Y1	CIBC 5.65% Preferred - sold 3800 shares @ $43.35 less commission $483.00		164,247.00
14.	July 28/Y1	Record gain on sale of CIBC shares	58,370.93	
15.	July 28/Y1	NS Power Holdings Inc. - sold 3000 shares @ $17.50 less commission $392.25		52,107.75
16.	July 28/Y1	Record loss on sale of NS Power Holdings Inc. shares		8,746.00
17.	July 28/Y1	Westcoast Energy 9.7% Bond - sold $20,000.00 @ $1.0800		21,600.00
18.	July 28/Y1	Record gain on sale of Westcoast Energy Bond	220.00	
19.	July 28/Y1	Bank of Nova Scotia - purchase 90 day term deposit @ 2.75% due Oct. 26/Y1	1,000,000.00	
	TOTALS		$2,146,023.07	$1,146,023.07
		AMOUNT UNDER INVESTMENT AS OF August 31, Year 1		1,000,000.00
				$2,146,023.07

ESTATE OF MARY SOPHIA YOUNG
CASH SUMMARY
For the Period January 21, Year 0 to August 31, Year 1

Capital Receipts	$1,541,029.71	
Capital Disbursements	-455,318.80	
CAPITAL ACCOUNT BALANCE	$1,085,710.91	$1,085,710.91
Revenue Receipts	$72,221.65	
Revenue Disbursements	-6,252.09	
REVENUE ACCOUNT BALANCE	65,969.56	65,969.56
TOTAL RECEIPTS		$1,151,680.47
Less amount under Investment as of August 31 Year 1		1,000,000.00
UNINVESTED CASH BALANCE		$151,680.47

Secure Capital Account
Balance as of August 31, Year 1 $151,680.47

ESTATE OF MARY SOPHIA YOUNG
STATEMENT OF TRUSTEE'S COMPENSATION
For the Period January 21, Year 0 to August 31, Year 1

Capital Receipts	$1,541,029.71		
Add unrealized original assets	178,462.57		
	$1,719,492.28	@ 2.5%	$42,987.31
Capital Disbursements	$455,318.80		
Add capital account balance	1,085,710.91		
Add unrealized original assets	178,462.57		
	$1,719,492.28	@ 2.5%	42,987.31
Revenue Receipts	$72,221.65	@ 2.5%	1,805.54
Revenue Disbursements	$6,252.09		
Add revenue account balance	65,969.56		
	$72,221.65	@ 2.5%	1,805.54
Care and Management Fees @ 2/5ths of 1% of $1,565,000.10 for 19 months ($6,260.00 per annum)			9,911.67
TOTAL TRUSTEE'S COMPENSATION			$99,497.37

ESTATE OF MARY SOPHIA YOUNG
STATEMENT OF UNREALIZED ORIGINAL ASSETS
As of August 31, Year 1

Templeton Growth Fund - 4090.100 units	$27,407.29
Exxon Corporation - 1400 shares @ US $71.125 (to CDN @ $1.5170)	151,055.28
TOTAL UNREALIZED ORIGINAL ASSETS	$178,462.57

ESTATE OF MARY SOPHIA YOUNG
STATEMENT OF PROPOSED DISTRIBUTION

Net Receipts (from Cash Summary)		$1,158,118.61
Add Value of Unrealized Assets		178,462.57
		$1,336,581.18
Less Trustee's compensation	$99,497.37	
Less GST on compensation	6,964.82	
Less balance in revenue account to be paid to Estate of Martha Young	65,969.56	
Less allowance for final tax clearance certificate	164,149.43	-336,581.18
TO BE DISTRIBUTED TO WBI BENEVOLENT FOUNDATION		$1,000,000.00

"FLAWED"

RELEASE OF ESTATE TRUSTEE WITH A WILL[5]

WBI BENEVOLENT FOUNDATION, of the City of Toronto, in the Province of Ontario, DOES HEREBY ACKNOWLEDGE that it has this day received of and from PAMELA LYONS, Estate Trustee of the last Will and Testament of MARY SOPHIA YOUNG, late of the City of Toronto, in the Province of Ontario, deceased, the sum of **ONE MILLION DOLLARS ($1,000,000)** in full satisfaction and payment of such sum or sums of money, legacies and bequests as are given and bequeathed to it under the last Will and Testament aforesaid and all interest accrued thereon.

AND THEREFORE, the said WBI BENEVOLENT FOUNDATION, does by these presents remise, release, quitclaim and forever discharge the said PAMELA LYONS, her heirs and estate trustee(s) of and from any and all actions, claims, accounts and demands whatsoever which it now has or ever had against the said PAMELA LYONS in respect of or in connection with the Estate of the deceased and does hereby agree to hold harmless the said PAMELA LYONS and indemnify her with respect to any claims which may be made against the Estate and for which the said PAMELA LYONS may be found liable.

WITNESS the corporate seal of WBI BENEVOLENT FOUNDATION duly attested by the hand of its authorized officer in that regard this   day of September, Year 1.

WBI BENEVOLENT FOUNDATION

per:_____

---

[5] CAUTION: This is a fictitious case study created by Deborah L. Campbell for teaching purposes. Deborah L. Campbell, M. Jasmine Sweatman of Miller Thomson LLP. Copyright 2003.

CHAPTER 5: CASE STUDY **185**

CASE STUDY COMMENTARY

You have now had an opportunity to review the estate accounts and release received from Pamela Lyons.

COVERING LETTER

- The tone of the letter could be considered unprofessional.
- See discussion regarding the position that the distribution will be made once the release is received.

FLAWED ACCOUNTS

There should have been a number of issues which you would wish to query before you would be in a position to consider executing the release. These are itemized below according to the appropriate estate accounting section.

STATEMENT OF ORIGINAL ASSETS

- Accrued interest does not appear to have been calculated on any of the bonds or debentures.
- Is the total of $151,055.28 for the Exxon Corporation shares in Canadian or US Dollars?
- A cross reference to the entry in the Capital Receipts detailing the realization of the respective assets would have been helpful.

CAPITAL RECEIPTS

- More information is required with respect to the receipt of $676,287.54 as the proceeds from the sale of 22 Sussex Drive.
- There should have been accrued interest on the Ford Credit, AGT and Canada Savings Bonds to the date of death.
- It appears the estate did not receive the semi-annual interest payment which would have been made on the AGT debenture in February, Year 0 or Canada Savings Bond interest when the bonds were redeemed in July, Year 0.
- Where did 2,560 Nortel shares come from?
- Why did the trustee sell 560 Nortel shares for $65,349 but only receive $2,765 for the remaining 2,000 shares?

- The deceased apparently held 1,700 BC Gas shares as of her date of death, however, only 1,000 shares were sold in August, Year 0. What happened to the remaining 700 shares — they are not listed in the Statement of Unrealized Assets.
- What happened to the remaining Bank of Nova Scotia shares — they are not listed in the Statement of Unrealized Assets.
- The deceased held 500 Toronto-Dominion Bank shares as of her date of death, however, 1,000 TD Bank shares were sold in July, Year 1. Where did the additional shares come from?
- The deceased held 2,470 Enbridge Inc. shares as of her date of death, however, the trustee sold 4,940 Enbridge shares in July, Year 1. Where did the additional shares come from?
- Why do the accounts include an adjusting entry of $7,653.36?
- More details with respect to the price per share and costs on the sale of the equities would have been helpful for comparison purposes.

CAPITAL DISBURSEMENTS

- Why are payments being made out of the Capital account to or for the benefit of the life tenant, Martha Young (Tartan Properties, Municipal Hydro, Bell Canada)?
- Further information should be requested with respect to the payments to the Receiver General for Canada identified as estate taxes in the amount of $2,271.87 and terminal taxes of $186,355.60.
- What were the payments made to William Young and Lillian Day for?
- Copies of all Lawless & Lyons accounts are required.

REVENUE RECEIPTS

- It appears that no dividends were received with respect to BCE Inc. shares.
- See comments under Capital Receipts with respect to Ford Credit, AGT Debenture and Canada Savings Bonds interest income.

REVENUE DISBURSEMENTS

- Why were fees paid to the Trust Company?
- The total on page 16 should be $6,252.09 and not $6,522.09.

INVESTMENT ACCOUNT

- Why did the trustee select and hold the Laidlaw and NS Power Holdings Inc. shares, resulting in capital losses to the estate of $12,580.38 and $8,746 respectively?

STATEMENT OF TRUSTEE'S COMPENSATION

- The compensation calculation requires adjustment for legal fees incurred that were, in effect, estate trustee duties.
- The compensation was pre-taken without prior approval or clause in the Will.
- The total compensation should be reduced by the amount pre-taken.
- Any amount taken in excess should be refunded with interest.
- Details with respect to calculation of estate value of $1,565,000.10 for purposes of the care and management fee are required.
- Compensation is claimed for transferring the assets of the deceased from herself as the deceased's court-appointed Guardian of Property to herself in her capacity as trustee. Prior to Mrs. Young's death, Pamela Lyons had likely already realized Mrs. Young's assets and had them under her control. These points suggest that adjustments are required to the compensation (see corrected Statement of Trustee's Compensation and Statement of Proposed Distribution for an appropriate result).
- Consider the "five factors" outlined in Chapter 3 and whether any of those factors result in a reduction in the compensation.

STATEMENT OF UNREALIZED ORIGINAL ASSETS

- There are a different number of Templeton Growth Fund units at the end of the accounting period than at the beginning, but no transactions related to this asset appear in the estate accounts.

STATEMENT OF PROPOSED DISTRIBUTION

- It appears that the trustee has pre-taken a considerable amount of compensation, therefore, any claim for outstanding compensation should be reviewed before additional compensation payments are made.
- Once the payments made to or for the benefit of the life tenant are transferred from Capital Disbursements to Revenue Disbursements, it

appears that there is a Revenue Account overdraft, therefore, further payments to the estate of the deceased life tenant are inappropriate.
- The allowance or holdback pending receipt of the final tax Clearance Certificate may be excessive.

MISSING INFORMATION

- The accounts do not include a Statement of Trustee's Investments.

FLAWED RELEASE

- It is from a standard release form.
- It indicates that the sum of $1,000,000 is in "full satisfaction" of the funds to which the Foundation is entitled from the estate, notwithstanding that this is an interim distribution and the trustee continues to hold $164,149.43 pending receipt of the final tax Clearance Certificate.
- It includes the charity's unlimited indemnity of the trustee.

COMMENTARY: LEGAL ACCOUNTS[6]

As a result of reviewing the flawed accounts, the Foundation requested copies of all legal accounts rendered by Lawless & Lyons. You have reviewed these accounts (which follow) and have the following comments:

- The total amount incurred on account of legal fees appears excessive.
- A significant portion of the fees were for services rendered by the trustee in her capacity as estate trustee rather than by the trustee in her capacity as solicitor for the estate (see accounts detailing in bold the activities undertaken as solicitor).
- The Foundation should request that the accounts be redone separating out those activities undertaken as solicitor and those undertaken as estate trustee.
- The accounts do not provide sufficient detail.
- The Foundation should request that the accounts also be redone to show the amount of time spent on each activity, who performed the activity, the hourly rate and the day that the activity was undertaken.

NOTE: In the sample legal accounts that follow, the activities noted in bold are normally carried out by the estate solicitor and not by the estate trustee. Only those activities should attach an account for legal services. The remaining activities (*i.e.*, those normally carried out by the estate trustee) are covered by the payment of trustee compensation.

---

[6] CAUTION: This is a fictitious case study created by Deborah L. Campbell for teaching purposes. Deborah L. Campbell, M. Jasmine Sweatman of Miller Thomson LLP. Copyright 2003.

LAWLESS & LYONS LLP

Barristers and Solicitors
123 Main Street
Anywhere, Ontario L5G 1K1
Telephone: (905) 525-1234
Facsimile: (905) 525-9150

February 28, Year 0

Pamela Lyons
Trustee of the Estate of Mary Sophia Young
123 Main Street
Anywhere, ON L5G 1K1

Re: Mary Sophia Young

TO FEES for professional services rendered in my capacity as Guardian of Property for Mary Sophia Young for the period from July 1, Year 1 to January 21, Year 0.

OUR FEE:	$40,000.00
G.S.T. ON FEE:	2,800.00
TOTAL DUE AND PAYABLE	$42,800.00

THIS IS OUR ACCOUNT HEREIN,

LAWLESS & LYONS LLP

per:

Pamela Lyons
E. & O.E.

Our G.S.T. Registration No. 000000000001

LAWLESS & LYONS LLP
Barristers and Solicitors
123 Main Street
Anywhere, Ontario   L5G 1K1

Telephone: (905) 525-1234
Facsimile: (905) 525-9150

April 30, Year 0

Pamela Lyons
Trustee of the Estate of Mary Sophia Young
123 Main Street
Anywhere, ON   L5G 1K1

Re: Estate of Mary Sophia Young

TO FEES for professional services including; **reviewing Will, documents, securities and other documents concerning the Estate; preparing notarial copies;** preparing inventory of assets; collecting and advising on assets; **preparing all documents required to apply to the Superior Court of Justice for Certificate of Appointment of Estate Trustee with Will; serving documentation on beneficiaries; filing all documents and obtaining Court Certificate;** ascertaining debts; advertising for creditors; reporting from time to time.

OUR FEE:	$3,950.00
G.S.T. ON FEE:	<u>276.50</u>
Sub-Total	**$4,226.50**
TOTAL FEE AND GST (Carried Forward)	$4,226.50

Disbursements:

Paid Court fee re Certificate of Appointment		$325.00
Photocopying	10.00 T	
Faxes:	2.00 T	

Long distance telephone charges   4.33 T
Courier   <u>6.00 T</u>   347.33

G.S.T. on Taxable (T) Disbursements   <u>1.56</u>

TOTAL DUE AND PAYABLE   <u>$4,575.39</u>

**THIS IS OUR ACCOUNT HEREIN,
LAWLESS & LYONS LLP**

per:

Pamela Lyons
E. & O.E.

Our G.S.T. Registration No. 000000000001

LAWLESS & LYONS LLP
Barristers and Solicitors
123 Main Street
Anywhere, Ontario L5G 1K1
Telephone: (905) 525-1234
Facsimile: (905) 525-9150

July 15, Year 0

Pamela Lyons
Trustee of the Estate of Mary Sophia Young
123 Main Street
Anywhere, ON L5G 1K1

Re: Estate of Mary Sophia Young
     Sale of 22 Sussex Drive, Ottawa

TO FEES for professional services rendered in connection with the sale of the above property including reviewing agreement of purchase and sale; drafting transfer, statutory declaration, direction with respect to closing proceeds, Statement of Adjustments; attending at Registry Office to exchange documentation and keys for sale proceeds; reporting to you and all other meetings, telephone discussions and correspondence not specifically set out above.

OUR FEE:		$2,975.00
G.S.T. ON FEE:		208.25
Sub-Total		$3,183.25
TOTAL FEE AND GST (Carried Forward)		$3,183.25
Disbursements:		
Photocopying	4.50 T	
Faxes	1.25 T	
Long distance telephone charges	3.37 T	
Courier	11.78 T	
Mileage charges	36.00 T	
Parking	9.00 T	65.90
G.S.T. on Taxable (T) Disbursements		4.61
TOTAL DUE AND PAYABLE		**$3,253.76**

THIS IS OUR ACCOUNT HEREIN,

LAWLESS & LYONS LLP

per:

Pamela Lyons
E. & O.E.

Our G.S.T. Registration No. 000000000001

LAWLESS & LYONS LLP

Barristers and Solicitors
123 Main Street
Anywhere, Ontario L5G 1K1

Telephone: (905) 525-1234
Facsimile: (905) 525-9150

July 30, Year 0

Pamela Lyons
Trustee of the Estate of Mary Sophia Young
123 Main Street
Anywhere, ON L5G 1K1

Re: Estate of Mary Sophia Young

TO FEES for professional services including: dealing with the Trust Company concerning various banking matters, including filing certified copies of Estate documents; discussing certain particular assets; taking custody of art collection and obtaining valuation of art collection; various banking matters including filing certified copies of estate documents; attending at bank to open Estate account, listing contents of three safety deposit boxes and finally accepting custody of contents of boxes; dealing with Beancounters concerning tax returns; dealing with brokers concerning securities; transferring securities; arranging for payment of bills; correspondence with and dealing with beneficiaries; dealing with claims of life tenant; arranging for several appraisals of property located at 22 Sussex Drive, Ottawa; meeting with real estate agent to list property for sale; consideration of various offers presented by real estate agent; negotiating and accepting offer; reporting from time to time.

OUR FEE: $7,250.00

G.S.T. ON FEE: <u>507.50</u>

Sub-Total $7,757.50

TOTAL FEE AND GST (Carried Forward) $7,757.50

Disbursements:

Photocopying	32.75 T	
Faxes	6.25 T	
Parking	3.75 T	
Long distance telephone charges	12.78 T	
Courier	16.00 T	
Certified Copies	12.00	83.53

G.S.T. on Taxable (T) Disbursements   <u>5.01</u>

TOTAL DUE AND PAYABLE   <u>**$7,846.04**</u>

THIS IS OUR ACCOUNT HEREIN,

LAWLESS & LYONS LLP

per:

Pamela Lyons
E. & O.E.

     Our G.S.T. Registration No. 000000000001

LAWLESS & LYONS LLP
Barristers and Solicitors
123 Main Street
Anywhere, Ontario L5G 1K1

Telephone: (905) 525-1234
Facsimile: (905) 525-9150

September 15, Year 0

Pamela Lyons
Trustee of the Estate of Mary Sophia Young
123 Main Street
Anywhere, ON L5G 1K1

Re: Estate of Mary Sophia Young

TO FEES for professional services including: receiving mail, opening mail and attending at bank to deposit estate cheques from time to time; organizing income tax receipts; dealing with claims of life tenant; reviewing investments; various discussions with brokers and arranging reinvestment of funds; preparing initial Statement of Original Assets; set up partial list of receipts and disbursements; estate account entries; follow up on missing month end statements; reviewing draft accounts to locate balancing errors and adjusting entries.

OUR FEE:	$16,650.00
G.S.T. ON FEE:	<u>1,165.50</u>
Sub-Total	**$17,815.50**
TOTAL FEE AND GST (Carried Forward)	**$17,815.50**

<u>Disbursements:</u>

Photocopying   67.00 T

Faxes:	18.00 T	
Long distance telephone charges	9.52 T	
Courier	8.00 T	102.52

G.S.T. on Taxable (T) Disbursements   7.18

TOTAL DUE AND PAYABLE $17,925.20

THIS IS OUR ACCOUNT HEREIN,

LAWLESS & LYONS LLP

per:

Pamela Lyons
E. & O.E.

Our G.S.T. Registration No. 000000000001

LAWLESS & LYONS LLP
Barristers and Solicitors
123 Main Street
Anywhere, Ontario L5G 1K1

Telephone: (905) 525-1234
Facsimile: (905) 525-9150

September 26, Year 0

Pamela Lyons
Trustee of the Estate of Mary Sophia Young
123 Main Street
Anywhere, ON L5G 1K1

Re: Estate of Mary Sophia Young

Disbursements:

Paid Court fee re Certificate of Appointment	$490.00	
Long distance telephone charges	4.07 T	$494.07
G.S.T. on Taxable (T) Disbursements		.28
TOTAL DUE AND PAYABLE		**$494.35**

THIS IS OUR ACCOUNT HEREIN,

LAWLESS & LYONS LLP

per:

Pamela Lyons
E. & O.E.

Our G.S.T. Registration No. 000000000001

LAWLESS & LYONS LLP
Barristers and Solicitors
123 Main Street
Anywhere, Ontario L5G 1K1

Telephone: (905) 525-1234
Facsimile:(905) 525-9150

November 30, Year 0

Pamela Lyons
Trustee of the Estate of Mary Sophia Young
123 Main Street
Anywhere, ON   L5G 1K1

Re: Estate of Mary Sophia Young

TO FEES for professional services including receiving mail, opening mail and attending at bank to deposit estate cheques from time to time; organizing income tax receipts; dealing with claims of life tenant; reviewing investments; various discussions with brokers and arranging reinvestment of funds; estate account entries; dealing with Beancounters concerning preparation and filing of income tax returns; reporting from time to time.

OUR FEE:	$11,500.00
G.S.T. ON FEE:	805.00
SUB-TOTAL	**$12,305.00**
TOTAL FEE AND GST (Carried Forward)	$12,305.00

Disbursements:

Photocopying   80.90 T

Faxes	23.25 T	
Long distance telephone charges	7.03T	
Courier	8.40T	
Postage	<u>9.25</u>T	128.83
G.S.T. on Taxable (T) Disbursements		<u>9.02</u>
TOTAL DUE AND PAYABLE		<u>$12,442.85</u>

THIS IS OUR ACCOUNT HEREIN,

LAWLESS & LYONS LLP

per:

Pamela Lyons
E.&O.E.

Our G.S.T. Registration No. 000000000001

LAWLESS & LYONS LLP
Barristers and Solicitors
123 Main Street
Anywhere, Ontario   L5G 1K1

Telephone: (905) 525-1234
Facsimile: (905) 525-9150

January 31, Year 1

Pamela Lyons
Trustee of the Estate of Mary Sophia Young
123 Main Street
Anywhere, ON   L5G 1K1

Re: Estate of Mary Sophia Young

TO FEES for professional services including: receiving mail, opening mail and attending at bank to deposit estate cheques from time to time; dealing with claims of life tenant; reviewing investments; various discussions with brokers and arranging reinvestment of funds; estate account entries; dealing with Beancounters to finalize income tax returns; reporting from time to time.

OUR FEE:	$9,500.00
G.S.T. ON FEE:	665.00
Sub-Total	**$10,165.00**
TOTAL FEE AND GST (Carried Forward)	$10,165.00

Disbursements:

Photocopying	58.80 T	
Faxes	23.35 T	
Long distance telephone charges	11.63 T	
Courier	10.08 T	103.86
G.S.T. on Taxable (T) Disbursements		7.27
TOTAL DUE AND PAYABLE		**$10,276.13**

THIS IS OUR ACCOUNT HEREIN,

LAWLESS & LYONS LLP

per:

Pamela Lyons
E. & O.E.

Our G.S.T. Registration No. 000000000001

LAWLESS & LYONS LLP
Barristers and Solicitors
123 Main Street
Anywhere, Ontario L5G 1K1

Telephone: (905) 525-1234
Facsimile: (905) 525-9150

March 31, Year 1

Pamela Lyons
Trustee of the Estate of Mary Sophia Young
123 Main Street
Anywhere, ON L5G 1K1

Re: Estate of Mary Sophia Young

TO FEES for professional services including receiving mail, opening mail and attending at bank to deposit estate cheques from time to time; dealing with claims of life tenant; reviewing investments; various discussions with brokers and arranging reinvestment of funds; estate account entries; reporting from time to time.

OUR FEE:	$3,500.00
G.S.T. ON FEE:	245.00
Sub-Total	**$3,745.00**
TOTAL FEE AND GST (Carried Forward)	$3,745.00

Disbursements:

Copies	15.25 T	
Postage	3.50 T	
Telephone	7.15 T	
Courier	5.00 T	30.90
G.S.T. on Taxable (T) Disbursements		2.16
TOTAL DUE AND PAYABLE		**$3,778.06**

THIS IS OUR ACCOUNT HEREIN,

LAWLESS & LYONS LLP

per:

Pamela Lyons
E. & O.E.

Our G.S.T. Registration No. 000000000001

LAWLESS & LYONS LLP
Barristers and Solicitors
123 Main Street
Anywhere, Ontario L5G 1K1

Telephone: (905) 525-1234
Facsimile: (905) 525-9150

May 31, Year 1

Pamela Lyons
Trustee of the Estate of Mary Sophia Young
123 Main Street
Anywhere, ON L5G 1K1

Re: Estate of Mary Sophia Young

TO FEES for professional services including: receiving mail, opening mail and attending at bank to deposit estate cheques from time to time; dealing with claims of life tenant; reviewing investments; various discussions with brokers and arranging reinvestment of funds; estate account entries; reporting from time to time.

OUR FEE:		$2,500.00
G.S.T. ON FEE:		175.00
Sub-Total		**$2,675.00**
TOTAL FEE AND GST (Carried Forward)		$2,675.00

Disbursements:

Copies	10.00 T	
Postage	4.92 T	
Telephone	17.64 T	32.56
G.S.T. on Taxable (T) Disbursements		2.28
TOTAL DUE AND PAYABLE		**$2,709.84**

THIS IS OUR ACCOUNT HEREIN,

LAWLESS & LYONS LLP

per:

Pamela Lyons
E. & O.E.

                              Our G.S.T. Registration No. 000000000001

LAWLESS & LYONS LLP

Barristers and Solicitors
123 Main Street
Anywhere, Ontario L5G 1K1

Telephone: (905) 525-1234
Facsimile: (905) 525-9150

June 30, Year 1

Pamela Lyons
Trustee of the Estate of Mary Sophia Young
123 Main Street
Anywhere, ON L5G 1K1

Re: Estate of Mary Sophia Young

TO FEES for professional services including: receiving mail, opening mail and attending at bank to deposit estate cheques from time to time; dealing with claims of life tenant; reviewing investments; various discussions with brokers and arranging reinvestment of funds; estate account entries; reporting from time to time.

OUR FEE:	$1,500.00
G.S.T. ON FEE:	105.00
Sub-Total	**$1,605.00**
TOTAL FEE AND GST (Carried Forward)	$1,605.00

Disbursements:

Copies	3.00 T	
Postage	.96 T	
Telephone	4.37 T	8.33
G.S.T. on Taxable (T) Disbursements		.58
TOTAL DUE AND PAYABLE		**$1,613.91**

THIS IS OUR ACCOUNT HEREIN,

LAWLESS & LYONS LLP

per:

Pamela Lyons
E. & O.E.

                        Our G.S.T. Registration No. 000000000001

LAWLESS & LYONS LLP
Barristers and Solicitors
123 Main Street
Anywhere, Ontario L5G 1K1

Telephone: (905) 525-1234
Facsimile: (905) 525-9150

August 30, Year 1

Pamela Lyons
Trustee of the Estate of Mary Sophia Young
123 Main Street
Anywhere, ON L5G 1K1

Re: Estate of Mary Sophia Young

TO FEES for professional services including: receiving mail, opening mail and attending at bank to deposit estate cheques from time to time; dealing with claims of life tenant; reviewing investments; various discussions with brokers and arranging reinvestment of funds; estate account entries; dealing with Beancounters to finalize T3 return; reporting from time to time.

OUR FEE:	$5,000.00
G.S.T. ON FEE:	350.00
Sub-Total	**$5,350.00**
TOTAL FEE AND GST (Carried Forward)	$5,350.00

Disbursements:

Copies	9.50 T	
Postage	3.75 T	
Telephone	17.69 T	30.94

G.S.T. on Taxable (T) Disbursements   <u>2.17</u>

TOTAL DUE AND PAYABLE   <u>**$5,383.11**</u>

THIS IS OUR ACCOUNT HEREIN,

LAWLESS & LYONS LLP

per:

Pamela Lyons
E. & O.E.

        Our G.S.T. Registration No. 000000000001

CASE STUDY COMMENTARY

As a result of asking questions about the flawed set of accounts and release and a period of negotiation, revised estate accounts detailing additions and corrections in bold were subsequently received. Now compare the corrected set of accounts utilizing the estate accounting section headings.

CORRECTED ACCOUNTS

Statement of Original Assets

- All issues appear to have been addressed and/or corrected.

Capital Receipts

- It may be necessary to request further information from the trustee. detailing why the 2,000 Nortel shares were held for an extended period of time while their value decreased.
- All other issues appear to have been addressed and/or corrected.

Capital Disbursements

- Unless the deceased made significant charitable gifts before her death, it is likely that the payment of $186,355.60 to the Receiver General for Canada would not be able to be reduced, notwithstanding the gift of the residue of her estate to your charity as a result of the intervening interest of Martha Young, the life tenant. In an estate where significant legacies or a large share of the residue are gifted to charities and the estate accounts indicate that terminal taxes have been paid, further information should be requested from the accountant preparing the return(s) to ensure that the charitable donations have been included or any amended tax returns incorporating the gifts are filed.
- The payment of estate taxes out of the capital account in the amount of $2,271.87 appears to be correct as the estate realized investments during the estate tax year which resulted in significant capital gains to the capital beneficiary.[7]
- For commentary on the Lawless & Lyons accounts see prior commentary.

---

[7] Note: an informal CCRA ruling may suggest that there may be some flexibility in this area.

Revenue Receipts

- All issues appear to have been addressed and/or corrected.

Revenue Disbursements

- The payments made to or for the benefit of the life tenant have been transferred to the Revenue account.
- The payments made to The Trust Company represent their custodial charges for holding the majority of Mrs. Young's assets pending the issuance of the Certificate of Appointment. The charges identified as "executors' work" have been applied against the compensation claimed by the trustee.
- The incorrect total was a typographical error and has been corrected.

Investment Account

- Occasionally in falling markets, investment losses do occur. Hopefully, the trustee has been able to provide information with respect to her investment plan which supports her decision to purchase and hold these investments.

Statement of Trustee's Compensation

- The compensation has been adjusted by refunds, payments made to the trustee and duplicate entries.
- In some estates, the amount of compensation calculated on the "*in specie*" transfer of assets (such as the Bank of Nova Scotia shares or the personalty) may also require review and/or negotiation.

Statement of Unrealized Original Assets/Trustee's Investments

- All issues appear to have been addressed and/or corrected.

Statement of Proposed Distribution

- It is up to the charity to determine whether or not it is appropriate to request that the estate of the life tenant reimburse the charity for the revenue overpayment.
- It appears that a settlement with respect to the compensation paid to the trustee in her capacity as Guardian of Property has been

negotiated. Each individual estate will have circumstances which will determine whether or not this is appropriate.
- All other issues appear to have been addressed and/or corrected.

Corrected Release
- A corrected release, addressing the issues raised, although not ideal, could be signed.

ALBERTA

The general principles stated in the Ontario commentary of this chapter also apply to Alberta personal representatives preparing an accounting for beneficiaries. However, some differences are worth mentioning. The differences affect, firstly, the amount of compensation paid to Pamela Lyons for acting as Mrs. Young's court-appointed guardian of property prior to Mrs. Young's passing; secondly, Pamela Lyons' ability to pre-take payment for acting as the guardian; and thirdly, Pamela Lyons' compensation for acting as the personal representative of the estate after Mrs. Young's passing.

COURT-APPOINTED GUARDIAN AND TRUSTEE COMPENSATION AND PRE-TAKING

In Alberta, a person appointed by the court to manage a dependent adult's property is called a trustee. If the dependent adult also needs his or her personal affairs managed, the court may appoint a guardian. These two appointments are made when an interested person applies to the court pursuant to the *Dependent Adults Act*.[8]

The *Dependent Adults Act* does not allow a trustee or guardian to pre-take compensation.[9] If a trustee or guardian would like to be compensated for performing such duties, he or she must make an application to the Court and seek the Court's approval for such payment.

Upon the death of the dependent adult, the Court-appointed guardian's and trustee's powers cease immediately and the personal representative named in the Will takes over control of the deceased's estate. If the Court-appointed guardian and trustee is the same person as the personal

---

[8] R.S.A. 2000, c. D-11.
[9] *Ibid.*, ss. 59 and 60.

representative named in the Will, he or she should seek the consent of the residuary beneficiaries of the Will before taking compensation for duties performed before the death occurred. If unanimous consent of the residuary beneficiaries cannot be obtained, the personal representative should make a Court application requesting the Court to approve his or her compensation.

PERSONAL REPRESENTATIVE'S COMPENSATION AND PRE-TAKING

If the amount of the personal representative's compensation is not fixed by the Will, by an agreement, or a contract, then the personal representative's compensation is determined by the Surrogate Rules[10] which sets out the general principles used to determine the compensation. The Surrogate Rules do not provide any percentages or dollar amounts for compensation. Instead, they provide the factors that should to be considered when setting the amount of compensation for a personal representative. One thing is certain — the size of the estate does not determine the size of the compensation.[11] Therefore, a large estate may not necessarily mean a large compensation fee.

In the case study in this chapter, the personal representative's duties were not particularly complex. Many of the tasks could have been delegated to the personal representative's secretary or paralegal, thus keeping fees reasonable. It is also important to recognize that a lawyer, when performing the administrative duties of a personal representative, cannot charge at the lawyer's hourly rate, but must reduce the rate.[12]

The Alberta Surrogate Court Committee established the "Suggested Fee Guidelines" for personal representatives. The Guidelines set fees based on percentages of the value of the capital receipts and revenue receipts. However, the Alberta Courts have clearly stated that these percentages should only be used as a guideline.

There are some services for which a personal representative cannot charge an estate, such as researching the law to calculate what fees the personal representative will seek. This is a service for the personal representative's benefit and not for the estate.

One of the facts of the case study, a fair request for compensation by the personal representative would be as follows:

---

[10] AR 130/95, Schedule 1, Part 1.
[11] *Sproule v. Montreal Trust Co.*, [1979] 2 W.W.R. 289 (Alta. C.A.).
[12] See Surrogate Rule 7 in Schedule 1, Part 1.

Capital

- 4% of the first $250,000 of capital;
- 3% on the next $250,000 of capital; and
- 1% on the balance of the capital of the estate.

Revenue Receipts

- 3% on all of the revenue receipts.

Care and Management

- 4/10 of 1% on the first $250,000 of capital;
- 3/10 of 1% on the next $250,000 of capital; and
- 2/10 of 1% on the balance of the capital of the estate.

For a further discussion on personal representative compensation in Alberta, refer to the Alberta portion of Chapter 3.

BRITISH COLUMBIA

Most of the commentary in this chapter also applies in British Columbia. The differences arise with respect to amounts that were paid to Pamela Lyons in her capacity as Court-appointed guardian of Mrs. Young's property (prior to Mrs. Young's death) and in her capacity as executor and trustee of Mrs. Young's estate.

COURT-APPOINTED GUARDIAN OF PROPERTY COMPENSATION

In British Columbia, a Court-appointed guardian of property is called a "committee". The compensation to be paid to a committee is determined by the Public Guardian and Trustee of British Columbia when the committee presents his or her committee accounts to the Public Guardian and Trustee for passing (approval). Committees are required to pass accounts on a regular basis, usually every two years. The Public Guardian and Trustee, which has developed policies with respect to the amounts of committee fees, will then provide information with respect to the current policy.

TRUSTEE'S COMPENSATION

The principles governing compensation for estate trustees are set out in Chapter 3. Generally, an estate trustee in British Columbia is entitled under the *Trustee Act*[13] to receive up to 5 per cent of the realized value of the original assets of the estate and of unrealized original assets (valued at the time the fees are being requested). The estate trustee will also receive 5 per cent of income receipts, plus an annual care and management fee of up to two-fifths of 1 per cent of the average market value of the assets for the year. The care and management fee is not usually requested or awarded if the estate is wound up within a year.

On the facts of the case study, a request for capital fees would be in the range of 2.5 – 4 per cent on the capital receipts. There would be a request of 5 per cent on the revenue receipts. The care and management fee requested would be similar to that set out in the case study.

---

[13] R.S.B.C. 1986, c. 464.

CHAPTER 5: CASE STUDY **215**

ESTATE OF MARY SOPHIA YOUNG

STATEMENT OF ESTATE ACCOUNTS
For the Period January 21, Year 0 to August 31, Year 1
(CORRECT VERSION OF ACCOUNTS)[14]

ESTATE TRUSTEE: Pamela Lyons

DATE OF DEATH: January 21, Year 0

DATE OF APPOINTMENT: May 18, Year 0

LAWLESS & LYONS LLP
Barristers and Solicitors
123 Main Street
Anywhere, Ontario L5G 1K1

---

[14] CAUTION: This is a fictitious case study created by Deborah L. Campbell for teaching purposes. Deborah L. Campbell, M. Jasmine Sweatman of Miller Thomson LLP. Copyright 2003.

ESTATE OF MARY SOPHIA YOUNG
STATEMENT OF ESTATE ACCOUNTS

For the Period January 21, Year 0 to August 31, Year 1

INDEX

	Page Nos.
Statement of Original Assets - January 21, Year 0	1 - 2
Capital Receipts	3 - 5
Capital Disbursements	6 - 8
Revenue Receipts	9 - 13
Revenue Disbursements	14 - 17
Investment Account	18 - 20
Cash Summary	21
Statement of Trustee's Compensation	22 - 23
Statement of Unrealized Original Assets - August 31, Year 1	24
Statement of Trustees' Investments – August 31, Year 1	24
Statement of Proposed Distribution	25

CHAPTER 5: CASE STUDY   1

ESTATE OF MARY SOPHIA YOUNG

STATEMENT OF ORIGINAL ASSETS

As of January 21, Year 0

DISPOSITION
Page Item

Bank Accounts

The Trust Company, Winnipeg, Manitoba Investment Administration Acct. No. 405-020460-1			
- Balance	$6,302.30	3	1
The Trust Company, Ottawa Main Branch, Ottawa, Ontario Chequing Acct. No. 354-595415	56.33	3	2

Bonds and Debentures

Canada Savings Bonds due Nov. 1, Year 4 - Principal	60,000.00	4	17
- accrued interest from Nov. 1 to Jan. 21/Y0	542.15	4	17
AGT Ltd. 9.5% Debenture due Aug. 24/Y4			
- Principal $25,000.00 @ $1.0490	26,225.00	5	42
- accrued interest from Aug. 24 to Jan. 21/Y0	969.52	3	7
Ford Credit Canada due April 8/Y0			
- Principal $55,000.00 @ $.98938	54,415.90	3	11
(includes accrued interest of $105.21 from Jan. 7 to Jan. 21/Y0)			

Stocks

Bank of Nova Scotia - 3000 shares @ $31.85	95,550.00	5	31,34
Bank of Nova Scotia - ex-dividend	630.00	3	3
Royal Bank of Canada - 1200 shares @ $76.20	91,440.00	5	36
Enbridge Inc. - 2470 shares @ $69.25	171,047.50	5	33,38
Enermark Income Fund - 2600.000 units @ $2.78	7,228.00	4	23
Teck Corporation, Class "B" - 200 shares @ $10.10	2,020.00	4	28
BC Gas Inc. New - 1700 shares @ $29.50	50,150.00	4	22
BCE Inc. - 2050 shares @ $60.60	124,230.00	5	39
TransAlta Corporation - 3500 shares @ $23.00	80,500.00	4	25

2 BEQUEST MANAGEMENT FOR CHARITABLE ORGANIZATIONS

		Page	Item
Exxon Corporation - 1400 shares @ US $71.125			
(to CDN @ $1.5170)	151,055.28		
First Australia Prime - 3500 shares @ $10.60	37,100.00	4	24
Toronto-Dominion Bank - 500 shares @ $62.25	31,125.00	4,5	20,35
Toronto-Dominion Bank - ex-dividend	170.00	3	4

Mutual Funds

Templeton Growth Fund - 3463.797 units @ $7.9125	27,407.29		

Real Property

22 Sussex Drive, Ottawa	750,000.00	4	18

Annuities

Trust Company Fixed Term Annuity	8,724.26	3,4	See *

Miscellaneous

CPP - January, Year 0	287.70	3	9
OAS - January, Year 0	410.82	3	9
Prior Year Income tax refund (estimated)	5,292.39	5	30
Globe & Mail - subscription refund	105.43	3	6
Continental Insurance Brokers - premium refund	434.16	4	21
Jewellery, Furniture, Art and personal effects	10,000.00	5	32
TOTAL ORIGINAL ASSETS	$1,793,419.03		

* Realization of Trust Company Fixed Term Annuity at Item Nos. 5, 8, 10, 13, 15, 16, 26, 27 and 29

ESTATE OF MARY SOPHIA YOUNG

CAPITAL RECEIPTS

For the Period January 21, Year 0 to August 31, Year 1

1.	Jan. 21/Y0	The Trust Company Investment Administration Acct. #405-020460-1 - Balance	$6,302.30
2.	Jan. 21/Y0	The Trust Company Chequing Acct. #354-595415 - Balance	56.33
3.	Jan. 27/Y0	Bank of Nova Scotia - ex-dividend	630.00
4.	Jan. 31/Y0	Toronto-Dominion Bank - ex-dividend	170.00
5.	Feb. 1/Y0	Trust Company Fixed Term annuity payment	186.10
6.	Feb. 16/Y0	Globe & Mail - subscription refund	105.43
7.	**Feb. 24/Y0**	**AGT Ltd. 9.5% Debenture** - accrued interest from Aug. 24 to Jan. 21/Y0	**969.52**
8.	Mar. 1/Y0	Trust Company Fixed Term annuity payment	186.10
9.	Mar. 7/Y0	Government of Canada - Jan/Y0 CPP payment	287.70 410.82
10.	Mar. 31/Y0	Trust Company Fixed Term annuity payment	186.10
11.	Apr. 8/Y0	Ford Credit Canada – investment principal - accrued interest Jan. 7 to Jan. 21/Y0	54,316.14 105.21
12.	Apr. 8/Y0	Lakeshore Lodge - refund of account overpayment	2,674.92
13.	May 6/Y0	Trust Company Fixed Term annuity payment	186.10
14.	**May 7/Y0**	**Record receipt of 2560 shares Nortel Networks as result of BCE Inc. corporate re-organization**	0.00
15.	May 31/Y0	Trust Company Fixed Term annuity payment	186.10

16.	June 30/Y0	Trust Company Fixed Term annuity payment	186.10
17.	July 2/Y0	Canada Savings Bonds – redeemed - **accrued interest from Nov. 1 to Jan. 21/Y0**	60,000.00 542.15
18.	July 15/Y0	Usually, Always, Wright - proceeds from sale of 22 Sussex Drive Sale Price $725,000.00 Less real estate commission -43,500.00 Less GST on real estate commission- -3,045.00 Less adjustments in favour of purchaser <u>-2,167.46</u>	676,287.54
19.	July 28/Y0	Nortel Networks - sold 560 shares @ $117.65 less commission $535.00	65,349.00
20.	July 31/Y0	**Toronto-Dominion Bank - record share split - now 1000 shares**	0.00
21	Aug. 6/Y0	Continental Insurance Brokers - insurance premium refund	434.16
22.	Aug. 9/Y0	BC Gas Inc. - sold **1700 shares** @ **$28.65** and 1000 shares @ **$28.75 less commission $739.21**	48,065.79
23.	Aug. 9/Y0	Enermark Income Fund - **sold 2600 units** @ **$4.06 less commission $360.01**	10,195.99
24.	Aug. 9/Y0	First Australia Prime Income Fund - **sold 3500 units** @ **$9.80 less commission $901.86**	33,398.14
25.	Aug. 9/Y0	TransAlta Corp. - **sold 3500 shares** @ **$21.05 less commission $999.34**	72,675.66
26.	Aug. 26/Y0	Trust Company Fixed Term annuity payment	186.10
27.	Aug. 31/Y0	Trust Company Fixed Term annuity payment	186.10
28.	Aug. 31/Y0	Teck Corporation - Class "B" - **sold 200 shares** @ **$12.95 less commission $325.00**	2,265.00
29.	Sept. 14/Y0	Trust Company Fixed Term annuity - balance	7,712.78

30.	Sept. 14/Y0	Government of Canada - prior year income tax refund	5,253.92
31.	Sept. 23/Y0	Record value of 2000 shares Bank of Nova Scotia for transfer in specie to beneficiaries	63,700.00
32.	Sept. 23/Y0	Record value of jewellery, furniture, art and personal effects to be transferred to beneficiaries	10,000.00
33.	June 30/Y1	Enbridge Inc. - record share split - now 4940 shares	0.00
34.	July 28/Y1	Bank of Nova Scotia - sold 1000 shares @ $38.25 less commission $267.50	37,982.50
35.	July 28/Y1	Toronto-Dominion Bank - sold 1000 shares @ $38.25 less commission $267.50	35,482.50
36.	July 28/Y1	Royal Bank of Canada - sold 1200 shares @ $81.30 less commission $267.50	97,292.50
37.	July 28/Y1	Nortel Networks - sold 2000 shares @ $1.65 less commission $535.00	2,765.00
38.	July 28/Y1	Enbridge Inc. - sold 4940 shares @ $32.75 less commission $267.50	161,517.50
39	July 28/Y1	BCE Inc. - sold 2050 shares @ $32.65 less commission $267.50	66,665.00
40.	July 28/Y1	Record gain on sale of CIBC 5.65% Preferred shares	58,370.93
41.	July 28/Y1	Record gain on sale of Westcoast Energy 9.7% Bond	220.00
42.	Aug. 24/Y1	AGT Ltd. Debenture redeemed	25,000.00
	TOTAL CAPITAL RECEIPTS		$1,608,693.23

ESTATE OF MARY SOPHIA YOUNG

CAPITAL DISBURSEMENTS

For the Period January 21, Year 0 to August 31, Year 1

1.	Jan. 25/Y0	Lakeshore Lodge - February rent	$3,897.50
2.	Jan.25/Y0	Central Health Services - paid outstanding account	130.01
3.	Feb. 28/Y0	Lawless & Lyons - paid account for services rendered as guardian of property (**Fee $40,000.00, GST $2,800.00**)	42,800.00
4.	Mar. 15/Y0	Bell Canada - paid outstanding account	13.14
5.	Mar. 15/Y0	Lakeshore Nursing Services - paid outstanding account	3,648.21
6.	Mar. 15/Y0	Central Health Services - paid outstanding account	187.79
7.	Mar. 17/Y0	Minister of Finance - paid probate fees	14,185.00
8.	Mar. 23/Y0	Lakeshore Funeral Chapel - paid funeral expenses	3,709.79
9.	Apr 30/Y0	Lawless & Lyons - **paid account for solicitors' services (Fee $3,950.00, GST & Disbursements $625.39)**	4,575.39
10.	May 2/Y0	Lakeshore Pharmacy - paid outstanding account	479.74
11.	July 15/Y0	Legacy payments to grandnieces and grandnephews as follows:	
		- Robert Day	5,000.00
		- Cheryl Day	5,000.00
		- Bruce Young	5,000.00
		- Janna Young	5,000.00
12.	July 15/Y0	William Young - **reimburse for funeral expenses paid on behalf of estate:**	
		- catering fees	378.20
		- newspaper notices	372.86
		- **minister honourarium**	400.00
		- **organist honourarium**	100.00
		-caretaker honourarium	40.00

13.	July 15/Y0	Sunnybrook & Women's College Health Sciences Centre - paid account	170.00
14.	July 15/Y0	Lawless & Lyons - **paid account for solicitors' services with respect to sale of 22 Sussex Drive, Ottawa**	3,253.76
15.	July 30/Y0	Lawless & Lyons - **paid account for services rendered as Estate Trustee** (Fee $7,250.00; GST & Disbursements $596.04)	7,846.04
16.	Sept. 15/Y0	Lawless & Lyons - **paid account for solicitors' services** (Fee $1,650.00, GST & Disbursements $225.20)	1,875.20
		- **paid on account of trustee's compensation** (Fee $15,000.00, GST $1,050.00)	16,050.00
17.	Sept. 22/Y0	EnRoute/Diners Club - paid outstanding account	67.43
18.	**Sept. 23/Y0**	Record value of shares transferred in specie to beneficiaries as follows:	
		- **Lillian Day** - 1000 shares Bank of Nova Scotia	31,850.00
		- **William Young** - 1000 shares Bank of Nova Scotia	31,850.00
19.	Sept. 23/Y0	Record value of jewellery, furniture, art and personal effects transferred to beneficiaries	10,000.00
20.	Sept. 26/Y0	Lawless & Lyons - **paid disbursement account**	494.35
21	Oct. 18/Y0	William Young - **reimburse for additional expenses as follows:**	
		- **internment of ashes $214.00**	
		- **St. George's Memorial Fund donation $500.00**	
		- **Rector, St. George's $50.00**	764.00
22.	Oct. 18/Y0	Lillian Day - **reimburse for appraisal costs**	440.50
23.	Nov. 4/Y0	Western Cemetery Lettering - paid marker engraving	292.11

24.	Nov. 30/Y0	Lawless & Lyons - **paid account for services rendered as Estate Trustee** (Fee $11,500.00, GST & Disbursements $942.85)	12,442.85
25.	Jan. 31/Y1	Lawless & Lyons - **paid account for services rendered as Estate Trustee** (Fee $9,500.00, GST & Disbursements $776.13)	10,276.13
26.	Feb. 1/Y1	Receiver General for Canada - terminal T1 taxes	186,355.60
27.	May 15/Y1	Beancounters - paid preparation terminal tax return	1,605.00
28.	June 30/Y1	Loss on sale of 1000 shares Laidlaw Inc.	12,580.38
29.	Mar. 31/Y1	Lawless & Lyons - **paid account for services rendered as Estate Trustee** (Fee $3,500.00, GST & Disbursements $278.06)	3,778.06
30.	May 31/Y1	Lawless & Lyons - **paid account for services rendered as Estate Trustee** (Fee $2,500.00, GST & Disbursements $209.84)	2,709.84
31.	June 30/Y1	Lawless & Lyons - **paid account for services rendered as Estate Trustee** (Fee $1,500.00, GST & Disbursements $113.91)	1,613.91
32.	July 28/Y1	Loss on sale of 3000 shares NS Power Holdings Inc.	8,746.00
33.	Aug. 30/Y1	Lawless & Lyons - **paid account for services rendered as Estate Trustee** (Fee $5,000.00, GST & Disbursements $383.11)	<u>5,383.11</u>
	TOTAL CAPITAL DISBURSEMENTS		<u>$445,361.90</u>

ESTATE OF MARY SOPHIA YOUNG

REVENUE RECEIPTS

For the Period January 21, Year 0 to August 31, Year 1

1.	Jan. 31/Y0	The Trust Company Investment Administration Account - interest	$8.80
2.	Feb. 15/Y0	First Australia Prime Income Fund - dividend	280.00
3.	Feb. 22/Y0	Enermark Income Fund - dividend	104.00
4.	Feb. 24/Y0	Royal Bank of Canada - dividend	552.00
5.	**Feb. 24/Y0**	**AGT Ltd. 9.5% Debenture - interest** from Jan. 22 to Feb. 24/Y0	217.98
6.	Feb. 28/Y0	BC Gas Inc. - dividend	476.00
7.	Feb. 28/Y0	The Trust Company Investment Administration Account - interest	.35
8.	Mar. 1/Y0	Enbridge Inc. - dividend	1,420.25
9.	Mar. 1/Y0	The Trust Company Investment Administration Account - interest	.02
10.	Mar. 7/Y0	The Trust Company - adjustment regarding Jan. 6/Y0 fees	302.34
11.	Mar. 10/Y0	Exxon Corporation - dividend (US $574.00)	828.57
12.	Mar. 15/Y0	First Australia Prime Income Fund - dividend	280.00
13.	Mar. 22/Y0	Enermark Income Fund - dividend	78.00
14.	Mar. 31/Y0	The Trust Company - estate account interest	1.49
15.	Apr. 4/Y0	TransAlta Corporation - dividend	875.00
16.	**Apr. 8/Y0**	**Ford Credit Canada - interest Jan. 22 to Apr. 8/Y0**	578.65
17.	**Apr. 15/Y0**	BCE Inc. - dividend	697.00
18.	Apr. 15/Y0	First Australia Prime Income Fund - dividend	280.00

19.	Apr. 20/Y0	Enermark Income Fund - dividend	78.00
20.	Apr. 28/Y0	Bank of Nova Scotia - dividend	630.00
21.	Apr. 30/Y0	Toronto-Dominion Bank - dividend	170.00
22.	Apr. 30/Y0	The Trust Company - estate account interest	36.78
23.	May 16/Y0	First Australia Prime Income Fund - dividend	280.00
24.	May 20/Y0	Enermark Income Fund - dividend	130.00
25.	May 24/Y0	Royal Bank of Canada - dividend	552.00
26.	May 31/Y0	BC Gas Inc. - dividend	501.50
27.	May 31/Y0	The Trust Company - estate account interest	48.09
28.	June 1/Y0	Enbridge Inc. - dividend	1,494.35
29.	June 10/Y0	Exxon Corporation - dividend (US $574.00)	798.19
30.	June 14/Y0	The Trust Company - reverse duplicate custodial fee	430.56
31.	June 15/Y0	First Australia Prime Income Fund - dividend	280.00
32.	June 21/Y0	Enermark Income Fund - dividend	78.00
33.	June 30/Y0	Teck Corporation - dividend	20.00
34.	June 30/Y0	The Trust Company - estate account interest	43.82
35.	July 2/Y0	TransAlta Corporation - dividend	875.00
36.	**July 2/Y0**	**Canada Savings Bond interest - Jan 22 to July 1/Y0**	**1,057.85**
37.	**July 4/Y0**	**Templeton Growth Fund - dividend**	**1,627.98**
38.	**July 15/Y0**	**BCE Inc. - dividend**	**697.00**
39.	July 16/Y0	First Australia Prime Income Fund - dividend	280.00
40.	July 18/Y0	First Australia Prime Income Fund - dividend	280.00
41.	July 20/Y0	Enermark Income Fund - dividend	78.00

42.	July 28/Y0	Bank of Nova Scotia - dividend	630.00
43.	July 31/Y0	Toronto-Dominion Bank - dividend	170.00
44.	July 31/Y0	The Trust Company - estate account interest	45.40
45.	Aug. 13/Y0	First Australia Prime Income Fund - dividend	280.00
46.	Aug. 24/Y0	Royal Bank of Canada - dividend	576.00
47.	Aug. 24/Y0	AGT Ltd. 9.5% Debenture - semi-annual interest	1,187.50
48.	Aug. 31/Y0	The Trust Company - estate account interest	10.18
49.	Sept. 1/Y0	Enbridge Inc. - dividend	1,494.35
50.	Sept. 10/Y0	Exxon Corporation - dividend (US $574.00)	849.80
51.	Sept. 16/Y0	Treasury Bill interest	765.26
52.	Sept. 17/Y0	Scotiabank - term deposit interest	109.48
53.	Sept. 20/Y0	The Trust Company - estate account interest	7.49
54.	**Oct. 15/Y0**	**BCE Inc. - dividend**	**697.00**
55.	Oct. 28/Y0	CIBC 5.65% Preferred - dividend	1,341.85
56.	Oct. 28/Y0	Bank of Nova Scotia - dividend	210.00
57.	Oct. 31/Y0	Toronto-Dominion Bank - dividend	170.00
58.	Nov. 15/Y0	Laidlaw Inc. - dividend	66.55
59.	Nov. 15/Y0	NS Power Holdings Inc. - dividend	622.50
60.	Nov. 15/Y0	Westcoast Energy 9.7% Bond - semi-annual interest	970.00
61.	Nov. 24/Y0	Royal Bank of Canada - dividend	576.00
62.	Nov. 25/Y0	Secure Capital - account interest	13.06
63.	Dec. 1/Y0	Enbridge Inc. - dividend	1,494.35
64.	Dec. 10/Y0	Exxon Corporation - dividend (US $574.00)	833.74
65.	Dec. 25/Y0	Secure Capital - account interest	57.45

66.	Jan. 15/Y1	BCE Inc. - dividend	**697.00**
67.	Jan. 25/Y1	Secure Capital - account interest	35.70
68.	Jan. 28/Y1	CIBC 5.65% Preferred - dividend	1,342.50
69.	Jan. 28/Y1	Bank of Nova Scotia - dividend	210.00
70.	Jan. 31/Y1	Toronto-Dominion Bank - dividend	170.00
71.	Feb. 15/Y1	Laidlaw Inc. - dividend	66.55
72.	Feb. 15/Y1	NS Power Holdings Inc. - dividend	622.50
73.	Feb. 24/Y1	Royal Bank of Canada - dividend	576.00
74.	Feb. 24/Y1	AGT Ltd. 9.5% Debenture - semi-annual interest	1,187.50
75.	Feb. 25/Y1	Secure Capital - account interest	19.42
76.	Mar. 1/Y1	Enbridge Inc. - dividend	1,494.35
77.	Mar. 10/Y1	Exxon Corporation - dividend (US $574.00)	846.65
78.	Mar. 25/Y1	Secure Capital - account interest	18.53
79.	**Apr. 15/Y1**	**BCE Inc. - dividend**	**697.00**
80.	Apr. 25/Y1	Secure Capital - account interest	12.75
81.	Apr. 28/Y1	CIBC 5.65% Preferred - dividend	1,342.50
82.	Apr. 28/Y1	Bank of Nova Scotia - dividend	210.00
83.	Apr. 30/Y1	Toronto-Dominion Bank - dividend	170.00
84.	May 15/Y1	Laidlaw Inc. - dividend	66.55
85.	May 15/Y1	NS Power Holdings Inc. - dividend	622.50
86.	May 15/Y1	Westcoast Energy 9.7% Bond - semi-annual interest	970.00
87.	May 24/Y1	Royal Bank of Canada - dividend	576.00
88.	May 25/Y1	Secure Capital - account interest	9.34
89.	June 1/Y1	Enbridge Inc. - dividend	1,494.35
90.	June 10/Y1	Exxon Corporation - dividend (US $574.00)	823.69
91.	June 25/Y1	Secure Capital - account interest	7.75
92.	**July 9/Y1**	**Templeton Growth Fund - dividend**	**4,810.16**

93.	July 15/Y1	BCE Inc. - dividend	697.00
94.	July 15/Y1	Scotiabank - GIC interest	30,150.00
95.	July 25/Y1	Secure Capital - account interest	7.82
96.	July 28/Y1	CIBC 5.65% Preferred - dividend	1,342.50
97.	July 28/Y1	Bank of Nova Scotia - dividend	210.00
98.	July 31/Y1	Toronto-Dominion Bank - dividend	170.00
99.	Aug. 15/Y1	NS Power Holdings Inc. - dividend	622.50
100.	Aug. 24/Y1	AGT Ltd. 9.5% Debenture - semi-annual interest	1,187.50
101.	Aug. 24/Y1	Royal Bank of Canada - dividend	576.00
102.	Aug. 25/Y1	Secure Capital - account interest	8.13
		TOTAL REVENUE RECEIPTS	**$84,696.27**

ESTATE OF MARY SOPHIA YOUNG

REVENUE DISBURSEMENTS

For the Period January 21, Year 0 to August 31, Year 1

1.	Feb. 1/Y0	Tartan Properties - rent	$1,000.00
2.	Mar. 1/Y0	Tartan Properties - rent	1,000.00
3.	Mar. 7/Y0	The Trust Company Market Value fee to Jan. 21	280.60
4.	Mar. 7/Y0	The Trust Company Security Trade fee to Jan. 21	21.74
5.	Mar. 10/Y0	Exxon Corporation - non-resident tax	86.09
6.	Mar. 15/Y0	Municipal Hydro - paid account	45.09
7.	Mar. 21/Y0	Bell Canada - paid account	23.29
8.	Mar. 31/Y0	The Trust Company - estate account overdraft charges	36.38
9.	Apr. 1/Y0	Martha Young - payment to income beneficiary	3,500.00
10.	Apr. 1/Y0	Tartan Properties - rent	1,000.00
11.	Apr. 5/Y0	The Trust Company - Fees for executors' work to Apr. 1/Y0 (Fee $1,000.00, GST $70.00)	1,070.00
12.	Apr. 6/Y0	The Trust Company - custodial fee - Feb. 20 to Mar. 19/Y0	428.00
13.	Apr. 13/Y0	The Trust Company - custodial fee - Jan. 21 to Feb. 19/Y0	413.02
14.	Apr. 21/Y0	Bell Canada - paid account	19.72
15.	Apr. 25/Y0	The Trust Company - custodial fee - Feb. 20 to Mar. 19/Y0	430.56
16.	Apr. 30/Y0	The Trust Company - estate account overdraft charges	21.69
17.	May 1/Y0	Martha Young - payment to income beneficiary	3,500.00

18.	May 1/Y0	Tartan Properties - rent	1,000.00
19.	May 17/Y0	Municipal Hydro - paid account	47.39
20.	May 21/Y0	Bell Canada - paid account	21.23
21.	June 1/Y0	Martha Young - payment to income beneficiary	3,500.00
22.	June 1/Y0	Tartan Properties - rent	1,000.00
23.	June 10/Y0	Exxon Corporation - non-resident tax	86.10
24.	June 14/Y0	The Trust Company - custodial fee - Mar. 20 to Apr. 19/Y0	430.56
25.	June 21/Y0	Bell Canada - paid account	18.16
26.	June 22/Y0	The Trust Company - Market Value fee	432.89
27.	July 2/Y0	Martha Young - payment to income beneficiary	3,500.00
28.	July 2/Y0	Tartan Properties - rent	1,000.00
29.	July 2/Y0	The Trust Company - chequing account service charges	9.20
30.	July 15/Y0	Municipal Hydro - paid account	54.17
31.	July 21/Y0	The Trust Company - Market Value fee	133.75
32.	July 21/Y0	Bell Canada - paid account	27.10
33.	July 25/Y0	First Australia Prime Income Fund - reverse duplicate entry	280.00
34.	Aug. 1/Y0	Martha Young - payment to income beneficiary	3,500.00
35.	Aug. 1/Y0	Tartan Properties - rent	1,000.00
36.	Aug. 21/Y0	Bell Canada - paid account	21.75
37.	Aug. 23/Y0	The Trust Company - Market Value fee	133.75
38.	Sept. 1/Y0	Martha Young - payment to income beneficiary	3,500.00
39.	Sept. 1/Y0	Tartan Properties - rent	1,000.00

40.	Sept. 12/Y0	Exxon Corporation - non-resident tax	127.47
41.	**Sept. 15/Y0**	**Municipal Hydro - paid account**	**54.47**
42.	Sept. 17/Y0	Westcoast Energy 9.7% Bond - paid accrued interest	664.38
43.	Sept. 20/Y0	The Trust Company - Market Value fee	133.75
44.	**Sept. 21/Y0**	Bell Canada - paid account	**22.50**
45.	Oct. 1/Y0	Martha Young - payment to income beneficiary	3,500.00
46.	Oct. 1/Y0	Tartan Properties - rent	1,000.00
47.	Oct. 21/Y0	Bell Canada - paid account	23.39
48.	Nov. 1/Y0	Martha Young - payment to income beneficiary	3,500.00
49.	Nov. 1/Y0	Tartan Properties - rent	1,000.00
50.	Nov. 17/Y0	Municipal Hydro - paid account	56.50
51.	Nov. 21/Y0	Bell Canada - paid account	27.65
52.	Dec. 1/Y0	Martha Young - payment to income beneficiary	3,500.00
53.	Dec. 1/Y0	Tartan Properties - rent	1,000.00
54.	Dec. 10/Y0	Exxon Corporation - non-resident tax	125.06
55.	**Dec. 21/Y0**	Bell Canada - paid account	**21.75**
56.	Jan. 4/Y1	Martha Young - payment to income beneficiary	10,000.00
57.	**Jan. 4/Y1**	Tartan Properties - rent	1,000.00
58.	**Jan. 18/Y1**	Municipal Hydro - paid account	63.44
59.	**Jan. 21/Y1**	Bell Canada - paid account	18.15
60.	**Feb. 1/Y1**	Martha Young - payment to income beneficiary	3,500.00
61.	**Feb. 1/Y1**	Tartan Properties - rent	1,000.00
62.	**Feb. 1/Y1**	Receiver General for Canada - paid estate taxes	2,271.87

63.	Feb. 21/Y1	Bell Canada - paid account	19.76
64.	Mar. 1/Y1	Martha Young - payment to income beneficiary	3,500.00
65.	Mar. 1/Y1	Tartan Properties - rent	1,000.00
66.	Mar. 10/Y1	Exxon Corporation - non-resident tax	130.10
67.	Mar. 15/Y1	Municipal Hydro - paid account	62.74
68.	Mar. 21/Y1	Bell Canada - paid account	27.60
69.	Apr. 1/Y1	Martha Young - payment to income beneficiary	3,500.00
70.	Apr. 1/Y1	Tartan Properties - rent	1,000.00
71.	Apr. 15/Y1	Beancounters - paid preparation of T3 return	650.00
72.	Apr. 21/Y1	Bell Canada - paid account	20.45
73.	May 1/Y1	Martha Young - payment to income beneficiary	3,500.00
74.	May 1/Y1	Tartan Properties - rent	1,000.00
75.	May 19/Y1	Municipal Hydro - paid account	47.54
76.	May 21/Y1	Bell Canada - paid account	22.73
77.	June 1/Y1	Martha Young - payment to income beneficiary	3,500.00
78	June 1/Y1	Tartan Properties - rent	1,000.00
79.	June 10/Y1	Exxon Corporation - non-resident tax	127.00
80.	June 21/Y1	Bell Canada - paid account	27.42
81.	July 1/Y1	Martha Young - payment to income beneficiary	3,500.00
82.	July 1/Y1	Tartan Properties - rent	1,000.00
83.	July 15/Y1	Municipal Hydro - paid account	71.50
84.	July 21/Y1	Bell Canada - paid account	<u>19.54</u>

TOTAL REVENUE DISBURSEMENTS $89,908.99

ESTATE OF MARY SOPHIA YOUNG

INVESTMENT ACCOUNT

For the Period January 21, Year 0 to August 31, Year 1

			PURCHASED	REDEEMED
1.	July 4/Y0	Templeton Growth Fund - dividend reinvested - received additional 152.862 units @ $10.65	$1,627.98	
2.	July 15/Y0	Scotiabank - purchase GIC for 1 year @ 4.5% due July 15/Y1	670,000.00	
3.	Aug. 9/Y0	Purchase $166,000.00 Treasury Bills @ $.99539 due Sept. 16/Y0	165,234.74	
4.	Aug. 18/Y0	Purchase Scotiabank Term Deposit for 30 days @ 3.0% due Sept. 17/Y0	44,400.95	
5.	Sept. 16/Y0	Treasury Bills matured		$165,234.74
6.	Sept. 17/Y0	Scotiabank term deposit matured		44,400.95
7.	Sept. 17/Y0	CIBC 5.65% Preferred - purchase 3800 shares @ $27.60 plus commission $996.07	105,876.07	
8.	Sept. 17/Y0	Laidlaw Inc. - purchase 1000 shares @ $19.25 plus commission $436.63	19,686.63	

9.	Sept. 17/Y0	NS Power Holdings Inc. - purchase 3000 shares @ $20.00 plus commission $853.75	60,853.75
10.	Sept. 17/Y0	Westcoast Energy 9.7% Bond due Nov. 15/Y4 - Principal $20,000.00 @ $1.0690	21,380.00
11.	June 30/Y1	Laidlaw Inc. - sold 1000 shares @ $7.50 less commission $393.75	7,106.25
12.	June 30/Y1	Record loss on sale of Laidlaw shares	12,580.38
13.	**July 9/Y1**	**Templeton Growth Fund - dividend reinvested - received additional 473.441 units @ $10.16**	**4,810.16**
14.	July 15/Y1	Scotiabank GIC matured	670,000.00
15.	July 28/Y1	CIBC 5.65% Preferred - sold 3800 shares @ $43.35 less commission $483.00	164,247.00
16.	July 28/Y1	Record gain on sale of CIBC shares	58,370.93
17.	July 28/Y1	NS Power Holdings Inc. - sold 3000 shares @ $17.50 less commission $392.25	52,107.75
18.	July 28/Y1	Record loss on sale of NS Power Holdings Inc. shares	8,746.00

20 Bequest Management for Charitable Organizations

19.	July 28/Y1	Westcoast Energy 9.7% Bond - sold $20,000.00 @ $1.0800		21,600.00
20.	July 28/Y1	Record gain on sale of Westcoast Energy Bond	220.00	
21.	July 28/Y1	Bank of Nova Scotia - purchase 90 day term deposit @ 2.75% due Oct. 26/Y1	1,000,000.00	

TOTALS $2,152,461.21 $1,146,023.07

AMOUNT UNDER INVESTMENT AS OF $1,006,438.14
August 31, Year 1

$2,152,461.21

ESTATE OF MARY SOPHIA YOUNG

CASH SUMMARY

For the Period January 21, Year 0 to August 31, Year 1

Capital Receipts	$1,608,693.23	
Capital Disbursements	-455,361.90	
CAPITAL ACCOUNT BALANCE	$1,163,331.33	$1,163,331.33
Revenue Receipts	$84,696.27	
Revenue Disbursements	-89,908.99	
REVENUE ACCOUNT BALANCE	($5,212.72)	-5,212.72
TOTAL RECEIPTS		$1,158,118.61
Less amount under Investment as of August 31 Year 1		-1,006,438.14
UNINVESTED CASH BALANCE		$151,680.47

Secure Capital Account
Balance as of August 31, Year 1 $151,680.47

ESTATE OF MARY SOPHIA YOUNG
STATEMENT OF TRUSTEE'S COMPENSATION
For the Period January 21, Year 0 to August 31, Year 1

Capital Receipts	$1,608,693.23		
Add unrealized original assets	178,462.57		
Less Lakeshore Lodge account overpayment	-2,674.92		
	$1,784,480.88	@ 2.5%	$44,612.02
Capital Disbursements	$445,361.90		
Add capital account balance	1,163,331.33		
Add unrealized original assets	178,462.57		
Less solicitors' accounts (Item # 9, 14, 16, 20)	-10,198.70		
Less compensation accounts (Item #3, 15, 16, 24, 25, 29-31, 33)	-102,899.94		
Less capital losses	-21,326.38		
	$1,652,730.78	@ 2.5%	41,318.27
Revenue Receipts	$84,696.27		
Less the Trust Company fee adjustment (Item #10)	-302.34		
Less duplicate entry (Item #40)	-280.00		
Less reimbursement of custodial fee (Item #30)	-430.56		
	$83,683.37	@ 2.5%	2,092.08
Revenue Disbursements	$89,908.99		
Less revenue account overdraft	-5,212.72		
Less The Trust Company fees	-2,838.62		
Less The Trust Company compensation claimed (Item #11)	-1,070.00		
Less duplicate entry (Item #33)	-280.00		
	$80,507.65	@ 2.5%	2,012.69
Care and Management Fees @ 2/5ths of 1% of average estate value of $1,565,000.10** for 19 months ($6,260.00 per annum)			9,911.67

TOTAL TRUSTEE'S COMPENSATION	$99,946.73
Less compensation fees paid to Lawless & Lyons to date (fees only)	-95,750.00
Less compensation fees paid to The Trust Company (fees only)	<u>-1,000.00</u>
BALANCE OF TRUSTEE'S COMPENSATION	**$2,971.73**

**Average Estate Value Calculated as follows: Original Estate Value	$1,793,419.03
Remaining Original Assets	$178,462.57
Total Receipts (see Cash Summary)	<u>1,158,118.61</u>
Remaining Estate Value	$1,336,581.18
AVERAGE	$1,565,000.10

ESTATE OF MARY SOPHIA YOUNG
STATEMENT OF UNREALIZED ORIGINAL ASSETS
As of August 31, Year 1

Templeton Growth Fund - 4090.100 units $27,407.29

Exxon Corporation - 1400 shares @ US $71.125 (to CDN @ $1.5170) 151,055.28

TOTAL UNREALIZED ORIGINAL ASSETS $178,462.57

ESTATE OF MARY SOPHIA YOUNG
STATEMENT OF TRUSTEE'S INVESTMENTS
As of August 31, Year 1

Templeton Growth Fund - 626.303 units $6,438.14

Scotiabank Term Deposit due October 26, Year 1 1,000,000.00

TOTAL TRUSTEE'S INVESTMENTS $1,006,438.14

ESTATE OF MARY SOPHIA YOUNG
STATEMENT OF PROPOSED DISTRIBUTION

Net Receipts (from Cash Summary)		$1,158,118.61
Add reimbursement of compensation claimed as Guardian of Property in accordance with agreement (Fee $30,000.00, GST $2,100.00)		32,100.00
Add Value of Unrealized Assets		<u>178,462.57</u>
		$1,368,681.18
Less balance of Trustee's compensation	$2,971.73	
Less GST on compensation	208.02	
Less allowance for final tax clearance certificate	<u>50,000.00</u>	<u>-53,179.75</u>

TO BE DISTRIBUTED TO WBI BENEVOLENT FOUNDATION <u>$1,315,501.43</u>

Chapter 6

Estate Litigation and Management

ONTARIO

INTRODUCTION

Litigious proceedings involving an estate revolve around the last Will of a deceased or claims made against the estate. Disputes over the validity of a Will, for example, between a beneficiary and the estate trustee, or between classes of beneficiaries, as well as claims by third parties can all arise during the administration of an estate.

The deceased, having drawn a testamentary instrument, will have chosen to leave assets to certain individuals (usually family members) and/or organizations (usually favourite charities). More than one Will may have been drawn during the testator's lifetime or at the same time (multiple Wills). Sometimes, the changes from one Will to another are significant and drastic. Family members may fall out of favour and are excluded, or "newfound" friends or caregivers are added as beneficiaries. Usually, the details and motivation for the changes are not communicated at the time to those who expect or assume to benefit. The ultimate result of the testator's choices and decisions may lead a disgruntled beneficiary, intended or not, to seek to have the Will set aside on the grounds of improper execution, undue influence, suspicious circumstances and/or lack of testamentary capacity, or claiming a debt owed by the deceased.

These allegations assert that the Court cannot assume that the Will is valid, but rather must be proven in "solemn form". When faced with an objection, the estate trustee as the fiduciary named to administer the estate on behalf of named beneficiaries, must respond to the objection. If a conflict is created by the nature of the allegation, then a neutral party, such as an estate trustee, appointed by the Court typically administers the estate during the litigation.

Please note that where these comments refer to Wills, they apply equally to Codicils.

TYPES OF ESTATE PROCEEDINGS

Under the rubric of "estate litigation", there are various categories of proceedings, each bringing its unique dynamics and burdens of proof: "lost" Wills, interpretation of testamentary instruments, challenges to testamentary instruments, statutory claims (including dependant support and family law act claims), claims for services rendered, appeals, taxation/assessment, administration (including passing of accounts).

Although the validity of a Will can be challenged for any number of reasons, the most common challenges are based upon improper execution, lack of testamentary capacity, and undue influence. Fraud is also a ground for challenge, but is less common. The onus for proving that a Will is valid rests with its proponents or the estate trustee. However, where a party alleges undue influence, that party bears the onus of establishing that undue influence was exerted over the testator. Further, once it has been established that the Will has been duly executed, a presumption of validity arises.[1] This presumption does not shift the burden of proof to the party attacking the Will, but tactically, those objecting will need to lead some evidence to rebut the presumption of validity before the Will can be successfully challenged. An allegation of invalidity is not sufficient to rebut the presumption that a properly executed Will is valid.[2]

"LOST" WILL

Sometimes, unfortunately, there is a risk that a Will which, in the opinion of some, disproportionately favours a charity (at the expense of family members whether beneficiaries or not), will be "overlooked", "misplaced" or even destroyed. The result is an apparent intestacy favouring the next-of-kin.

In Ontario, the *Rules of Civil Procedure* provide a mechanism for the proving of lost or destroyed Wills.[3] By way of application, the validity and contents of a Will that have been lost or destroyed may be proven using affidavit evidence without *viva voce* (in person) evidence where all those

---

[1] *Vout v. Hay*, [1995] 2 S.C.R. 876.
[2] *Ibid.*
[3] R.R.O. 1990, Reg. 194, Rule 75.02.

with a financial interest in the estate consent to the proof, or as may otherwise be provided by the Court in an Order Giving Directions.

INTERPRETATION OF TESTAMENTARY INSTRUMENTS

One of the most common types of estate proceedings is an application for the opinion, advice and direction of the Court regarding an ambiguous provision in a testamentary instrument. Common applications concern defining a class of beneficiaries, identifying beneficiaries, and defining certain assets.

In Ontario, under section 60 of the *Trustee Act*[4] an estate trustee may seek the Court's assistance on interpretation issues, and be exonerated from liability for acting upon the opinion, advice and direction obtained from the Court. This "protection", however, does not mean that an estate trustee should seek the Court's assistance for every "little" matter. The Courts have frowned upon estate trustees who bring applications requesting direction on how they should exercise their discretion. In such cases, the Courts have refused to interfere, stating that the estate trustee should make the decision in the circumstances.

Generally, in order to interpret a testamentary instrument, the Court will "sit in the armchair of the testator" — examine the instrument as a whole and determine the most reasonable interpretation in the circumstances.

THE *CY-PRÈS* DOCTRINE

In the particular case of charities, a unique application seeking the opinion, advice and direction of the Court revolves around the misnaming or misidentifying of a charity or clarifying the purpose of a gift that is impossible or impractical to administer. Such an application will invoke the *cy-près* doctrine (a loose translation from Roman French meaning "as near as possible")[5] which has been around since the medieval period. Traditionally, the Courts have fostered charitable activities by upholding charitable gift intentions whenever possible. Therefore, in order for the Court to avail itself of the *cy-près* doctrine using the Court's inherent jurisdiction over charities, the deceased must have had a general charitable intent.

---

[4] R.S.O. 1990, c. T.23.
[5] This doctrine is not to be confused with the application of the principles in *Saunders v. Vautier*, (1841) 4 Beav. 115, 41 E.R. 482 which is an application to wind-up a trust.

The policy rationale is that if a person intended to benefit the public (via a charity) then the Courts should honour that intention by ensuring that the benefit is upheld. Hence, in a misnaming situation, the Courts will identify the charity with the closest name and objects; where the gift is impossible to carry out, the Courts will modify it so that it can be carried out.

There are a variety of types of *cy-près* applications. One is where the beneficiary named is non-existent. This can arise where the "named" organization does not and never did exist. In this case, the Court will entertain extrinsic evidence going to the testator's intention, his or her relationship to various competing organizations and circumstances surrounding the taking of the Will instructions. After examining the evidence, the Court will decide which organization the testator intended to benefit. In such cases, where enough is at stake, it is possible that the solicitor who drafted the Will could be brought into the litigation on the basis that the solicitor should have accurately determined who the testator intended to benefit and ensure that the organization's proper legal name was used.

For example, in *Royal Trust Corp. of Canada v. Hospital for Sick Children*,[6] the testator decreed that the residue of his estate should go to the "Crippled Children's Hospital" in Toronto and in Vancouver in equal shares. The "Crippled Children's Hospital" in Toronto never existed. The executor applied to the Court to interpret the Will to determine the beneficiary of the half share allocated to the "Crippled Children's Hospital" in Toronto.

There were a number of Ontario charities whose purpose was to treat or assist in the treatment of crippled children when the Will was executed. The Hospital for Sick Children, the Ontario Society for Crippled Children, Bloorview Children's Hospital, Hugh MacMillan Rehabilitation Centre, and the Crippled Children's Committee of the Rameses Shrine Temple, Toronto all responded to the application. As these charities had agreed in advance to the proportionate share each would receive, the main question for the Court was whether these organizations came within the general description of "crippled children's hospital". The Court found that there was a "definite charitable intention expressed by the testator" and that it was to benefit crippled children in Toronto.[7] The Court agreed that these

---

[6] (1997) 17 E.T.R. (2d) 57 (B.C.S.C.).
[7] *Ibid.*

charities fell within that general description and satisfied that charitable intention.[8]

A second type of application relates to successor beneficiaries. Sometimes the passage of time between when the Will was executed and the death of the testator, can see the merger or transferring of assets and operations from the named organization to another.

In *Conforti Estate v. Conforti*,[9] the testator left the residue of his estate to the Sacred Heart Child and Family Centre. Shortly before he died, the Centre transferred its assets and operations to the Aisling Centre in Scarborough and ceased operations. The Centre had been operated by the Order of Sisters of St. Joseph.

The Court was asked to determine who was entitled to the residue — the Aisling Centre, the Order of Sisters of St. Joseph, or the deceased's relatives. The Court found a general charitable intent and that the gift did not fail just because of the legal "disappearance" of the Centre. The *cy-près* doctrine required the residue to fulfil the testator's objects "as near as possible". As the Aisling Centre was fulfilling those objects now, it was held to be the recipient of the residue.

A third type of application is where there is an omission in determining the extent of the gift to charity. For example, in *Urquhart Estate (Trustee of) v. Urquhart*,[10] the testatrix had failed to insert the amounts she intended to go to each of the three charities named. The question was whether this made the gifts void for uncertainty. The Court held that it did not, finding that the use of the "=" sign meant that the testatrix wanted the three charities to share equally.

A fourth type of application is to remedy terms that are contrary to public policy. It could be with the passage of time that the conditions imposed on the gift are no longer socially acceptable. For example, where the recipients of a university scholarship are stated to be limited to "White Male, Catholic, British Subjects". Such a condition would be considered repugnant and contrary, not only to public policy but also the university's anti-discriminatory policy.

In *Canada Trust Co. v. Ontario Human Rights Commission*,[11] the Ontario Court of Appeal held that the *cy-près* doctrine could be used to remove race, colour, creed and ethnic origin restrictions on charitable gifts so that the gift could be administered in accordance with contemporary public

---

[8] Ibid.
[9] (1990), 39 E.T.R. 32, [1990] O.J. No. 1660 (Ont. Gen. Div.).
[10] [1999] O.J. No. 4585 (Ont. Sup. Ct.) (QL).
[11] (1990), 74 O.R. (2d) 481 (C.A.), rev'g. (1987), 61 O.R. (2d) 75 (H.C.J.).

policy. In so doing, the Court of Appeal recognized that the public interest would not be "promoted by the creation of a charity that by the lapse of time cease[d] to be useful".[12]

Likewise, the gift may contain too precise limitations. These limitations can cause problems if they are inconsistent with the charity's objects. A charity would not be able to accept the gift with the limitation as it would result in the charity acting outside the scope of its authority. In such a case, an application could be brought to determine whether the Court can invoke the *cy-près* doctrine or its inherent scheme approval power to modify the terms of the gift.

Another variant of the use of the *cy-près* doctrine is to request the Court to modify the administrative terms of a charitable trust in order to further its charitable objects. In *Killam Estate v. Dalhousie University*,[13] the Court was asked to relieve the trustees from the Will provision which restricted them to pay only income to beneficiaries. The trustees sought the Court's approval for the implementation of an agreement between the trustees and beneficiaries that would provide for combined capital and income payments to the beneficiaries. The Court agreed on the basis that "the alterations were in the best interests of the beneficiaries and for the better administration of the trust".[14]

Accordingly, using this doctrine provides an opportunity to "save" the gift. However, sometimes the Courts will refuse to apply the doctrine — often where there is insufficient charitable intent by the testator or where the application is brought as a matter of expediency.

In such cases, that particular gift "fails", and the property in question reverts to the estate to be distributed in accordance with the Will (usually, this means the gift falls into residue and forms part of the property to be distributed to the residuary beneficiaries). For example, if the residue is to be divided among three organizations and one of the organizations is non-existent (and there was insufficient evidence for the Court to identify that organization), then the residue, instead of being divided in three equal shares, would be divided in half.

Hence, although a helpful doctrine, the *cy-près* doctrine does not always work. In *Re Stewart Estate*,[15] the Court was faced with an interesting twist. The testator left $10,000 to the local YMCA. The language of the

---

[12] *Ibid.*, at 498, quoting a comment by John Stuart Mill in A.W. Scott and W.F. Fratcher, eds., *The Law of Trusts*, 4th ed. (Boston: Little, Brown & Co., 1989).
[13] [1999] N.S.J. No. 492 (N.S.S.C.) (QL).
[14] *Ibid.*, at para. 81.
[15] (1999) 88 A.C.W.S. (3d) 278 (P.E.I.S.C.T.D.), *per* DesRoches J.

bequest was general with no prohibition as to its use. He also directed that his housekeeper be allowed to reside in his house until her death. The estate was cash poor, so it was not able to make the bequest to the YMCA until the house was sold which could not happen until the housekeeper died. By the time that happened, the YMCA had ceased operations — the directors had resigned and it had significant liabilities. However, it was still incorporated and still existed in a legal sense.

The Court held that the estate could not rely upon the *cy-près* doctrine to direct the gift to another similar charity which was operational (as the estate trustee wanted to do) because the YMCA still "existed". The estate was required to pay the $10,000 to the Board of the YMCA knowing that it was not going to be used for philanthropic purposes, but rather to pay off creditors.[16]

In *Cumberland Trust v. Maritime Electric Co.*,[17] a charitable trust received monthly payments on a lease that had been granted in 1853 to the Charlottetown Gas Light Company for the life of a 999 year lease. The trust sought to have the lease amended by increasing the annual rent, adding a term limiting the unexpired portion of the lease to 20 years, and empowering the trust to terminate the lease on reasonable notice.

The Court rejected the application, noting that the original objects could still be carried out even if in a diminished capacity due to the low rental payments. It also noted that the *cy-près* doctrine could only be exercised where the objects were either impossible or impractical to carry out.[18]

In *Re Baker*,[19] the residue was left to the Northwestern General Hospital "to be used for the general purposes of the said hospital". After the testator's death, the hospital incorporated a foundation for the purposes of holding funds to advance medical research and education. Another charitable organization was also subsequently created in the name of the testator and his wife for the purposes of operating a nursing home and daycare centre.

The trustees brought an application to permit the residue of the testator's estate to be paid to the foundation. The application was on consent of all but the Public Trustee, who opposed. The Court, after noting its inherent jurisdiction to vary trusts, stated that it was a limited jurisdiction

---

[16] In such a case, it would have been helpful if the Will had been drafted to specify that the gift was only to happen to a registered and operational entity and would otherwise fail or be directed to another institution if that was not the case.
[17] [2000] P.E.I.J. No. 1 (P.E.I.S.C.T.D.) (QL).
[18] *Ibid.*, at para. 54.
[19] (1984), 47 O.R. (2d) 415 (Ont. H.C.J.).

"based upon the principle of aiding the preservation of the trust property and the administration of the trusts".[20] In this particular case, the Court was being asked (in its view) to vary the trust for the sake of expediency and that was not within the court's jurisdiction.

Procedurally, in Ontario, such applications are made pursuant to Rule 14.05(3) of the *Rules of Civil Procedure*. Typically, the estate trustee serves the application (*i.e.*, gives notice) on all organizations that are either similar in name or in object to that which the testator appears to want to benefit.

At this stage, the organization must decide whether to participate. It should also check to see whether the deceased had any connection to the organization — *i.e.*, were they on a mailing list, receiving a newsletter or materials or had they (or their spouse) made a donation. Where that search shows a connection to the organization, the more likely the organization will benefit from participating in the process. Of course, it also depends on who else responds.

An organization should seek the guidance of counsel in this decision-making process. If the organization decides to participate, it will require the assistance of counsel as evidence from the organization, participation in negotiations and making submissions to the Court is required.

With respect to the costs of these kinds of applications, the general trend is for the costs to be paid by the estate. The estate trustee's costs are borne by the estate. Generally, with respect to the competing beneficiary costs, the Court takes the position that the matter required the assistance of the Court and, as such, the litigation was no one's "fault".[21] However, be aware that more frequently, a beneficiary who is clearly the appropriate recipient may take the position that the other organizations are "taking advantage" of the ambiguity and, if unsuccessful, should bear their own costs. A further variation is to argue that the costs should be borne in the same proportions as the gift is allocated. Again, the question of cost is a matter of negotiation and ultimately the discretion of the Court.

The doctrine of *cy-près* is a rule of Will construction where the court may end up effectively altering the terms of the Will. Accordingly, these applications should not be taken for granted.

---

[20] *Ibid.*, at 415-416.
[21] Note that as a further variant, at times, the solicitor who drafted the Will will be named a party to the litigation, and, in the appropriate case, may be responsible for the costs.

WILL CHALLENGES

The next-of-kin may prefer an intestacy to a Will with a charitable bequest. They may, accordingly, seek to defeat the Will in order to create a total or partial intestacy, by challenging the Will on the basis set out in the subsequent sections.

Such an application, if successful, would eliminate the charitable interest as charities do not benefit under the intestacy distribution rules. In Ontario, the *Succession Law Reform Act*[22] provides the distribution scheme upon an intestacy:

- Where the deceased is survived by a spouse and no children, the spouse is entitled to the deceased's property absolutely.
- Where the deceased is survived by a spouse and children, the deceased's spouse is entitled to a preferential share of $200,000.
- Where the value of the estate does not exceed this preferential share, the spouse is entitled to the property absolutely.
- Where the value of the estate exceeds the preferential share, the spouse receives the preferential share and the residue is split 50/50 between the spouse and one surviving child. Where there are two or more children, the spouse receives the preferential share and one-third of the residue and the remaining two-thirds is split amongst the surviving children.

A valid testamentary document must be testamentary (*i.e.*, the free expression of the testator's wishes with respect to the distribution of his estate upon death) and conform to the statutory execution requirements. A document will represent the testator's "free expression" if he had knowledge of and approved its content, had testamentary capacity and was not exposed to undue influence.

A challenge to a Will's validity seeks to overturn the last testamentary instrument of a deceased. The most frequent grounds for challenging are non-compliance with the execution requirements set out in Part I of the *Succession Law Reform Act*, lack of testamentary capacity, or the presence of undue influence. Although less common, fraud and forgery may also be raised.

---

[22] R.S.O. 1990, c. S.26, Part II, ss. 44-46 and 68; See also O. Reg. 54/95.

PROPER EXECUTION

Typed or Processed Wills

In Ontario, the proper execution of a typed or processed testamentary document must satisfy several requirements.

Section 3 of the *Succession Law Reform Act*, states that a Will must be in writing, whether mechanically or by hand. Section 4(1)(a) requires that the Will be signed at the end by the testator, and section 4(1)(b) requires that the testator "makes or acknowledges the signature in the presence of at least two attesting witnesses present at the same time". Finally, section 4(1)(c) states that "two or more attesting witnesses must subscribe" the Will in the testator's presence. Although most Wills are customarily dated, this is not a formal validity requirement.

There is some flexibility to the requirement that the Will be signed at the end by the testator. First, in the event that a testator, due to illness or other circumstances, has difficulty in forming a signature, making a mark can be an adequate substitute, as long as the mark is intended to have the effect of a signature.[23] The use of a mark applies even if another party assists the testator in making his or her mark.

Second, even if the testator is unable to make a mark, under the *Succession Law Reform Act*, someone else may sign on behalf of the testator if the testator is present and so directs.[24] Usually, the person signing in the presence and by the direction of the testator signs in the testator's name, but it is also acceptable for such person to sign his or her own name.[25] Ideally, the party assisting the testator in making his or her mark or signing on the testator's behalf should be a disinterested person (*i.e.*, not a beneficiary or the spouse of a beneficiary). Otherwise, the validity of the Will would likely be called into question.

Third, an incorrect placement of the signature (*i.e.*, not at the end) does not usually invalidate the entire Will, although it may invalidate portions of it. As a rule, the signature of the testator should be placed immediately at the end of the Will. If it is not at the end, any sections following the signature are typically not valid.[26] Similarly, any additions made after the Will is signed are invalid.[27]

---

[23] *Re White*, [1948] 1 D.L.R 572 (N.S.S.C.).
[24] Section 4(1)(a).
[25] *Re Deeley and Green* (1929), 64 O.L.R. 535.
[26] *Succession Law Reform Act*, s. 7(2).
[27] *Ibid.*, s. 7(2).

The attestation criterion requires that two or more people witness the testator's signature, and then swear or affirm that they have done so.[28] This is why the testator must sign before either of the witnesses do and in the presence of both witnesses, since otherwise, the witness cannot really attest to having witnessed anything.[29] Witnesses must have attained the age of majority and be mentally capable. They must not be direct beneficiaries or the spouses of beneficiaries,[30] although an executor can be a witness.

If a beneficiary does act as a witness, the Will does not automatically become invalid, but the gift to the beneficiary or to a person claiming under the beneficiary will be void unless the witness or spouse satisfy the Court that neither of them exercised "undue influence on the testator".[31] The onus of proving no such influence rests with the beneficiary.

The witnesses must actually see the execution and will be called upon to swear an Affidavit of Execution at the time of the Application for a Certificate unless the affidavit was previously sworn. It is also prudent to have no one else in the room at the time of execution in order to minimize allegations of undue influence.

Where a Will must be formally proved in open court, with notice to all interested parties, the procedure is known as "proof in solemn form". This procedure may arise where, both witnesses to a testamentary instrument cannot be located or are dead, or where the document being put forward as the last testamentary instrument is not the original, as well as if the testamentary instrument is being challenged. In general, formal proof requires that the due execution of the document and the testamentary capacity of the testator be established through witness testimony before a judge.

Once the estate trustee (as the person with the obligation to propound the Will) has proven that the Will was executed properly, there arises a "rebuttable presumption" that the testator knew and approved the contents of the Will. The Court will then presume, in the absence of any evidence to the contrary, that the Will was made by a competent person. This means that the deceased was "of age" and had testamentary capacity.[32]

---

[28] Ibid., s. 4(1).
[29] Chesline v. Hermiston (1928), 62 O.L.R. 575.
[30] Succession Law Reform Act, s. 12(1).
[31] Ibid., s. 12(3).
[32] Note that at law there are different levels of capacity, some more onerous than others. One is the level required for executing testamentary documents — hence, the term "testamentary capacity". For a more detailed description, see Chapter 2.

Holograph Wills

Holograph Wills enjoy an exemption from the formal execution requirements of a typed Will. While a holograph Will must still be in writing and signed by the testator, no witnesses or attestations are required.[33] However, a holograph Will must be entirely handwritten by the testator. It is not sufficient for a testator to type his or her own Will and then sign it without being in the presence of two qualified witnesses.

WILL CHALLENGES

A person is entitled to distribute their assets as he or she sees fit. A testator has an absolute right to choose his or her beneficiaries without accountability to anyone, along with the right to change his or her mind as many times as he or she pleases so long as the capacity to make a Will exists.[34] Although a criterion of testamentary capacity is having an appreciation of the obvious beneficiaries such as spouse and children, a testator is not obliged to benefit any potential beneficiary. Thus, a testamentary instrument will not be invalidated by the mere fact that the testator has, for example, "cut out" a child or has disposed of his estate in a seemingly eccentric manner.

Nonetheless, acting in an eccentric manner makes it more likely that a challenge will be made by the obvious beneficiary who was excluded. Further, where testamentary capacity of the testator is called into question, such eccentric behaviour can be a factor that the Courts will consider. In particular, if the Will in question constitutes an unexplained and radical departure from prior Wills, it might be regarded as "suspicious".[35]

Age and Testamentary Capacity

In addition, in order for any Will (either typed or holograph) to be valid, the testator must generally have been over 18 years of age and of sound mind at the time the Will was made.[36]

Exceptions to the age requirement exist for minors who, when the Will was drawn, were members of the Armed Forces or sailors at sea or in the

---

[33] *Succession Law Reform Act*, s. 7(2). A detailed discussion of holograph Wills can be found in Chapter 2.
[34] *Visnjak v. Jakovich*, [1985] B.C.J. No. 1427 (S.C.) (QL) at para. 88; *Rufenack v. Hope Mission Slavic Gospel Assn.*, [2002] A.J. No. 1490 (Q.B.) (QL).
[35] *Re Poirier Estate*, [1944] S.C.R. 152.
[36] *Banks v. Goodfellow* (1870), L.R. 5 Q.B. 549.

course of a voyage; were or had been married; or were contemplating marriage to a specific person whom they subsequently marry.[37]

Testamentary capacity means that at the time of making the Will, the deceased had a sound disposing mind; that is, they understood the nature and quality of what they were doing in the sense that they knew and understood the nature of the claims of any person who might or should share in their estate, the extent of their property and the consequences of their wishes being carried out.

There is no absolute test of capacity as capacity is a continuum. The degeneration of capacity is usually a process that evolves over time. The test of a sound disposing mind is that the testator understood the nature and effect of the testamentary act, knew the extent of the property of which was being disposed, appreciated those who were obvious beneficiaries, and comprehended the claims (*i.e.*, by dependants) which should be given effect.[38] In simplest terms the question is "Did the testator fully understand and approve of the contents of his or her Will?"

The classic statement of the criteria used to describe the degree of mental capacity necessary to make a Will was established in *Banks v. Goodfellow*. In other words:

- did the testator understand of his or her own volition and initiative the nature of making a Will and its effects? (*i.e.*, what the Will is for and why it is being made);
- appreciate the nature and extent of his or her holdings?; and
- appreciate the claims to persons that he or she would be expected to benefit, either through legal or moral obligation?

Capacity is, accordingly, ultimately a question of fact.

Knowing the extent of one's property does not necessarily mean that the testator must have known the precise value of his estate and all assets. However, the testator should have had a general idea what assets comprise his or her estate and their approximate value.

The burden of proof to show that the testator had testamentary capacity rests on the estate trustee as the person propounding a Will. As such, the estate trustee must establish that the deceased had testamentary capacity when the Will was made.

The point at which the testator gave instructions is relevant to determining testamentary capacity, not the time at which the Will was

---

[37] *Succession Law Reform Act*, s. 8.
[38] *Banks v. Goodfellow* (1870), L.R. 5 Q.B. 549.

executed. At the time of giving instructions, the testator need only to understand what he or she is doing (*i.e.*, making a Will) and that he or she is completing that which he or she had previously instructed their lawyer to do.[39] Accordingly, before drafting a Will, it is expected that the lawyer will have had detailed discussions with the testator, particularly with regard to these issues, not only to assist in proper drafting but also to form a judgement as to whether testamentary capacity exists. If there is any doubt regarding capacity, the lawyer should consider having the client assessed. Even if there is doubt, the Court (in Ontario) has suggested that the lawyer should still draft the Will.[40] But, if there is no doubt that the client is incapable, then the Will should not be drafted.

Finally, it should be noted that at common law there is a presumption that a person has capacity. This means that the onus of proving the lack of capacity rests on those who raise the allegation and the onus of proving that the alleged incapacity did not affect the disposition of the property is on those supporting the Will.[41]

Suspicious Circumstances/Due Execution

A valid Will is one which has been freely executed by a testator who knew, understood and approved of its contents. The doctrine of suspicious circumstances dictates that whenever a Will is prepared under circumstances which raise genuine suspicions that it does not express the mind of the testator, the Court will not declare the Will to be valid unless the suspicions are removed.[42] This doctrine most commonly arises in cases where the beneficiary has been involved in the preparation of the Will.

The existence of suspicious circumstances does not mean that undue influence existed at the time. However, in successful undue influence cases, it is the cumulative effect of these suspicions that usually leads to a finding of undue influence. The issue of undue influence is aroused by the suspicious circumstances.

Suspicious circumstances can arise out of the circumstances of the preparation of the Will, the capacity of the testator, or factors suggesting

---

[39] *Re Seabrook* (1978), 4 E.T.R. 135 (Ont. Surr. Ct.); *Hall v. Bennett Estate* (2001), 40 E.T.R. (2d) 65 (Ont. S.C.J.); *Milsom v. Holien* (2001), 40 E.T.R. (2d) 77 (B.C.S.C.); and *Bourne Estate v. Bourne* (2000), 32 E.T.R. (2d) 164 (Ont. S.C.J.), supp. reasons at (2000), 32 E.T.R. (2d) 173 (Ont. S.C.J.).
[40] *Hall v. Bennett Estate* (2001), 40 E.T.R. (2d) 65 (Ont. S.C.J.).
[41] *Re Kryskiw*, [1954] O.W.N. 717 (Surr. Ct.); *Robins v. National Trust Co. Ltd.*, [1927] 2 D.L.R. 97 (Ont. P.C.), amended [1927] 1 W.W.R. 881.
[42] *Eady v. Waring* (1974), 2 O.R. (2d) 627 (C.A.); *Vout v. Hay*, [1995] 2 S.C.R. 876.

that the free will of the testator was overborne by acts of pressure. In practical terms, these factors affect the burden of proof. Generally, the burden is satisfied when the Will has been proven to have been duly executed. This presumption will hold unless the party challenging the Will leads some evidence to rebut the presumption of validity. One way to challenge the presumption is to point to suspicious circumstances that call capacity, knowledge or approval of the Will into question. If proven successful then the presumption of validity is rebutted.

The circumstances surrounding the preparation of the Will, which tend to call into question the capacity of the testator or suggest that his free will was overcome by undue influence, coercion or fraud, do not normally constitute an exclusive basis for challenging a Will, but are considered within the context of undue influence or lack of testamentary capacity. The presence of suspicious circumstances, however, if significant, may rebut the presumption (once due execution is proven) that the testator knew and approved the contents of the Will.

Generally, a properly executed Will means that there was sufficient testamentary capacity. If suspicious circumstances have been shown, then the onus reverts to those propounding the Will to satisfy the Court of the deceased's testamentary capacity. Thus, it is up to the estate trustee to lead cogent evidence of capacity, knowledge and approval proven on a balance of probabilities.

For these and other reasons, in drafting a Will, a solicitor should always inquire as to the identities of any obvious beneficiaries, review any former Wills, and take copious notes of the reason or reasons why an obvious beneficiary was excluded. Sometimes, the Will itself will state that the testator appreciates that the son or daughter may expect to share in the estate, but that for a particular reason he or she is not being included. The notes should also explain any major changes from the previous Will and contain comments about the testator's testamentary capacity.

Other evidence the court will consider in determining testamentary capacity are the observations of people familiar with the testator, including any medical professionals who might have cared for the testator, and friends and neighbours. Evidence about the capacity of the testator, and in particular, any recent deterioration, could be very influential.

Undue Influence

Since a valid Will must represent the testator's true intentions, a Will can be attacked on the basis that another party (usually someone who somehow otherwise benefits) has imposed their will upon the testator, so that the Will does not truly represent the true wishes of the testator.[43] Establishing undue influence requires more than showing that somebody attempted to persuade or pressure the testator to dispose of the estate in a particular fashion that was not their own. In other words, there must not only be influence, but influence that is undue, or that amounts to coercion. Although not easy to show, the hallmark of undue influence is the domination of the testator by another. For example, a request or even repeated requests for a gift may not be sufficient to constitute undue influence, but threatening adverse consequences if the request is not granted would likely constitute undue influence. Other examples of undue influence can arise when a third party, rather than the testator, instructs the solicitor in preparing the Will, or when next-of-kin or others "cocoon" the testator and prevent contact with others.

It is noteworthy that unlike due execution and testamentary capacity, when a Will is challenged on the basis of undue influence, the onus rests on the party seeking to attack the Will to prove his or her claim.

Despite the number of times this ground of attack is raised, it is difficult to successfully challenge a Will on the basis of undue influence. Therefore, typical objections when challenging a Will are made on all three grounds.

Fraud

Where it is proven that the Will was procured by fraud, it will be invalid. An example of fraud would be where someone forged the deceased's signature on the Will. As with undue influence, the onus of proving fraud rests with the party alleging it. Proving fraud is extremely difficult and more naturally attracts cost penalties if unproven. Accordingly, allegations of fraud are not raised as a matter of course.

CLAIMS AGAINST THE ESTATE BY SPOUSES, DEPENDANTS, AND NEIGHBOURS

This type of litigation does not relate to the validity of the Will, the capacity of the testator or the construction of the Will. These proceedings presume the Will is valid, that the testator had sufficient capacity and that the intentions are clear.

---

[43] *Wingrove v. Wingrove* (1885), 11 P.D. 81.

Rather, these claims assert that the claimant is entitled to relief (*i.e.*, money) from the estate. Some of the remedies are provided by legislation, such as for the support of surviving spouses and dependants. Again, the legislation does not invalidate the Will — it merely permits the Court, on the ground of public policy as reflected in the legislation, to modify the testator's intended scheme of distribution.

Spousal Election

Given the regime regarding rights of succession to estates as between spouses, in Ontario, the *Family Law Act*[44] may also give rise to litigation during the administration of the estate. This type of litigation is akin to typical family law litigation.

Section 5(2) of the *Family Law Act* states that:

> When a spouse dies, if the net family property [as defined in the statute] of the deceased spouse exceeds the net family property of the surviving spouse, the surviving spouse is entitled to one-half the difference between them. This is called the surviving spouses' entitlement under the statute.

This election is meant to ensure that surviving spouses are not "disinherited" upon the death of their spouse. The decision must be made quickly as the election must be filed with the Court within six months of the date of death. Once the election is filed, then the claim proceeds between the surviving spouse and the estate. Where the surviving spouse has been named as estate trustee and wishes to make this election, he or she should not assume the role of estate trustee because they would be placing themselves in a conflict position.

Where the deceased spouse has left a Will, the surviving spouse is put to the election[45] of taking the share to which he or she is entitled under the Will (or under the rules of intestate succession) or to receive one-half of the spouse's net family property. The Will can expressly provide that the surviving spouse may have his or her entitlement under the Will in addition to his or her entitlement under section 5(2).

The surviving spouse must make this election within six months of the date of death (unless the time limit is extended by Court Order). If the election is not filed within the time limit, the surviving spouse is deemed to have elected to take their interest under the Will. This option will most

---

[44] R.S.O. 1990, c. F.3.
[45] *Ibid.*, s. 6(5).

often be chosen when the deceased spouse leaves nothing or very little to the surviving spouse under their Will.

The spouse's entitlement has priority over the gifts made in the deceased spouse's Will, a person's right to a share of the estate under intestate succession and an Order for dependant support (except for a child) made under the *Succession Law Reform Act*[46] (discussed below).

Accordingly, where there is a surviving spouse, no distributions are usually made within six months of the death unless the surviving spouse agrees in writing to the distribution (or it is authorized by the Court).

Dependant Support or Relief Claims

Claims can also be made under Part V of the *Succession Law Reform Act* for dependant support claims.

Where a deceased has not made adequate support provision (whether testate or intestate) for any dependants, Part V of the *Succession Law Reform Act* permits the Court to order appropriate support out of the estate of the deceased. Any person who qualifies as a "dependant" under the statute may make a claim for support alleging that the deceased failed to adequately take care of them financially in the Will. The statute provides an expansive definition of dependant[47] and includes any individual whom the deceased was supporting at the time of death or whom the deceased may have had an obligation to support prior to their death.

In determining the amount and duration of support, the Court will consider the statutory factors set out in section 62. The claim applied against all estate assets defined by section 72 of the *Succession Law Reform Act*. Hence, this application can significantly reduce or possibly eliminate the bequest to charity.

The public policy rationale is similar to that for the spousal election. The deceased is expected to know and look after those he or she supported during his or her lifetime. The deceased should have provided for his or her dependants in their estate plan. The fact that they did not means that the estate must bear that burden.

A dependant support claim must be filed within six months of the date of the grant of the Certificate of Appointment.[48] Again, these claims proceed along similar lines of a support application in the context of

---

[46] *Family Law Act*, R.S.O. 1990, C. F.3, s. 6(12).
[47] The definition in s. 57 includes spouse or same-sex partner, parent, child (includes relationships of *in loco parentis*), or sibling of the deceased.
[48] *Succession Law Reform Act*, s. 61.

spousal and child support cases upon marriage breakdown, once the preliminary hurdle of proving the applicant is a dependant has been met. If successful, the estate would be faced with a Court Order requiring it to provide support (as determined) to the applicant. These types of claims may, therefore, have a significant impact on the beneficiaries and their entitlement in the estate.

When an estate is faced with a spousal election or dependant support claim, the estate trustee must deal with the claim before any distribution can be made. Although the application can be made with the consent of the Court after the six-month period has expired, the claim can only be exercised against the estate assets remaining undistributed at the time of the application. Accordingly, an estate trustee will normally wait out this limitation period (unless absolutely sure there is no possibility of a claim being made), before making any distributions. A beneficiary should, therefore, generally expect to wait at least six months before receiving a distribution.

Services Rendered Claims

Claims by third parties such as housekeepers, neighbours and caregivers, for "services rendered" may also be made. In these claims, the person alleges that the deceased promised to leave them something in their Will, in return for which the neighbour or friend assists the deceased during their lifetime.

Another example of a services rendered claim is a claim by a person who acted as an attorney under a power of attorney during the lifetime of the deceased. The attorney may file a claim for compensation for services rendered to the date of death.

If the attorney is also the estate trustee and submits a claim to the estate, then the attorney is in conflict and a substitute estate trustee should be appointed to act as estate trustee.

In the context of estate accounting, before approving the accounts, when such a claim is made, a beneficiary should ask for a copy of the power of attorney document for review. The deceased's intention as to compensation may be expressed in the document. Some standard form powers of attorney documents (especially if between family members) contain an express provision that there is to be no compensation.

Other types of claims that may be made are by other creditors (*i.e.*, mortgagors, under contract, promissory notes). These types of claims are different in that they are based in the common law either from the law from the court of equity or under contract, not statute. The claimant must prove that he or she is either owed the funds (*i.e.*, breach of contract) or is entitled to be compensated for the effort undertaken. In the case where the terms of the services rendered are clear (*i.e.*, the Court finds a contract (oral or written) that states that the claimant was to receive $10/hr), then the court will enforce the contract once the claimant has proven the terms of the contract and shown that they have satisfied their end of the contract. Where the relationship is less clear, the Court will fix a reasonable fee for the services rendered if satisfied that, in fact, the services were rendered. This is called compensating the claimant on a *quantum meruit* (*i.e.*, based on merit) basis. In the case of housekeeping services, for example, an hourly rate of $7-10 may be reasonable.

In Ontario, these claims proceed like any other type of civil litigation proceeding (although recognizing the additional procedure under the *Estates Administration Act*[49]). The claimant issues a Statement of Claim, the estate through the estate trustee defends the claim by filing a Statement of Defence. Once these pleadings are in place, then the framework of the litigation is set and the parties proceed through the various interlocutory steps as set out in the *Rules of Civil Procedure*. Where these claims are brought outside the Greater Toronto Area (Ontario) for an amount less than $5,000 or brought inside the Greater Toronto Area for an amount less than $10,000, they will be considered claims brought in Small Claims Court and the parties must follow the procedures set out for that Court. For claims in Ontario over the Small Claims Court limit but under $25,000, the Simplified Rules under the *Rules of Civil Procedure* will be followed. These Rules are intended to simplify or shorten the steps in the litigation with a view of achieving early resolution.

The estate trustee typically defends these claims on behalf of the estate with a view of only paying a reasonable amount, if justified, to the claimant. The costs of the litigation and the goal of avoiding protracted litigation are factors that will influence the amount paid. Accordingly, a beneficiary, charitable or otherwise rarely becomes involved in the day-to-day process of litigating these claims. It may be, however, that family members or friends who are also beneficiaries may have information relevant to the litigation and so may be requested in that capacity to act as witnesses. It is rare for a charity to have such kind of information. Having said that, a charity, when advised of litigation, should consider whether it has any information that may be relevant to the litigation, and if so, pass it on to the estate solicitor. For example, if the charity had a long-standing relationship with the donor, it could be that the donor mentioned during a

---

[49] R.S.O. 1990, c. E.22.

donor visit that he or she was greatly appreciative of the services received from the housekeeper and that he or she intended to leave a gift to the housekeeper as well as the charity. Such kind of information should (even if not requested) be communicated in writing to the estate solicitor.

In Ontario, the legal costs are not automatically covered by the estate. As with civil litigation matters, the costs should follow the event. Generally speaking, this means that if the claimant is unsuccessful, the estate solicitor should request that the claimant bear some or all of the estate's costs. A beneficiary should watch for this opportunity as too often in estate proceedings, the estate solicitor fails to see the comparison to civil litigation proceedings and does not take advantage of the *Rules of Civil Procedure*, such as making an offer to settle at the appropriate time.

Where the claimant is successful, he or she will request that their costs be borne by the estate. The Court will in its discretion determine whether this is appropriate. The estate trustee's costs are normally always borne by the estate (*i.e.*, the capital of the estate). However, a beneficiary should be aware that if it was obvious that the claimant would be successful, yet the estate solicitor did not recommend making an offer to settle, or, in some way, failed to attempt to mediate or resolve the litigation in order to minimize costs, then a case could be made that the costs should not in whole or in part be borne by the estate. Further, a beneficiary can take the position that the estate solicitor's costs are excessive.

In certain circumstances, if discussion does not resolve these issues, a beneficiary can (even if the legal account had been paid) request that the legal accounts be assessed. For these reasons, a beneficiary, especially a residuary beneficiary, should request regular reports and copies of the legal accounts, monitor the litigation, ensure the proper process is being followed and keep check of the costs being incurred. Consulting with the other beneficiaries and utilizing the assistance of counsel is also advisable as there are strategic factors that come into play on the issue of costs.

The power to deal with these claims rests with the estate trustee (with the assistance of counsel). However, as a practice, it is common for the estate trustee to seek the consent of the beneficiaries on the major decisions that may have to be made — for example, deciding to accept or make an offer to settle, or going to trial. In these cases, the beneficiaries may be called upon to "cast a vote" on the options presented. It is suggested that a beneficiary insist that the estate solicitor present the background evidence to the litigation, discuss the options available and provide a recommended course of action before requesting that the beneficiary "cast their vote". A beneficiary should not delay in seeking out the information needed to make a decision (or in making a decision) as often, the estate solicitor and estate trustee will proceed on the basis of the majority of the "votes" cast; unanimity is not required. A beneficiary should also consult with the other beneficiaries and with their own counsel for advice, if necessary.

Sometimes, a charitable residuary beneficiary will be asked to agree to "give" a sum (from their residue share) to the friend, housekeeper or family member who was "forgotten" in the Will. The estate trustee when making the request, may indicate that he or she knows the deceased wanted to benefit the person and that they would have been included in the Will if only the deceased had "gotten around" to adding them. These requests should be considered carefully. Although there are many nuances to such a request, and the questions to ask and decision-making process vary depending on the circumstances, the general rule is that this should not be done. Despite the good will potentially generated by agreeing to the request, the charity's obligation is to ensure that the deceased's wishes are carried out. For whatever reason (and it is not for the estate trustee or the charity to guess), the person was excluded or not added. Where the situation is that the person will (if the request is rejected) assert a claim against the estate, then a charity (after confirming this) has more flexibility in agreeing to the request. In this case, the charity is compromising or settling potential or actual litigation.

STEPS IN AN ESTATE ACTION

In Ontario, as of January 1, 1995, Rules 74 and 75 of the *Rules of Civil Procedure*,[50] replaced the former *Estate Rules*, altering both the terminology and the procedure to be followed in estates matters. Generally, Rule 74 addresses itself to non-contentious proceedings, whereas Rule 75 deals with contentious proceedings. These rules and accompanying forms provide a comprehensive code of procedure, some of which may, in particular, assist charities in resolving litigious issues.

First, however, it is useful to explain the litigation process generally and the remedies available. In summary, these steps include:

- notification;
- response;
- application or motion for directions;

---

[50] R.R.O. 1990, Reg. 194.

- interlocutory procedures that assist in gathering evidence, such as production of relevant documentation, and examination for discoveries; and
- resolution by settlement (*i.e.*, negotiation or mediation) and/or hearing or trial.

NOTIFICATION

Generally speaking, anyone who will be affected by a Court proceeding should be made aware of it (unless the Court Rules provide otherwise). In Ontario, it is a broad class of persons who may become involved in an estate proceeding. The *Rules of Civil Procedure* state that any person who has a financial interest in the estate has a right to be given notice of any proceeding concerning the estate.

Orders for Assistance

Can anything be done where there is a Will under which a person is or suspects that he or she is a beneficiary and the testator has died but no notification has been received?

In Ontario, assistance may be sought from various sources. One source is section 9 of the *Estates Administration Act*, which states that if the applicant reasonably believes that someone has a testamentary instrument, the Court will compel that person to produce it. To be successful, the applicant only has to prove that he or she has a reasonable belief that that person has such a document. If the person or institution does not answer the Order and is later found to have had such a document in his or her possession, he or she could potentially be found in contempt of court. Sections 44 and 45 of the *Estates Administration Act* also provide another "short-cut" procedure.

Another tool is to apply for a Court Order compelling the person to prove the testamentary instrument. This procedure allows a person with a financial interest in the estate to move the administration forward where the person named as estate trustee is not.

The most common source for assistance in Ontario comes from the *Rules of Civil Procedure* in the form of Orders for Assistance. These Rules provide procedural assistance depending upon the nature of the issue. There are a number of orders that can be sought by any party appearing to have a financial interest in an estate. These orders were a major innovation of the new Rules, as quite often, it was difficult and expensive to "kick-start" the administration of an estate. Almost all of these orders can be sought by way of an *ex parte* (without notice) motion and are relatively inexpensive. These provisions have a low standing threshold — anyone who appears to have a financial interest in an estate may apply to the Court.[51]

Order to Accept or Refuse the Appointment

Under Rules 74.15(1)(a) and (b) of the *Rules of Civil Procedure*, a motion (Form 74.36) can be sought to compel the named estate trustee to accept or refuse the appointment. This Order is useful in situations where the named estate trustee delays or fails to apply for a Certificate of Appointment. It is also useful where it is suspected that the named estate trustee is administering the estate and there is concern that he or she is doing so with an invalid Will. Compelling the named estate trustee to accept or refuse the appointment allows the process of opposing the estate trustee's appointment or challenging the validity of a Will to begin. Such an Order forces the application process for a Certificate of Appointment. If the named estate trustee fails to respond to the Order, they are deemed to have renounced their right to act. Upon application, any Notice of Objection on file takes effect, and a Will challenge may proceed. Rule 74.15(1)(b) provides for a similar motion (Form 74.37) where there is no Will.

Further, there is some point in insisting upon probate as the application requires the estate trustee to swear an oath that they will administer the estate on a timely basis and account as necessary.

Rule 74.15(1)(c) of the *Rules of Civil Procedure* also deals with the situation where the named estate trustee is either unable or unwilling to act, or where there is no named estate trustee. The applicant who proposes to be appointed estate trustee needs to secure the consent of beneficiaries who together are entitled to the majority of the assets of the estate at the time of death. In the event that these beneficiaries are slow to file their consents or objections, an interested party may move for an Order requiring them to do so. If, after an Order to Consent or Object to a Proposed Appointment (Form 74.38) has been issued, any beneficiary who fails to respond within the requisite time frame is deemed to have consented to the appointment.

---

[51] Rule 74.15(1) of the *Rules of Civil Procedure* details a number of these types of orders and only a few are highlighted.

Order to Beneficiary Witness

In the event that a beneficiary or the spouse of a beneficiary acts as a witness to the Will, any gifts or legacies to the beneficiary in question are at risk of being invalidated. Rule 74.15(1)(f) of the *Rules of Civil Procedure* deals with this problem by allowing the Court to require the witness to bring a motion asking the Court to find that no improper or undue influence was exerted on the testator by the beneficiary witness. Usually, the second witness will also be called upon to confirm that there was no undue influence in the execution of the Will. If a beneficiary fails to bring a motion within the required time frame after an Order to Beneficiary Witness (Form 74.40) is issued, the estate trustee may seek an Order declaring that any gift or bequest to the beneficiary is void.

Order to Former Spouse

Section 17 of the *Succession Law Reform Act* provides that where a spouse is appointed estate trustee, any bequest to a spouse or a clause conferring an appointment power upon a spouse are automatically revoked upon divorce or annulment, unless the Will expresses an intention to the contrary. If the testator's marriage has been terminated, a motion can be made under Rule 74.15(1)(g) of the *Rules of Civil Procedure* to order a former spouse to take part in the proceedings and, in particular, require a determination of the former spouse's interest, if any, in the estate. If the former spouse fails to respond to an Order to Former Spouse (Form 74.41), the issues are determined without the input of the former spouse and he or she is bound by any decision that is reached in his or her absence.

The remaining Orders for Assistance under Rule 74.15(1) of the *Rules of Civil Procedure* arise only after an estate trustee has been appointed and involve motions to force the estate trustees to act in certain ways. Some examples follow.

Order to File Statement of Assets

Anyone with a financial interest in the estate can seek to have the estate trustee file a statement of the assets with the Registrar, outlining all the assets of the estate and their approximate value. Once such a statement has been filed, further particulars can be requested under Rules 74.15(1)(d) and (e) of the *Rules of Civil Procedure*. The motion for further particulars is the only one of the Orders for Assistance that is required to be brought upon notice to the estate trustee under Rule 74(15)(2). This

Order requires the estate trustee to file with the Court a statement detailing the nature and value of all estate assets at the date of death to be administered by the estate trustee.

Order for Further Particulars

After receiving the above statement, this Order requires the estate trustee to provide "further particulars by supplementary affidavit or otherwise as the court directs".

Order to Pass Accounts

Rule 74.15(1)(h) of the *Rules of Civil Procedure* allows a party with a financial interest in the estate to force the estate trustee to pass accounts. This is another easy method to obtain financial information about the estate. Sometimes (in the right circumstances), this Order can be obtained so that the value of the estate can be ascertained to determine whether a challenge is worthwhile.[52]

Notice of Commencement of Proceedings

One such remedy is to request notice of when such an application for a Certificate of Appointment is made. Rule 74.03 of the *Rules of Civil Procedure* allows anyone with a financial interest in the estate to file a Request for Notice of Commencement of Proceeding with the Registrar any time before a Certificate of Appointment of Estate Trustee is issued. This Notice is prepared without notice and filed over-the-counter. Some standard language follows:

> I, [name], object to the issuance of a Certificate of Appointment of Estate Trustee without notice to me because I have concerns that: the purported last Will of the deceased was not properly executed, the deceased lacked testamentary capacity, the deceased did not have knowledge of and approve of the contents of the Will or was subjected to undue influence.
>
> The nature of my interest in the estate is that I am entitled to [amount of share] of the residue of the estate pursuant to a prior Will of the deceased.

---

[52] Further, other *Rules of Civil Procedure* also provide a person who has a financial interest in the estate with other procedural remedies, before or at the time an Application for a Certificate of Appointment has been made.

In Ontario, where there is a Will, one or more of the parties named as estate trustee will apply for a Certificate of Appointment of Estate Trustee with a Will under Rule 74.04 of the *Rules of Civil Procedure*. Although not mandatory, obtaining a Certificate of Appointment is useful because it constitutes the only recognizable legal evidence of the Estate Trustee's authority. This process, however, allows those who oppose the Will or appointment to object.

Once the Application for Certificate of Appointment of Estate Trustee has been made, the *Rules of Civil Procedure* outline a number of motions that can be brought by interested parties at this stage. Usually, these are considered contentious estates proceedings and hence are found in Rule 75.

Formal Proof of Testamentary Instrument

If a person dealing with an Ontario Will is considering challenging it but does not yet have sufficient information to do so, that person can avail themselves of Rule 75.01 of the *Rules of Civil Procedure*. Under this Rule, any person can apply to have the document that is being put forward as the deceased's Will formally proven (*i.e.*, proven in solemn form) in order to have the Court declare that the Will is valid after hearing evidence surrounding the execution of the Will.

Objection to Issuing a Certificate of Appointment

Under Rule 75.03 of the *Rules of Civil Procedure*, an interested party can oppose an application for a Certificate of Appointment of Estate Trustee by filing a Notice of Objection (formerly called a *caveat*) with the Registrar any time before the Certificate is issued.

In order to have standing to file a Notice of Objection, the objector must have some potential financial interest in the estate. Further (quite obviously), if a Certificate of Appointment of Estate Trustee has already been issued, a Notice of Objection can no longer be filed.

The purpose of this Notice of Objection is to ensure that nothing is done with the estate without notice to the objector. The filing of the Notice of Objection prevents the issuance of the Certificate until the Objection is withdrawn. Once on file, the estate is effectively frozen until the objection is removed. No Certificate of Appointment can be issued and (technically) no assets can be distributed.

The Notice sets out the interest of the objector in the estate, and the grounds upon which any challenge to the Will are to be based. Once the

Notice of Objection is filed, it is valid for three years and can be withdrawn by the person who filed it at any time.

Upon being filed with the Court, the Registrar notifies the applicant estate trustee who then must serve a Notice of Objection (Form 75.1) on the objector. Once the objector has received the Notice to Objector (Form 75.3), he or she has 20 days to file a Notice of Appearance (Form 75.4). Failing this, the objection will be removed and the application will proceed without further notice to the objector. Once a Notice of Appearance has been filed, the applicant has 30 days to move for directions (these motions are discussed below).

The failure to file a Notice of Appearance within the stated time period results in the application to prove the Will proceeding as if the Notice of Objection had not been filed. In other words, if a Notice of Appearance is not filed, the Court will proceed to issue the Certificate of Appointment and the Will challenge is over.

Revocation of Certificate of Appointment

Once a Certificate has been issued, anyone with a financial interest in the estate can move under Rule 75.04 of the *Rules of Civil Procedure* to have it revoked on the grounds that it was obtained by error or fraud, or that it is no longer valid, or for any other reason. This procedure may be used, for example, where one wants to oppose the choice of estate trustee, even if one does not intend to challenge the validity of the Will.

Return of Certificate of Appointment

Under Rule 75.05 of the *Rules of Civil Procedure*, the Court may order the return of the Certificate of Appointment to the Court where the validity of the testamentary instrument for which the certificate is challenged or where an application has been made to have the certificate of appointment revoked.

An Order for the Return of the Certificate of Appointment of Estate Trustee is a necessary first step if one wishes to challenge the validity of a Will after a Certificate has already been issued. This step must be taken to prevent any distribution of estate assets pending the resolution of a challenge to the Will. Otherwise, the estate trustee, Certificate in hand, could continue to administer the estate as if no challenge were pending. Without the Certificate, an estate trustee who continues to act and deal with the estate as trustee does so at their personal peril.

Upon service of the Order, the estate trustee is required to return the original grant to the Court and their right to act is suspended until the issues are resolved. The estate trustee will return the Certificate of Appointment by depositing it with the Registrar.

Once the challenger obtains an Order for the return of the Certificate, he or she must move for directions within 30 days, or the Certificate may be released to the estate trustee, who can resume the administration of the estate. If the challenger proceeds with a motion for directions, the Certificate will not be released until the challenge is concluded. At that time, an Order releasing the Certificate is needed.

APPLICATION OR MOTION FOR DIRECTIONS

Once an objection has been made, the estate is considered in litigation. This litigation must be managed. In Ontario, the next procedural step unique (as compared to other forms of litigation) to estate matters is the motion or application for directions using Rule 75.06 of the *Rules of Civil Procedure*. This is an important motion or application.

An interested party who wishes to challenge the Will must bring such a motion or application if the estate trustee does not do so. The Order for Directions will be brought by way of a motion if proceedings have already been commenced. An Application for Certificate of Appointment of Estate Trustee is considered to be an originating process, so that in most cases, the Order for Directions will be pursued by way of a motion. In the event no proceedings are underway, an application is required.

An application or motion for directions can be brought whenever there is an issue concerning the administration of the estate that needs to be resolved in order for the administration to continue.

The motion or application for directions serves a function similar to that of the pleadings in other types of litigation. It is a procedural motion in that it sets out the issues, the parties and their relative positions; timelines for the completion of the various steps in the litigation; whether mediation will take place; and usually confirms certain powers of the estate trustee or estate trustee during litigation to obtain relevant documentation, such as medical records. Accordingly, each party should ensure that his or her interest in the estate is set out, as well as all the grounds for challenging the Will.

As outlined above, the most common bases of challenge are formal validity, testamentary capacity, and undue influence. Recall that suspicious circumstances do not constitute a separate basis for challenge. Rather, they will raise the spectre of one of the other criteria of validity not being met.

All interested parties in an application or motion for directions must be served at least 10 days in advance of the hearing. Typically, the time frame is much longer. Upon such a motion, the Court may direct that the issues be decided at trial; determine who the parties to the proceedings are; decide who will be served with the Order Giving Directions (Form 75.8 or Form 75.9) and by what method and in what timeframe; appoint an estate trustee during litigation; order the parties to mediation; or impose any other procedure that is just under the circumstances.

As a general rule, pleadings are not required in Will challenges because all the issues will have been identified in the Order for Directions. This potential absence of pleadings is one of the distinguishing features of estate litigation as compared to other kinds of civil litigation in which the pleadings set the parameters of the action. In estate litigation, one must be careful to ensure that all bases of challenge are included in the Order for Directions, because it is this document, and not the pleadings that guide the subsequent litigation. If, however, a Statement of Claim is filed, the defendant must also file a Statement of Defence as with ordinary civil litigation. Failing this, the defendant who does not file a Statement of Defence will no longer be considered to be a party to the proceedings, will receive no further notice and will not be included in any settlement discussions. If one wishes, however, one can file a Statement of Submission of Rights to Court rather than a Statement of Defence in response to a claim.

Finally, in Ontario, any party having a financial interest in an estate may apply at any time for directions or move for directions to bring any matter before the court. Rule 14.05(3) of the *Rules of Civil Procedure*, sets out the framework that may include:

14.05(3)(a) the opinion, advice or direction of the court on a question affecting the rights of a person in respect of the administration of the estate of a deceased person or the execution of a trust;

(b) an order directing executors, administrators or trustees to do or abstain from doing any particular act in respect of an estate or trust for which they are responsible;

(c) the removal or replacement of one or more executors, administrators or trustees, or the fixing of their compensation;

(d) the determination of rights that depend on the interpretation of a deed, will, contract or other instrument, or on the interpretation of a statute, order in council, regulation or municipal by-law or resolution;

(e) the declaration of an interest in or charge on land, including the nature and extent of the interest or charge or the boundaries of the land, or the settling of the priority of interests or charges;

(f) the approval of an arrangement or compromise or the approval of a purchase, sale, mortgage, lease or variation of trust...

Upon receipt of the Notice, the Registrar is required to notify the party of the commencement of any proceedings related to the estate. The Notice is valid until a Certificate of Appointment of Estate Trustee is issued or for three years unless renewed.

In response to receiving notification of a proceeding, a beneficiary may ignore the proceeding at his or her own peril, retain counsel and file a Notice of Appearance, or submit his or her rights to the Court.

Notice of Appearance

If named a beneficiary in the proceeding, that party will be served (*i.e.*, notified of the proceeding) with the Application or Motion (unless service is dispensed with by Court Order or under the Rules). Once served, a party has a choice.

In Ontario, the beneficiary can decide to respond to the proceeding and participate in it as a party by serving and filing a Notice of Appearance. In order to do so, the beneficiary can only respond through counsel.

Submitting One's Rights

An alternative to filing a Notice of Appearance and unique to estate proceedings in Ontario, is the option of enjoying limited participation in the litigation without becoming a party to the proceeding. This option, available under Rule 75.07 of the *Rules of Civil Procedure*, is to submit one's rights to the court. If a beneficiary does not want (or need) to participate as a full status party, then the party would typically submit their rights to the Court either on a motion for directions respecting the conduct of the application for a Certificate of Appointment or by filing a Statement of Submission of Rights with the court in response to a statement of claim filed by the plaintiff in compliance with the Order Giving Directions.

A beneficiary who has submitted his or her rights to the Court is not a party to the litigation. Although not considered a full status party to the proceeding, the beneficiary is entitled to certain notification, such as notice of the time and place of trial, if any; a copy of the judgment when the matter is decided; and the opportunity to approve or reject any settlements arrived at by the parties. Further, no consent matter can be approved without the consent of all individuals submitting their rights to the Court, or proof that they have been served and have failed to object.

A beneficiary who submits his or her rights is not vulnerable to costs being awarded against them (except to the extent they are payable from the estate), but is also not allowed to seek costs, is entitled to notice of the trial and a copy of the judgment, and has the right to participate in any settlement discussions.

As an example, in a case where the issue relates to the residue clause, all residuary beneficiaries and legatees receive notice. The matter concerns the interpretation of the residue clause, a matter that the legatees have no direct interest in and accordingly, may choose to "submit their rights" to the Court.

The ability to submit one's rights to the Court is a process unique to Ontario estate matters. It allows that person to avoid the need to fully participate in the litigation thus retaining the right to participate in any settlement arrangements. Given the availability in Ontario, a charitable beneficiary should really never not respond.

Estate Trustee During Litigation

Any party having a financial interest in an estate may apply or move for directions to bring any matter before the Court. By so doing, and where it is clear that the estate "will be going into litigation", the Court (at a party's request or on its own initiative) may appoint a "neutral" person to act as estate trustee during the litigation. The role of this appointment is to ensure that the administration of the estate is continued by a neutral party until the litigation is resolved.

The general rule is that a party unconnected with the litigation is the most proper person to be appointed. This rule excludes beneficiaries with an interest in the outcome of the litigation and named estate trustees. Therefore, the parties should attempt to find a neutral person who would be willing to act. Typically, a trust company is appointed. Sometimes, however, this is not so easy. In the appropriate circumstances, the parties will agree to (subject to Court approval) the appointment of the named estate trustee as estate trustee during litigation on the understanding that no assets will be distributed during the litigation.

An estate trustee during litigation can administer the assets, and ensure that all investments are protected, but is not entitled to distribute the estate in any way. Once the litigation is concluded, the estate trustee during litigation automatically loses his or her authority to act. Once the litigation is resolved, the role ends (subject to any issue over compensation and the subsequent passing of accounts).

In Ontario, for example, if an estate trustee is prevented from acting by way of a Notice of Objection, Revocation or Return of the Certificate of Appointment, an estate trustee during litigation should likely be appointed to administer the estate assets pending the resolution of the litigation. If such an application is granted under Rule 74.10 of the *Rules of Civil Procedure* a Certificate of Appointment of Estate Trustee During Litigation will be issued by the Court.

In other provinces, these neutral parties may be called *administrators pendent lite* or administrators pending litigation.

After an Order for Directions or an Order for Assistance has been received, the parties will then "settle into" the litigation. Typically, the Order Giving Directions outlines the procedural steps the parties must take as well as the substantive issues that form the dispute between the parties. The Order will also typically include the deadlines the parties must meet in an attempt to keep the litigation moving.

It is at this stage that the position of the parties is crystallized. Therefore, it is also at this stage that parties with a common interest should make a final push to retain lead counsel. This may give rise to the issue of retainers and cost arrangements. Caution is suggested when faced with a request for a charity to execute a retainer letter and/or contribute to a financial retainer. Professional advice is advisable.

In Ontario, the *Rules of Civil Procedure* also set out the procedure, documentation required, parties to be served and deadlines to be met with respect to these applications.

Interlocutory Procedures

Once the framework of the litigation has been established, the next step is to attend to the gathering of the evidence relevant to the issues being litigated.

Production of Documents

One such step involves collecting the relevant documents and providing them to all parties, a process called the exchange of productions. For example, if there is a dispute as to the capacity of the testator at the time he or she executed his or her Will, the exchanged documents would include the deceased's medical records. The documents are exchanged in an organized fashion using an affidavit of documents that lists, usually in chronological order, all of the relevant documents.

With respect to charities, it is not common for a charity to have any relevant document to the deceased. However, with the increased sophistication in record keeping, it is becoming more common for charities to be able to search for records relating to the deceased, such as a history of giving donations or being on a mailing list. This documentation is helpful in supporting the argument that the deceased intended to give to charity as it was consistent with his or her pattern of behaviour before death.

Examination for Discovery

Once the documents are exchanged, the next step is the examination for discovery. An examination for discovery is a process whereby the relevant parties, under oath, are subjected to a series of questions which, if relevant, must be answered. Discoveries usually take place on "neutral territory", for example, in the office of an official examiner who provides a reporter to record the questions asked and the answers given. The transcripts, which set out in written form the evidence given by the deponent during the discovery can then be ordered. The evidence provided by the witness at discovery can then be used (for or against) the witness at the trial.

This process not only provides the parties with the opportunity to ask questions and flesh out the other side's story, but also allows counsel to assess the credibility of the various witnesses. As it is typical in estate matters for individuals who are not directly connected to the deceased to have relevant information, quite often, those third parties will also be subjected to the discovery process even though they are not parties to the litigation. In particular, it is quite common for the deceased's physician or his solicitor to be subjected to discovery. In such cases, the estate usually bears the costs of having the witness and their solicitor attend the discovery.

It is at the end of the discovery process that the parties have a clear understanding of the various positions. It is also typically the first opportunity for the parties to determine the strengths and weaknesses of their case and whether this matter should proceed to trial. As this process can be costly, it is prudent for classes of beneficiaries who share the same interest to consider retaining a common solicitor (who must, in Ontario, consider Rule 2.04 of the *Rules of Professional Conduct*) to act for those common interests.

Resolution – Settlement or Trial

Good counsel throughout the course of litigation will always be thinking about ways to resolve the litigation and will actively suggest ways to achieve this. This onus falls on all counsel in the normal course, but in estate proceedings, falls more heavily on the solicitor for the estate.

There are a number of avenues open to assist the resolution process. One method is to begin negotiations. This can be done at any time during the course of the litigation, although, quite often, the parties involved will want to have a measure of comfort with the expected evidence before seriously entering into negotiations.

Another method is through more formal alternative dispute resolutions. Such mechanisms include mediation and arbitration. Mediation is the most common in Ontario.

Mediation

Mediation is the most popular form of alternative dispute resolution and is mandatory in certain parts of Ontario. It can occur at any time in the process (once the framework is established), but typically, there is a natural pause during the litigation where it is most effective.

On January 4, 1999, Rule 24.1 of the Ontario *Rules of Civil Procedure* came into effect, establishing the Ontario Mandatory Mediation Program for civil, non-family, case managed actions. On September 1, 1999, Rule 75.1 came into effect, bringing estates, trusts and substitute decisions matters into the Program. The Program, introduced as a pilot in Toronto and Ottawa-Carleton, is expected to expand. Accordingly, all estates, trusts and substitute decisions commenced in Ottawa or Toronto after September 1, 1999 have proceeded to mediation unless there was a Court-ordered exemption.

Rule 75.1.05 of the *Rules of Civil Procedure* provides that within 30 days after the last day for serving notice of appearance, a motion for directions relating to the conduct of the mediation must be brought. Typically, the Order with respect to mediation will appear in the Order Giving Directions wherein the court may direct such matters as:

- the issues to be mediated;
- who has carriage of the mediation;
- the time-frame for conducting the mediation;
- which parties are required to attend the mediation in person (referred to under the rule as "the designated parties");

- how the parties required to attend the mediation are to be served by the mediator with a notice of the mediation; and
- how the cost of the mediation is to be apportioned among the designated parties.[53]

After the Order is obtained, the parties have the first choice on selecting the mediator — selected from either the court roster or privately. If the parties fail to select a mediator within 30 days, the party with carriage of the mediation will file a request for an assignment of mediation. Under Rule 75.1.07(5) of the *Rules of Civil Procedure*, the Coordinator then assigns a mediator from the roster and provides the mediator with a copy of the Order Giving Directions. Once chosen or assigned, the mediator must immediately fix a date for the mediation and, at least 20 days before that date, serve on every designated party a notice (Form 75.1B) of the place, date and time of the mediation.

Once the mediator is in place, the parties can focus on preparing a mediation brief. The brief under the mandatory rules must be served on the parties and filed with the mediator at least seven days prior to the mediation. The mediation brief (Form 75.1C) must contain a statement of issues.

Where the mediation cannot proceed because, for example, a designated party failed to attend within the first 30 minutes or statements of issue were not provided, the mediator will cancel the session and file a Certificate of Non-Compliance. Once filed, the party with carriage of the mediation must bring a motion for further directions within 15 days after the date fixed for the mediation session. At that motion, the Court may order a timetable for the proceeding and strike out documents, as well as award costs. The mediator may also charge a cancellation fee in accordance with the fee payable by the party in default.

If the mediation proceeds, then within 10 days of the mediation the mediator must file a report under Rule 75.1.12(2) of the *Rules of Civil Procedure* with the Coordinator.

The mediators' fees for mediations under Rule 75.1 are set by regulation under the *Administration of Justice Act*.[54] The fee regulation includes:

---

[53] See Rule 75.1.05(4)(a) to (f).
[54] R.S.O. 1990, c. A.6, as am. S.O. 2000, c. 26, Sched. A, s. 1. See also O. Reg. 451/98, amended to O. Reg. 241/01.

- a table that sets out the following maximum fees that may be charged for the session depending upon the number of parties:
  - up to $600 plus G.S.T. for a mediation session involving two parties;
  - up to $675 plus G.S.T. for a session involving three parties;
  - up to $750 plus G.S.T. for four parties; and
  - up to $825 plus G.S.T. for five parties or more;
- a provision relating to apportioning fees (each party is required to pay an equal share of the fees, unless the court orders otherwise);
- a provision relating to the parties agreeing to fees for continuing the mediation beyond the mandatory three hour session; and
- a provision relating to cancellation fees, including the failure to provide a Statement of Issues and for the failure to attend.

Mediation is proving to be quite successful in Ontario today. Although seen as an additional step by some, it allows the parties to get together and discuss their version of events and creates the opportunity to settle at an early stage. The likelihood of settlement is increased with mediation. Even if the mediation is unsuccessful on that particular day, it often serves to allow the parties to assess their opponent, to narrow the issues and to lead to further dialogue after the mediation that quite often leads to settlement. Although there are costs associated with mediation, they are usually less than the costs of trial.

PRE-TRIAL AND TRIAL

Yet another way in which the litigation may be resolved is by hearing or trial. Usually, this is the last resolution measure and will only take place if the other methods of resolution, such as negotiation and mediation have failed to solve the issues. The hearing or trial takes place before a judge. It is the last step (aside from any appeals) in the litigation process. It is also the most expensive step.

If the matter is proceeding to trial, then the parties will indicate this to the other side and the Court by "setting the matter down for trial". In Ontario, this is accomplished by serving and filing a trial record. Once the trial record is received, it is "put into the trial system" and the Court will schedule one last attempt to resolve the matter by scheduling a pre-trial.

A pre-trial is mandatory and is a process whereby counsel for the parties meet with a judge in chambers to discuss the matter and obtain the judge's view as to the likely outcome at trial. The parties are required to be available for the pre-trial. If the pre-trial fails to settle, the trial is scheduled.

APPEAL

After the trial, the judge who heard the case will deliver his or her judgment by way of reasons, usually written. Any party who is not satisfied with the decision can bring an appeal within a certain amount of time to the Court of Appeal.

The decision to appeal must be made very carefully. At a minimum, it serves to lengthen the administration of the estate and the cost consequences can be significant. The Court of Appeal is not prone to reversing decisions of trial judges, especially where the trial judge made judgment calls on the evidence or the credibility of the witnesses.

THE PLAYERS

Estate Trustee

The estate trustee is charged with administering the estate. Typically, this means calling in and converting the deceased's assets, ascertaining liabilities, discharging obligations and distributing the estate in accordance with the testamentary instrument or, if an intestacy, in accordance with the *Succession Law Reform Act*.[55]

During litigation, the role that the estate trustee plays depends on the nature of the litigation. Where the matter is one of Will interpretation (and this may not always be contentious litigation), the estate trustee will participate in the proceeding, but is relatively non-partisan. The estate trustee's obligation to the Court is to present the evidence and the law on both sides of the issue so that the Court may determine what the testator intended and so that the estate trustee can obtain clarity and direction from the Court as to the proper administration of the estate.

The trustee's role in these types of cases is not to contend for any particular outcome, or to defend his or her own position or interests. Thus, in presenting materials to the Court, estate trustees should confine themselves to presenting the facts and law. They might also review the various possible interpretations of the law or of the Will, and outline the practical consequences of each interpretation on the disputing parties, but should not advocate any particular interpretation. In other words, the

---

[55] R.S.O. 1990, c. S.26, Part III.

materials and argument of the estate trustee should assist the Court as much as possible in delineating the issues and setting out the relevant law, without compromising their neutral position.

Although the competing interests are usually independently represented and fully argued, the estate trustee has the primary responsibility to the Court to prepare and file the required materials, setting out a brief summary of the facts and an overview of the law, without taking a position. As the estate trustee is expected to be neutral, being only interested in clarifying his or her obligations by determining the proper interpretation of the testamentary instrument or the appropriate instrument to be guided by in administering the estate, where he or she has not acted improperly their costs are usually payable out of the estate on a full indemnity basis.

The estate trustee is in an unusual position in the event of a Will challenge. Where the challenge is directed at the Will, the role of the estate trustee is to defend the last Will and testament of the deceased. This means the estate trustee must take a more active role and clearly oppose the challenge being made. The estate trustee in these cases is not expected to be neutral. Acting neutral would, in fact, be seen by the beneficiaries to that Will as contrary to the estate trustee's duty to propound the Will. In these cases, the beneficiaries may not be separately represented by counsel as the expectation is that the estate trustee will vigorously defend the Will, and by so doing, defend their interests as beneficiaries under that Will.

Minors, Unborns and Unascertaineds

In Ontario, the Children's Lawyer represents the interests of minor and unborn or unascertained beneficiaries.[56] This Office is served (given notice of the proceedings) whenever there are minor beneficiaries and unborn or unascertained beneficiaries. If any of those interests need to be represented, a representative (lawyer) from that office will attend and participate as a full status party.

Mentally Incapable Persons

In Ontario, the Public Guardian and Trustee's primary role in testate estate administration is to represent the interests of mentally incapable individuals who are not represented by guardians of property or attorneys

---

[56] See Rule 74.04(5).

acting under a power of attorney (Rule 74.05(6)). As this office now has limited resources or staff to act on behalf of charities whose interest is determined, it places all responsibility on the charity.

With the recent changes to the Ontario *Rules of Civil Procedure* (*i.e.*, Rule 74.04), an estate trustee is <u>not</u> required to serve the Office where there is a charitable interest unless there is a "problem", such as, the charity cannot be located, the purpose of the gift cannot be fulfilled or the gift has been renounced.

The Beneficiary

The role of the beneficiary depends upon the type of beneficiary and their interest under the Will. The factors to consider as a charitable beneficiary are discussed at the end of this chapter.

Costs in Estate Litigation

> There is, perhaps, too much litigation in this province growing out of disputed wills. It must not be fostered by awarding costs lightly out of the estate. Parties should not be tempted into a fruitless litigation by a knowledge that their costs will be paid by others.[57]

> There is no hard and fast rule stating that costs of all parties must always be paid out of the estate. Each case is to be considered on its own merits.[58]

All litigious proceedings ultimately require consideration of the legal costs incurred by the parties involved. The general rule in litigation is that the unsuccessful party should pay the costs of the successful party (and of course, their own costs). This rule aims to caution litigants to ensure that only those matters that require judicial interference reach trial so that limited judicial and client resources are used effectively.

In Ontario, the award of costs remains a matter of judicial discretion guided by statutory provisions such as section 131 of the *Courts of Justice Act*[59] which states:

> 131(1) Subject to the provisions of an Act or rules of court, the costs of and incidental to a proceeding or a step in a proceeding are in the discretion of the court, and the court may determine by whom and to what extent the costs shall be paid.

---

[57] *Logan v. Herring* (1900), 19 O.P.R. 168 (trial decision) *per* Boyd C. at 170.
[58] *Biggins v. Rock*, [1990] O.J. No. 601 (Ont. Surr. Ct.) (QL).
[59] R.S.O. 1990, c. C.43.

Rule 57.01 of the Ontario *Rules of Civil Procedure* sets out the factors which the court may consider in exercising its discretion under section 131. In addition to the result and any written offer to settle, the factors that are to be considered under Rule 57.01 include:

(a) the amount claimed and the amount recovered in the proceeding;

(b) the apportionment of liability;

(c) the complexity of the proceeding;

(d) the importance of the issues;

(e) the conduct of any party that tended to shorten or lengthen unnecessarily the duration of the proceeding;

(f) whether any step in the proceeding was,
 (i) improper, vexatious or unnecessary, or
 (ii) taken through negligence, mistake or excessive caution;

(g) a party's denial or refusal to admit anything that should have been admitted;

(h) whether it is appropriate to award any costs or more than one set of costs where a party
 (i) commenced separate proceedings for claims that should have been made in one proceeding, or
 (ii) in defending a proceeding separated unnecessarily from another party in the same interest; and

(i) any other matter relevant to the question of costs.

A court is not prevented, however, under Rule 57.01(2) of the *Rules of Civil Procedure*, from awarding costs against a successful party in a "proper" case.

In estate proceedings, all of these factors are relevant; some more than others. For example, apportionment of liability is not as important as testamentary instrument interpretation or challenge cases usually ending in an all or nothing result. A testator either did or did not have capacity. A testator either was unduly influenced or was not. There can be no sharing of fault. In contrast, whether a party took an unnecessary step can have a significant impact, especially, for example, where the evidence discloses that the testator had capacity, yet the party objecting continues to pursue the position that capacity was lacking.

The general consensus among practitioners may be that in estate matters, Courts have traditionally departed from the usual cost rule, whereby the unsuccessful party pays the costs of the successful party, such that the estate, not the unsuccessful party, bears the costs. This perception is an assumption (although counsel is starting to recognize the belief and refer to a trend away from that principle). The case law does not justify the perception or assumption. In fact, it demonstrates that there was never such a trend — only exceptions for those cases where the cause of the litigation was the fault of the testator or those interested in the residue, or if there was sufficient reason to question either the execution of the Will, the capacity of the testator, or to allege undue influence or fraud. In addition, there has not been a "trend away" from awarding costs out of the estate; indeed there has never been such a trend (unless the comments were intended to be limited to cases falling under the exceptions).

The case law does not provide for a general rule that costs will be paid out of the estate as the perception among practitioners and some judges would suggest — not unless an exception applies. The determination of costs in an interpretation case is fairly straightforward. Absent wrongdoing by a party, in matters of interpreting a testamentary instrument, costs of all the parties will be paid out of the estate, including those of the applicant/estate trustee on a full indemnity basis, unless the actions of the estate trustee went beyond assisting the court and taking a neutral position. Sometimes, the costs of the other parties will also be on a solicitor and client basis if that scale is justified in the Court's view. Interpretation cases are seen as arising out of the "fault of the testator" and accordingly, he or she is to "blame" for requiring the matter to be determined by the Court. Accordingly, the estate should bear the full costs of the reasonable and necessary judicial inquiry. In matters that settle prior to adjudication, as part of the settlement, each party will, most times, receive some or all of their costs from the estate. But where the application was devoid of merit and motivated by other concerns (*i.e.*, family animosity), costs can be used to penalize.

In Will challenge cases, the guiding parameters are that costs will generally be paid by the losing challenger where the facts show upon a reasonable investigation that the challenge would fail, there was no evidence adduced in support of the challenge, where the challenger acted improperly, or where the challenge was unsubstantiated on the evidence. The losing challenger will typically be required (directly or indirectly) to bear his or her own costs only (and not those of the successful party) where he or she acted reasonably, there was doubt or suspicions which justified the plea, the issue was fairly argued or there was an honest difference in opinion, or the challenger was entitled to have a judicial inquiry.

As dependant support or spouse election cases do not concern issues of capacity, execution or interpretation/construction, costs should follow the event. Costs should follow the normal costs consequence unless good reason exists to depart from the general rule. The case law also suggests that good reason to depart from the normal rule such that costs are paid out of the estate, the other side pays or no costs are awarded, include parties' agreement, precipitate action of estate trustees, public policy suggesting otherwise (*i.e.*, where the unsuccessful party was acting as litigation guardian), abuse of process, or the testator was found to be at fault.

In administration cases, the costs of the estate trustee are normally paid by the estate on a full indemnity basis, assuming the costs are reasonable. Absent good reason (*i.e.*, the *mala fides* of the estate trustee) to order otherwise, the Court will determine reasonableness by considering such things as the size of the estate and the result achieved. Although an estate trustee acting properly is entitled to costs, it does not follow that the other parties will also get their costs paid by the estate.

As with any matter, appeals may be brought after a determination of any interlocutory matter or final resolution by trial. The usual appeal rules apply. In Ontario, however, pursuant to section 10 of the *Estates Act*,[60] matters falling under this statute may be appealed to the Divisional Court. In practice, appealing directly to the Court of Appeal is common.

The costs of unsuccessful appeals are more closely scrutinized by the Court than costs of an original action which fails. There is a higher risk on appeal that, if unsuccessful, the costs of the appeal will usually be borne by, or awarded against, the unsuccessful appellant. More than at first instance, costs will follow the event. Where the estate trustee appeals, and subsequently fails, the Court is not likely to be sympathetic and order costs to follow the event. The case law is fairly consistent that the costs of an appeal will follow the event and be borne by the unsuccessful appellant, unless there is "good reason" to order otherwise.

When making an award of costs, the Court may fix them in a lump sum (without being bound by the tariffs) or order them to be assessed by an assessment officer. Rule 57.01(3) of the *Rules of Civil Procedure* codifies that power. In Ontario, the practice is to fix costs. This avoids delay, the added cost of an assessment and "cleans the slate". In fixing costs, the Court is not conducting an assessment.

An assessment is the review of the itemized charges and determining, based on the circumstances of the case, whether the charge is reasonable in the circumstances. The factors considered by an assessment officer in exercising his or her discretion are set out in Rule 58.06(1) of the *Rules of Civil Procedure*.

---

[60] R.S.O. 1990, c. E.21.

Where costs are to be paid out of a fund or estate, Rule 58.08(2) of the *Rules of Civil Procedure* provides that the assessment officer may "direct what parties are to attend and may disallow the costs of the assessment of any party whose attendance was unnecessary". A party's attendance will be deemed unnecessary where its interest "is small, remote or sufficiently protected by other interested parties".

In Ontario, it should be pointed out that the courts may not be influenced by the other cost rules in the *Rules of Civil Procedure*. For example, the Court stated in *Re Olenchuk Estate*[61] that Rule 49.10 (offer to settle rule) does not apply in estate matters as it is "incompatible" to "apply rules designed to encourage [the] settlement of adversarial and contentious proceedings".[62]

However, as the Court in that case considered (*i.e.*, as a factor under Rule 57), the fact that offers had been made in looking at the parties' *bona fides*, this rule is still an important consideration. Further, as a general rule, offers to settle should be at least contemplated, if not made, regardless of the impact (or lack thereof) of the *Rules of Civil Procedure*.

In summary, the general rule in litigation is that the unsuccessful party should pay the costs of the successful party (and, of course, their own costs). The same general rule applies in estate litigation. Costs in estate proceedings are still discretionary as modified by the two principles. In other words, if an argument could reasonably be made that an unsuccessful party's course of conduct had good and sufficient grounds, such that a judicial inquiry was required, then, at worst, the losing party would likely be relieved from paying the costs of the successful opponent and, at best, would (also) get some or all of his or her costs paid by the estate.

IMPACT AND CONSEQUENCES OF THE ESTATE BEING IN LITIGATION

Impact on Beneficiaries

Challenging a Will has a direct impact on the beneficiaries in a number of ways. First, it invariably reduces the total value of the assets available for distribution to the beneficiaries because at least some of the costs of litigation (depending on the issue litigated and the circumstances of litigation) will be paid out of the estate. Without a doubt, the estate trustee's costs of propounding the Will are paid by the estate. Will

---

[61] *Ibid.*, at 150.
[62] (1991), 43 E.T.R. 146 (Ont Gen. Div.).

interpretation costs are typically also paid by the estate. Costs of reasonable challenges can also be paid (partially or totally) out of the estate.

Second, litigation delays the distribution of all or part of the estate, as distributions may have to be frozen until the challenge is dealt with.

Third, the result of the challenge can improve, worsen, or destroy a given beneficiary's entitlement. For next-of-kin, invalidating a Will can often serve to increase their proportionate share of an estate. This is especially so for spouses, who receive favourable treatment under the intestate succession regime in Ontario. For more distant beneficiaries, including friends and charities, litigation often adversely affects their share, or renders gifts to them void altogether. Unlike close relatives, charities are not entitled to a share of the estate in the event of an intestacy.

Of course, this is not always the case. In some cases, invalidating the most recent testamentary instrument will not result in an intestacy, but in the upholding of an earlier Will, which may provide for a greater share of the estate than the more recent Will. Further, some litigation is between charities or other individuals where there are errors made in naming them in the Will. In these circumstances, the likely result of the litigation is not an intestacy, but merely the choosing of one beneficiary over another or the sharing of the interest among those that participate.

CONFLICT OF INTEREST

As with all matters, being aware of the issue of conflict of interest is paramount. Estate litigation is no exception. An example of a conflict is where parties adverse in interest to each other are represented by the same lawyer. The potential for conflict can arise as between the solicitor who prepared the Will and the beneficiary; the estate solicitor and estate trustee; the estate trustee and beneficiary; and even beneficiary and beneficiary, to name a few.

A solicitor, in particular, is required to be attuned to the possibility of conflict and discuss this with their client. When a conflict develops, a solicitor is usually required to remove him or herself from the matter and is generally precluded from acting for anyone in the litigation. The consequence of a conflict can sometimes mean that in smaller towns, the parties have to venture further afield to find independent representation.

A charity should also be alert to the possibility of conflict and not be shy in inquiring whether a particular party or lawyer is in a conflict. The risk of proceeding in light of a conflict is that neither party is adequately represented.

Charities' Perspective and Response

Charities, by virtue of being a beneficiary of someone's estate, can become involved in estate litigation for various reasons including outdated estate plans; inadequate estate planning; poorly drafted documents; the nature of the estate assets; and conflicts between the beneficiaries and the personal representatives of the deceased. The extent to which a charity becomes involved may be, however, more discretionary. The charity's experience, reporting structure and organization framework often impacts the role played.

There are, however, key differences between charities and other litigants. Some include the following:

- *Form and structure*: Charities come in a variety of forms and governing structures.
- *Directing minds*: The directing mind of a charity is usually a board of directors. The members of the board of directors are volunteers. Although well meaning individuals, they may have a limited understanding of their legal duties and responsibilities and the litigation process. There may not be access to legal counsel with the relevant and necessary expertise in estate matters.
- *Inherent Court Jurisdiction*: Regardless of structure, a charity is subject to certain controls imposed by statute and the common law. A Court retains an inherent jurisdiction over the affairs of a charity. The public guardian and trustee also has statutory control.
- *Restrictions*: A charity is limited by its charitable objects. Although its objectives may change over time, a charity must constantly be aware of the limited framework of its charitable objectives. Acting outside that framework is unauthorized and can lead to the revocation of the charities' charitable status — its raison d'etre.
- *Degree of knowledge*: A charity involved in estate litigation is usually once removed from the factual background to the dispute. Although charities have a self-interest in the outcome of the litigation (or else they would not be participating), they typically have very little knowledge of the events or facts being challenged. A charity is typically less familiar with family history and dynamics.
- *Public Perception*: An aware charity is always conscious of its public image. Maintaining a positive image in the mind of the public and the charity's community is fundamental. Such considerations colour a charity's reaction and attitude. However, knowing the importance of maintaining this image with the public may lead to being taken

advantage of by the other parties (and their counsel) involved in the litigation.

The most common types of estate proceedings that involve a charity are Will challenges, Will interpretations (including *cy-près* applications), and passing of accounts.

A charity may be named in a Will to receive a legacy or part or the entire residue. As a beneficiary, even if only as legatee, a charity is entitled to notice of any estate proceeding which may affect its entitlement or require its consent and is entitled to participate in the resolution of these issues.

There are several ways in which a charity may be involved in an estate dispute. First, a charity may decide to "submit its rights" (see earlier discussion on submitting one's rights). Like any other beneficiary, a charity may decide to leave the "battle" to the other beneficiaries. By submitting its rights, the charity is not required to retain counsel or participate in the process, thereby neither exposing it to costs directly nor entitling it to costs. The charity, however, retains the right to participate in any settlement discussions and must consent to any settlement.

Second, a charity may decide to monitor the litigation and not be an active participant. A charity may self-monitor the litigation in-house or with the assistance of outside counsel. In some charities, internal governance requires the staff person to bring every aspect of the litigation (not just the information required to make a decision) to the attention of the board; in other cases, the staff person has the discretion and delegated responsibility to make the basic decisions. Depending on the structure of the organization, many layers of decision makers may have to be consulted, which, in turn, results in timing issues.

Third, a charity may decide to be an active participant. Factors which may cause a charity to be more active include being the sole beneficiary or the only charity who believes in the "cause", unhappiness with the handling of the matter by the solicitor for the estate, and where the other charities' beneficiaries have agreed to let it (through its counsel) take the lead.

FACTORS TO CONSIDER

There are several factors which affect when and why a charity may participate. The following list is not intended to be exhaustive:

- *Adequate representation*: A charity must ensure that it is an informed participant. This means that it should know the facts leading up to the proposed litigation, the remedial options or relief being sought by the various parties, the identity and positions of the other parties, the alternatives to litigation, the anticipated outcomes of the litigation, and the likelihood of cost recovery. A charity should expect that good counsel would provide this information to their client. A staff person handling the litigation should ensure that he or she has the requisite authority to retain and instruct counsel. It may be that a by-law or board resolution is needed.
- *The duties*: A charity faces and owes certain duties. The directors must act in good faith and in the best interests of the organization. A director has a duty of knowledge, a duty of care, a duty of skill and prudence, a duty of diligence, a duty to manage, and a duty to act in their scope of authority. The staff person, correspondingly, must carry out the organization's policies in the best interests of the organization. The organization has a duty to its members and a duty to the donor or testator. All of these duties culminate in a duty to investigate, a duty to defend and, where necessary, a duty to compromise. These duties should significantly influence a charity's approach to making decisions and participation in any alternative dispute resolution process.

There is also the public duty. There is a reason for charities in our society. As noted by the Court in *Public Trustee v. Toronto Humane Society*:[63]

> The basic justification for the existence of a charity in the legal sense is that it confers a public benefit of a nature recognized by the courts as such. In return for that benefit, charitable institutions have been accorded certain legal immunities and advantages. Originally, these pertained largely to matters of mortmain and perpetuities, and a judicial bent to ensure that such gifts did not fail. Latterly, a principal advantage has been the right to receive contributions which may be deducted by the donor for income tax purposes...it must be recognized that this loss of revenue reflects on the taxpayers as a whole, so that it may properly be said that all taxpayers contribute to every charity to a greater or a lesser extent.

This public duty requires a charity to act in certain ways. For example, a charity should ensure issues are resolved promptly, actively canvass alternative dispute resolution methods, avoid acting unreasonably or

---

[63] (1987), 60 O.R. (2d) 236 at 251-52 (H.C.J.).

aligning themselves with unreasonable positions, and minimize the appearance of charity fighting charity.[64] The public duty also requires that charities be responsive and proactive as necessary, scrutinize the administration (and refrain from formal passing of accounts where not required), urge reasonable compromise and be prepared to seek costs against unreasonable parties, seek out similarly situated organizations with a view of co-operating, and consolidate legal representation and expenses. A charity should also adequately investigate legal matters to form an educated assessment of the issue and ultimate course of action, and be flexible and consistent.

- *The philosophy of the organization*: Each charity has its own culture and decision making philosophy. Some charities are more aggressive or are seen to be more aggressive than others. To a large extent, this perception of "aggression" is unfair as it is more likely the result of the charity being more informed of their rights and more inclined to defend those rights.
- *The public relations aspect of the matter*: Charities are particularly sensitive to the public relations aspect of any decision that has to be made. They are also sensitive to the family of the deceased and are genuinely concerned about the family's perception of their actions. The manner in which the charity conducts itself will be scrutinized by the other parties, the Public Guardian and Trustee and the Court. A balance between defending the right to a gift and being reasonable in the circumstances must be found and maintained. Acting at either end of the spectrum can have repercussions on the charity's image and consequent donor base.

    This does not mean that a charity will not "fight" if it believes "in the cause" or if it believes that some moral stance should be taken. A charity does not appreciate being "threatened" with such comments as "I'll go to the press", or "You should feel fortunate that the deceased left you anything", or "By the way, if it weren't for me suggesting your organization, you would not have received anything", or "Everybody else has agreed, so why can't you".
- *The number of residuary beneficiaries*: The fewer the residuary beneficiaries, the more likely that the participation by the charities will be more balanced. It should be possible (and encouraged) for one counsel to represent the common interests of the charities. This

---

[64] After all, the important thing is to ensure that the charitable intent is confirmed, not necessarily to ensure that your particular organization is the recipient of that intention over another.

eliminates duplication of legal fees and makes the channels of communication more efficient. The larger the number of residuary beneficiaries, the more complicated and unbalanced the involvement of the charities. A charity may decide, given the number of other charities involved, to take a back seat and let others deal with the litigation. Other charities may decide the opposite — if they are involved, they can direct the process more and retain some measure of control over costs and the issues.

- *Ability to work with others*: If the opportunity exists to join forces with similarly interested charities, this influences the decision to participate. If charities of like mind can agree on joint representation and course of action, then not only are the costs shared, but the costs overall are reduced. Courts appreciate this — the failure of charities to consolidate legal representation has been the subject of adverse judicial comment.[65] Claims for excessive costs are often trimmed.[66]
- *Size of the charity*: A smaller charity will have fewer resources to participate in protracted litigation. It will have less discretion to tie up resources for the payment of legal fees and will generally be more anxious to have the matter resolved. The larger charities have more resources, and more importantly, more experience with litigation and hence are more understanding of the time frames and unpredictability of litigation.
- *Timing*: Each charity will have a fiscal year-end and it may vary from one to the other. Depending on how the fiscal year goes (this may also depend on the size of the organization), this may impact the decision making process.
- *Access to advisors*: Some charities have access to counsel — someone they have developed a relationship with and whom they can call if they have a legal question or a matter that is or appears to be headed towards litigation or mediation. These charities may also have a budget for legal fees. Some charities' regular counsel are volunteer lawyers who give advice on a *pro bono* basis. Those charities who do

---

[65] *Southam v. Royal Trust Corp. of Canada*, [2000] B.C.J. No. 684 (B.C.S.C.) (QL). In this case, three charities with a similar interest retained separate counsel on a British Columbia *Wills Variation Act* R.S.B.C. 1996, c. 490 application. On the issue of costs, the Court considered the fact that the three charities had not joined forces and had insisted on separate representation.

[66] *Dodds Estate v. Northside United Church*, [1994] O.J. No. 4202 (Ont. Gen. Div.) (QL). In this case, the gross estate was $650,000 and the combined claims for counsel fees exceeded $28,000. The Court, on this *cy-près* application regarding 16 per cent of the residue, awarded the estate trustees $3,500 in costs and the three competing charities $5,000, noting at para. 10 that:

> Any enthusiasm for litigation at the expense of others ought to be tempered with a view of preserving the disputed funds for the benefit of the beneficiary.

not have legal budgets or who have not developed a relationship with counsel tend to be less active. A charity is encouraged to develop relationships with the legal community in order to ensure access to any advice they may need in the future. It is even suggested that the failure to develop such a relationship could be a breach of a charity's obligation to its stakeholders and board of directors.

- *The failure to meet obligations*: A charity should remember the consequences of failing to respond or act in accordance with its obligations. It must remember the supervisory power of the Public Guardian and Trustee and the inherent jurisdiction of the Courts. In Ontario, for example, the Public Guardian and Trustee enjoys broad powers over charities under the *Charities Accounting Act*[67] and the *Public Inquiries Act*.[68] Under section 6 of the *Charities Accounting Act*:

> 6(1) Any person may complain about the manner in which a person or organization has solicited or procured funds by way of contribution or a gift from the public for any purpose, or as to the manner in which any such funds have been dealt with or disposed of.

If such a complaint is made, the Act provides the procedure to be followed to allow the court to authorize the Public Guardian and Trustee to conduct an investigation. If so ordered, the Public Guardian and Trustee has not only the powers that may be given in the Order but also the powers of a commission under Part II of the *Public Inquiries Act*.[69]

The power of the Court's inherent jurisdiction over charities is demonstrated in the case of *Public Trustee v. Toronto Humane Society*.[70] In that case, the Court was concerned about the use of charitable funds for political purposes and improprieties in the election and operation of the board of directors. The Court concluded that the Humane Society was a trustee or fiduciary and accountable to the Public Guardian and Trustee. The Court held that the directors themselves were also fiduciaries and accountable to the obligations and members of the charity, and (in part) appointed a representative to have full access to the Humane Society's books and records. The Court empowered this representative to oversee the election of a new board of directors at the next annual meeting.

Estate litigation is distinctive. The person in the best position to interpret the Will and know the wishes of the testator is the deceased, who

---

[67] R.S.O. 1990, c. C.10.
[68] R.S.O. 1990, c. P.41.
[69] See also *Stahl v. Ontario Society for the Prevention of Cruelty to Animals* (1989), 70 O.R. (2d) 355 (Ont. Div. Ct.).
[70] (1987), 60 O.R. (2d) 236 (H.C.J.).

is not around to explain or defend his or her decisions. This fact colours the litigation.

In estate litigation matters, the following points should be remembered:

- Nobody should assume that a charity is not interested or unsophisticated — many charities have access to counsel and have the confidence to assert their rights.
- A charity should be respected like any other beneficiary. It has equal rights to ask questions and receive information and a charity tends to be reasonable and fair.
- Charities are sensitive to the donor/deceased and upholding his or her denotative intent. They believe in simply defending a valid will and, if treated right, can be a strong ally.
- A charity should be given a complete copy of the Will, even if only receiving a legacy.
- A charity, like any other beneficiary, is entitled to complete and regular reports on the status of the administration even while waiting for the Clearance Certificate.
- Where there are numerous charities, they should be encouraged to obtain representative counsel for the group — it can be like herding cats if the group is not organized and acting with a unified thrust and it can affect the course of the litigation.

From the perspective of the legal professional, given the continuous potential of estate litigation, safeguards should be put in place to ensure that a record of all relevant matters is kept in case of a Will challenge potentially years after the work was done. In particular, a legal advisor should bear in mind the three grounds upon which Wills are most often challenged: due execution, testamentary capacity and undue influence. Of these, only the proper execution of the Will lies almost wholly within the control of the legal professional.

Finally, with any piece of litigation, the issues of privacy, confidentiality and privilege of all the parties involved must always be kept in mind and may be addressed in the Order for Directions. That privilege is not necessarily transferred to the next-of-kin or personal representative of the deceased. In estate matters, these issues deserve special attention.

ALBERTA

INTRODUCTION

As previously discussed, common examples of estate litigation include formal proof of a Will, contested motions for advice and directions, *Dependants Releif Act*[71] applications, and the like. Litigious proceedings involving an estate are on the increase for several reasons. For example, families are becoming more complex, with second marriages and common law relationships. Thus, estates are also becoming larger and more complex.

In estate litigation, the Courts are often called on to decide issues involving equitable and moral claims, and are required to exercise their discretionary power to grant or refuse relief based on imperfect evidence. The Courts, are therefore liberal when it comes to curing procedural defects and irregularities, and tend to deal with the substance and merits of the issue, rather than focusing on procedure, thereby deciding an issue based on technical matters.

APPOINTMENT OF A PERSONAL REPRESENTATIVE TO HANDLE ESTATE LITIGATION

Rule 43 of the Alberta Rules of Court[72] provides:

> Trustees, executors or administrators may sue and be sued on behalf of or as representing the property or estate of which they are trustees, or representatives without joining any of the persons beneficially interested in the trust or estate, and shall be considered as representing those persons.

Before an estate can be sued, or the estate can initiate litigation, a personal representative must be formally appointed by the Court. If a personal representative is named in a Will, but has not applied for a Grant of Probate, he or she will have to do so before the litigation can proceed. If a Will does not exist, then an interested party, usually a family member, will have to make an application to the Court for a Grant of Administra-

---

[71] The title and chapter number of the *Family Relief Act*, R.S.A. 2000, c. F-5 were amended by the *Adult Interdependent Relationships Act*, S.A. 2002, c. A-4.5, s. 35 to the *Dependants Relief Act*, S.A. 2002, c. D-10.2. The *Adult Interdependent Relationships Act* came into force on June 1, 2003, except for s. 17 which came into force on January 1, 2003 and except for sections 26, 52, 60 and 71 which are not yet in force as of June 2003.

[72] AR 390/68.

tion. Until there has been a formally appointed personal representative, there is no status for the estate to commence proceedings.[73]

The correct procedure for an estate wishing to commence litigation is to issue an originating document, only after there has been a formally obtained Grant of Probate, Letters of Administration, Letters of Administration With Will Annexed, or a Court Order appointing an Administrator *ad litem* or Court-appointed representative of the estate.

Likewise, before an estate can be sued, a personal representative must be appointed. If a grant has not been obtained, or no one has come forward and agreed to obtain a grant, counsel should first attempt to take steps to encourage the named personal representative in the Will, or the next-of-kin entitled, to apply for and obtain the appropriate grant from the Court. A creditor is also ranked as a party entitled to apply for a Grant of Administration under Surrogate Rule 11(2)(j).[74]

If the executor (or on an intestacy, the next-of-kin entitled to apply for a grant), has not applied for and received a Grant of Letters of Administration or a Grant of Probate, then the party wishing to sue the estate may make an application to the Court to appoint an administrator *ad litem* of the estate, who will be given the authority to deal with the intended action.

An administrator *ad litem* will defend the claim on behalf of the estate and may take any steps that a defendant would be entitled to take in an action, including third party proceedings and action by way of counterclaim. However, there is a distinction between the appointed administrator of an estate who has all of the powers the deceased had, and the administrator *ad litem*. An administrator *ad litem* is appointed for the purposes of the civil action and may not administer or distribute the estate in any way.

The administrator *ad litem* has limited powers, and may defend and counterclaim in the specific action for which he or she was appointed, however, they may not generally commence civil proceedings in this capacity.[75] A Court-appointed administrator *ad litem* is obliged to act, in the best interests of the estate of the deceased person for whom he or she has been appointed.

---

[73] See *Public Trustee (Alberta) v. Larsen* (1964), 49 W.W.R. 416 (Alta. S.C., App. Div.); and *Stout Estate v. Golinowski* (2002), 100 Alta. L.R. (3d) 5 (C.A.), rev'g. (1999), 77 Alta. L.R. (3d) 119 (Q.B.).

[74] See the Alberta *Trustee Act*, R.S.A. 2000, C. T-8, s. 46, regarding the appointment of a judicial trustee.

[75] See *Farish v. Papp* (1957), 23 W.W.R. 690 (Alta. S.C.); *Joncas v. Pennock* (Alta. App. Div.); and *Public Trustee (Alberta) v. Larsen* (1964), 49 W.W.R. 416 (Alta. S.C., App. Div.)

In seeking an administrator *ad litem*, counsel for the intended plaintiff may consider appointing:

- A lawful next-of-kin, personal representative, or even beneficiaries, if known, residing in the jurisdiction. It is usually in their personal interest to successfully defend or minimize any judgment as against the estate. This is particularly appropriate where the administrator *ad litem* must actively attend in costly or complex litigation. Prior to making the application to appoint an administrator *ad litem*, the person should be notified and their consent should be obtained.[76]
- A barrister and solicitor residing in the judicial district of the intended action, willing to act, may also be appointed.
- The Public Trustee for the Province of Alberta may consent to act, so long as the appointment is limited and they are not required to actively conduct the lawsuit, and the Plaintiff's solicitor agrees to certain conditions relating to procedure.[77]

It is also important to review the *Limitations Act*,[78] which sets out the limitation period when suing an estate. If the limitation period for filing the necessary pleadings has passed, an application to the Court can be made, seeking the Court's approval to take curative measures. Whether relief will be granted will depend on the facts of each case.[79] The Alberta Supreme Court in *Bauer v. Hyland*[80] permitted a statement of claim to be amended to refer to the estate of the deceased, after the limitation period had expired.

CONTESTED CLAIMS PROCEDURE

When an estate is dealing with a contested claim, the procedure is governed by section 41 of the *Administration of Estates Act*[81] and by Surrogate Rules 95 and 96.

---

[76] See *Harder v. Fedorak* (1982), 13 E.T.R. 39 (B.C.S.C.): the Court may appoint a person not consenting, although lack of consent is a factor the Courts look at in determining whom to appoint.
[77] *Public Trustee Act*, R.S.A. 2000, c. P-44, s. 19(5): consent of public trustee to appointment is always necessary.
[78] R.S.A. 2000, c. L-12, subs. 3(2)(c).
[79] See *Durand v. Hamilton* (1981), 32 B.C.L.R. 373 (B.C.S.C.); and *Jawanda v. Parsons* (1983), 147 D.L.R. (3d) 372 (B.C.S.C.).
[80] (1977), 2 A.R. 246.
[81] R.S.A. 2000, c. A-2.

Where the question of enforceability of a debt or claim against an estate arises, the personal representative should ask the residuary beneficiaries if the claim appears valid. If the beneficiaries agree to reject the claim, the personal representative should serve the claimant with a Notice of Contestation[82] which will advise the claimant if the claim is contested in whole or in part.

The procedural time limits for such claims are triggered when the claimant receives the Notice of Contestation. Therefore, it is recommended that the Notice of Contestation is personally served on the claimant. Section 41(1) and (2) of the *Administration of Estates Act* requires the claimant to file with the Court, and serve on the personal representative a statement of their claim by preparing a specific form, supported by an affidavit,[83] 60 days from receipt of the Notice of Contestation. If the claimant misses the 60 day limitation, the claim is "forever barred".[84]

Chambers applications involving an estate can be presented *ex parte* to the Court, so long as all of the necessary consents have been obtained. If the personal representative cannot get the beneficiaries to agree as to how to deal with the claim, he or she can make a Court application and allow the Court to adjudicate. Since this application is initiated by a notice of motion, it will be dealt with summarily in chambers, so long as there are no serious questions of fact in dispute.

When the Court hears such summary applications, it expects, and is entitled to, sufficient evidence being placed on the record confirming both its jurisdiction and that the order being sought is based on sufficient filed evidence to justify the order granted. Such evidence is usually put before the Court in the form of affidavits and/or legal briefs. Summary applications are expeditious and less costly. However, counsel should be aware of the limitations of proceeding by affidavit evidence in chambers.

Where material facts are in dispute, and there is contrary evidence before the Court, or where factually related issues become excessively complex, the Court is unlikely to dispose of the matter summarily in chambers. Instead, it may direct that the matter be dealt with in a special chambers application where both affidavit evidence and *viva voce* evidence (witnesses testifying under oath) is allowed, or the Court may direct a trial of an issue and request that pleadings be filed. The question of whether a summary procedure is appropriate lies in the discretion of the Court.

---

[82] Surrogate Form C 11.
[83] See Surrogate Form C 12 and Surrogate Rule 96.
[84] *Ibid.*, s. 41(2).

Surrogate Rule 64 allows the Court to direct a trial of any issues in dispute, if it deems that this is appropriate.

One of the characteristics of estate practice and estate litigation is the large number of potentially interested parties. Where the application involves an administrative matter, or interpretation of a document, counsel must identify all those affected in any way whatsoever, either actually or potentially, and serve all of the interested parties with the application.

Where a large number of beneficiaries have an identical interest, it may be possible to take practical steps to avoid duplication of counsel if possible. If a solicitor is already representing one or two members of a large class, the unrepresented interested persons may recognize the advantages in having the same solicitor represent them. There are provisions in the Surrogate Rules for the appointment of a representative for a particular class. This does not preclude any particular beneficiary from appearing with their own counsel, but it may have a bearing when costs are dealt with.

If an application is not urgent, caused for example by statutory limitations, it is recommended that counsel select a returnable date far enough in advance to allow all interested parties an opportunity to be properly served, to retain legal counsel, and to deal with other preliminary matters. Subsequent adjournments may also be necessary for a number of justifiable reasons. Estate litigation is often delayed because of the numerous parties involved.

The personal representative should be aware that he or she must administer the estate to the benefit of both the beneficiaries and creditors, both of whom the personal representatives owe a fiduciary duty. In internal disputes involving opposing parties interested in the estate, the personal representative should take the position of "informed neutrality" and ought not to argue on behalf of, or appear for, any of the beneficiaries.

As a final note, the Surrogate Rules may not deal with all matters relating to estate litigation. Surrogate Rule 2(1) states that if the Surrogate Court Rules do not address any matter, then the Alberta Rules of Court shall apply to the estate application before the Court, and will resolve the matter not otherwise dealt with by the Surrogate Rules.

EVIDENCE AND CORROBORATION IN ESTATE LITIGATION[85]

Corroboration is dealt with in section 11 of the Alberta *Evidence Act*,[86] which provides:

---

[85] These comments apply to estate litigation in Ontario.
[86] R.S.A. 2000, c. A-18.

In an action by or against the heirs, next of kin, executors, administrators or assigns of a deceased person, an opposed interested party shall not obtain a verdict, judgment or decision on that party's own evidence in respect of any matter occurring before the death of the deceased person, unless the evidence is corroborated by other material evidence.

The question that often arises is whether there is sufficient corroboration. The question was addressed in *Stephenson v. McLean Estate*.[87]

Examinations for Discovery

In Alberta, personal representatives who do not have a personal knowledge of the facts in issue are not required to seek and obtain information that will enable them to answer questions at examinations for discovery. However, personal representatives are required to disclose all information they have, even if it is hearsay evidence, as he or she is an officer of the Court whose purpose in estate litigation is to advance justice.

The general rule is that beneficiaries are not subject to examinations unless they are a party to the action or there are special circumstances that would further the administration of justice if the beneficiaries were to be examined.[88]

INVOLVEMENT OF BENEFICIARIES IN ESTATE LITIGATION

Settlement of Claims

It is always prudent for the personal representative to obtain the instructions and agreement from all the beneficiaries to settle a claim involving the estate, whether the claim is by or against the estate, and even if a personal representative has legal counsel.

Surrogate Rule 4 allows the personal representative to make an application to the Court for advice and directions "at any time". This type of application might be used by the personal representative when seeking an order approving a settlement.[89]

If a beneficiary insists on being permitted to participate in the litigation, there are provisions in the Alberta Rules of Court to allow them to be joined as a party to the action.[90]

---

[87] (1977), 4 Alta. L.R. (2d) 197 at 209-210 (S.C.).
[88] See *Re Cantalini* (1965), 49 D.L.R. (2d) 518 (Alta. S.C.); see also *Kryczka v. Kryczka* (1979), 17 A.R. 263 (Surr. Ct.): a person who was a witness to the Will is examinable.
[89] *Trustee Act*, s. 21.
[90] See Rules 38(6), 44 and 45.

COSTS IN ESTATE LITIGATION

It is highly recommended that counsel representing a personal representative in estate litigation obtain authorizations and consents from all beneficiaries interested in the estate prior to undertaking litigation on behalf of the estate, or defending a specific action against the estate. This is important because the general rule is that it is in the Court's discretion to decide if the personal representative is personally liable for the costs of the estate litigation.

For instance, where an administrator commenced proceedings on behalf of his father's estate, which was insolvent, the unsuccessful administrator was personally held liable for the costs.[91]

APPLICATIONS PURSUANT TO THE DEPENDANTS RELIEF ACT

Introduction

Testamentary freedom is the traditional principle used in the law of succession. This means that a testator is free to leave his or her estate to whomever they wish. However, this principle has been modified by family relief legislation because there may be legal and moral claims against the deceased which the Court will recognize on public policy grounds, even if the deceased did not. The difficult challenge for the Courts is to balance the wishes of the deceased against the legal and moral claims the dependants may have against the estate.

Family relief legislation differs significantly in each province. The general purpose of the legislation is, however, the same: to provide authority to the Courts to vary a Will if the circumstances warrant a variation. Some provinces look only at the financial needs (legal claim) of the applicant, while other provinces, such as Alberta, also enforce the moral obligation (moral claim) the deceased owed a dependant or dependants. Care must therefore be taken when relying on family relief decisions made outside Alberta.

In the 2002 fall session of the Legislature the Government of Alberta passed Bill 30-2, the *Adult Interdependent Relationships Act*. The intention of this Bill is to create legal status for adult interdependent partnerships for persons who live in relationships of interdependence and meet certain criteria, whether or not the relationships are conjugal. This status is similar

---

[91] *Shafer v. Jones* (1950), 2 W.W.R. 625 (Alta. S.C.); and *Duncan Estate v. Baddeley*, [2000] A.J. No. 1193 (C.A.) (QL) (re: new trial on damages). Refer also to Chapter 3 for a further discussion on costs in estate litigation.

to the legal consequences of marriage under some 68 statutes. Proclaimed in June of 2003, Bill 30-2 amends 68 statutes in Alberta including the *Family Relief Act* which has been renamed the *Dependants Relief Act*.[92]

Claims Under the Dependants Relief Act

The *Dependants Relief Act* gives the Court a discretionary authority to rewrite the deceased's Will after his or her death, and to recognize the claims made by the deceased's dependants. The *Dependants Relief Act* does not give dependants a proprietary right to a share of the deceased's estate, or to any particular asset. Instead, the act gives the Courts discretion to consider the Will of the deceased, or if a Will does not exist, the division of the deceased's estate pursuant to the *Intestate Succession Act*,[93] in light of both the provisions contained in the *Dependants Relief Act* and the principles of interpretation that have developed in the case law since the enactment of the legislation.

Before discussing the new categories of dependants who may soon be able to make a claim under the *Dependants Relief Act*, it is important to review the criteria the Court will use in determining whether a claimant is a dependant of the deceased.

The Supreme Court of Canada's decision in *Tataryn v. Tataryn Estate*[94] is the leading Canadian authority on family relief legislation.

It established the following:

- The Court must ask whether the Will makes adequate provision for a dependant, and if not, order what is adequate.
- The Court has broad discretion in the search for "contemporary justice".[95]
- The issues protected by the *Dependants Relief Act* are "adequate, just and equitable" provision for spouses/dependants and testamentary autonomy.
- What is sufficient to maintain a spouse/dependant (the need-maintenance approach is not appropriate, rather a Court must look to

---

[92] One amendment to the *Dependants Relief Act* is the addition of an "adult interdependent partner" in the definition of dependants who may make a claim against the deceased's estate.
[93] R.S.A. 2000, c. I-10.
[94] (1994), 3 E.T.R. (2d) 229.
[95] *Ibid.*, at 239.

the legal responsibilities which existed during the testator's lifetime and the moral duties owed to the spouse/dependant).

The Alberta Courts have ruled that the principles of *Tataryn* apply in Alberta.[96]

Who May Make a Claim Under the Dependants Relief Act

Section 3(1) of the *Dependants Relief Act* states:

3(1) If a person

(a) dies testate without making in the person's will adequate provision for the proper maintenance and support of the person's dependants or any of them, or

(b) dies intestate and the share under the *Intestate Succession Act* of the intestate's dependants or of any of them in the estate is inadequate for their proper maintenance and support,

a judge, on application by or on behalf of the dependants or any of them, may in the judge's discretion, notwithstanding the provisions of the will or the *Intestate Succession Act*, order that any provision that the judge considers adequate be made out of the estate of the deceased for the proper maintenance and support of the dependants or any of them.

A dependant is defined in section 1 of the *Dependants Relief Act* as including:

(i) the spouse of the deceased,

(ii) a child of the deceased who is under the age of 18 years at the time of the deceased's death, and

(iii) a child of the deceased who is 18 years of age or over at the time of the deceased's death and unable by reason of mental or physical disability to earn a livelihood.

There are two ways to be considered an adult interdependent partner under the new Act: either by living with another person in a relationship of interdependence for three years or more, or by entering into an agreement with another person, which would abridge the three year requirement to the date of the agreement. The agreement is provided for in the Regulations to the *Dependants Relief Act*. The three year requirement may also be abridged if the parties have a child by birth or adoption.

---

[96] See: *Siegel v. Siegel Estate* (1995), 35 Alta. L.R. (3d) 321, 10 E.T.R. (2d) 178 (Q.B.); *Webb v. Webb Estate* (1995), 28 Alta L.R. (3d) 110 (Q.B.); *Re Sheremata Estate*, [1998] A.J. No. 344 (Surr. Ct.); *Stang v. Stang Estate*, [1998] A.J. No. 261 (Q.B.); and *Dupere (Next Friend of) v. Spinelli Estate* (1998), 229 A.R. 137 (Surr. Ct.).

The requirement that the adult interdependent partner live in a relationship of interdependence with another person is also assessed. Whether a relationship of "interdependence" is assessed based on criteria such as whether the parties (i) share one another's lives, (ii) are emotionally committed to one another and (iii) function as an economic and domestic unit. Whether the parties function as "one economic and domestic unit" is assessed by criteria such as the existence of a conjugal relationship; the degree of exclusivity in the relationship; conduct and habits relating to the household and living arrangements; the degree to which the partners hold themselves out as one economic and domestic unit; the extent of direct and indirect contribution to each other's mutual well-being; the degree of financial dependence; care and support of children; and ownership, use and acquisition of property.[97]

As discussed in Chapter 1, an adult interdependent relationship may exist between persons of the same sex or opposite sex. A spouse and an adult interdependent partner of the deceased cannot both make a claim against the estate. For example, if the deceased was married at the time of his or her death, he or she could not have entered into a valid adult interdependent partner agreement. If the deceased was living with his or her spouse at the time of his or her death, they could not have an adult interdependent partner by ascription (the three year requirement) because the deceased could not have lived both with the spouse and the adult interdependent partner simultaneously. However, a deceased who did not live with his or her spouse, may be considered to have had an adult interdependent partner if he or she lived with another person for three years or more, prior to his or her death, but in that case, only the adult interdependent partner may make a claim against the estate.

One of the most important differences between the *Family Relief Act* and the *Dependants Relief Act* is that under the *Family Relief Act*, only a legally married spouse of the deceased, whether they were living together or not, could make a claim against the estate. Now, the legally married spouse may be barred from making a claim under the *Dependants Relief Act*, where only the adult interdependent partner will have such a right.

If the Court is faced with considering a spouse's claim under the *Dependants Relief Act*, the Court will apply different criteria than if it was considering a claim by an adult interdependent partner.

When the Court is considering a claim made by the spouse of the deceased, it will first look at what it would have awarded the spouse under

---

[97] *Ibid.*, s. 1(2)(a)-(i).

the *Divorce Act*[98] had the spouse applied to divorce the deceased prior to his or her death. The Courts will go through this exercise to establish a line between the rights that the spouse could have asserted against the testator before death, and those that can be awarded against the estate.[99]

When the Court is considering a claim made by an adult interdependent partner, the *Divorce Act* will not apply as it is a federal statute that only applies to married parties. The Court, in deciding what is proper maintenance for the adult interdependent partner, will use the same criteria it did when deciding what is proper maintenance for a spouse. The category of proper maintenance is much wider than adequate maintenance and is to be determined based on the following factors:

> the size of the [testator's] estate, the size of the testator's family, the age[s] of [the testator's] dependants, the station in life of the testator and his [or her] dependants, the character and views of the testator, the wishes of the testator, if his [or her] failure to perform [his] duty is due to omission or oversight, the relative needs and deserts of the claimants, the possibility of changes in existing circumstances, the future value of money and rates of interest, the opinions and wishes of a just and wise [parent] about the education and mode of life of the children of the [parent] and the testator, the situation arising when the testator has been married more than once, the personal income of the [testator's] dependants; the competing moral claims on the bounty of the testator… [and] the health and mental capacity of [the testator's] dependants.[100]

In defining what is "proper maintenance and support of the dependants", Alberta Courts have consistently rejected the approach that would leave the dependants only maintained and no more, and that would leave the dependants with no claim on the property of the deceased.[101] It is assumed that the Court's position will be the same when considering what is proper maintenance for an adult interdependent partner who has made a claim against the estate pursuant to either a constructive or resulting trust, an unjust enrichment or *quantum meruit* claim.[102]

---

[98] R.S.C. 1985, c. 3 (2nd Supp.).
[99] See *Siegel v. Siegel Estate*, [1996] 3 W.W.R. 247, 35 Alta. L.R. (3d) 321, 10 E.T.R. (2d) 178, 177 A.R. 282 (Q.B.); and *Stang v. Stang Estate*, [1998] A.J. No. 261, 58 Alta. L.R. (3d) 201 (Q.B.).
[100] *Siegel v. Siegel Estate*, [1996] 3 W.W.R. 247 at 266, citing *Re Protopappas Estate* (1987), 78 A.R. 60, 25 E.T.R. 241 (Q.B.) and *Re Lawther Estate*, [1947] 1 W.W.R. 577 (Man. K.B.).
[101] *Ibid.*, at 258.
[102] Refer to the section entitled "Relationship of Dependants Relief Act and Matrimonial Property Act Claims, Dower and Intestacy" for a further discussion on the two-step approach used by Courts when considering a spouse's claim under the *Dependants Relief Act*.

Procedure/Forum and Initiating Documents for Claims Under the Dependants Relief Act

Under the *Dependants Relief Act*, applications are made to the Court of Queen's Bench (Surrogate Matter) by Notice of Motion. The affidavit in support of the application should be detailed and should address the factors considered by *Siegel v. Siegel Estate* and *Re Protopappas Estate* as they apply to each particular case.

Such an application may also be brought on behalf of a dependant adult by the Court-appointed guardian or trustee of the estate of the dependant adult, by a parent, or by the Public Trustee (on behalf of a minor or dependent adult). If the application is brought by a parent on behalf of a minor, it is recommended that the application be framed in the name of the minor, by their next friend.

Included in the category of respondents to such an application is the personal representative of the estate, as well as the beneficiaries, whether the beneficiaries are by an intestacy or under the Will. The Public Trustee should be served with the application if the applicant or estate beneficiary is a minor or a dependant adult. Service is required on all parties who may be affected by the application, and no order may be made by the Court until it is satisfied that adequate notice has been given to all interested parties.

Where there is more than one dependant (*i.e.*, both a spouse/adult interdependent partner, and either a minor child(ren) or adult dependent child(ren)), the Court has said that it must balance the interests of all the dependants. Generally, a spouse/adult interdependent partner is considered to have a higher moral claim than the child(ren), but each case is generally unique and is decided on its particular facts.

Limitation Periods

Section 15 of the *Dependants Relief Act* states that all applications must be made within six months from the date the Grant is issued. The *Dependants Relief Act* allows the Court to extend the limitation period, however, a late claim against the estate can only affect the undistributed portion of the estate. Generally, the Court will only grant leave to file outside the six month time period, when it considers it just. The Court will not grant leave if to do so would create an injustice to the parties.

Section 17 of the *Dependants Relief Act* provides that the personal representative shall not distribute any portion of the estate for six months from the date of the grant unless the personal representative has consent of all of the dependants or a Court Order. The *Dependants Relief Act* does, however, allow for reasonable advances for maintenance to dependants who are beneficiaries. Once the executor receives notice of an application under the *Dependants Relief Act*, the executor cannot distribute the estate without a Court Order.

Where the estate consists of assets with an extremely changeable value, for example, speculative investments, the value of the estate at the time of the application is the value the Court finds most useful when making a decision on dependant's relief.

Effect of Agreements, Waivers and Releases on Dependants Relief Act Claims

The Courts have found that any attempt to contract out of the *Dependants Relief Act* is void as being against public policy. This is in contrast to, for example, being able to contract out of a dower and the *Matrimonial Property Act*,[103] which allows a party to waive such rights. Even if a dependant has signed an agreement, waiver or release of the right to make a family relief type of claim, a dependant is not barred from making such an application. The Court may, however, consider the waiver or release when hearing the application.

The traditional rule in estate matters was that costs were paid out of the estate, particularly where the application was caused by the actions or inactions of the deceased. In *Dependants Relief Act* cases, the traditional rule is generally followed. However, in the past few years, the Alberta Courts have, on occasion, moved away from the traditional rule and awarded costs against the party who was unsuccessful in Court.

MATRIMONIAL PROPERTY ACT

The *Matrimonial Property Act* was designed to govern the division of matrimonial property after a marriage breakdown. The general principle is that if a surviving spouse could have made a claim under the *Matrimonial Property Act* immediately prior to the death of his or her spouse, then that surviving spouse has the right to make a claim against the estate of the deceased spouse, subject to certain strict time limitations. For example, if a husband dies and his wife could have brought a *Matrimonial Property Act* claim just before his death, then her right survives, and she can bring the

---

[103] R.S.A. 2000, c. M-8.

claim against the property in the husband's estate. If any one of the spouses dies after a *Matrimonial Property Act* action has been commenced, then their action will survive.

The general *Matrimonial Property Act* presumption of equal distribution applies to claims made against an estate unless it appears to the Court that it would not be just and equitable to do so. The death of a spouse or the contents of the deceased spouse's Will are not relevant facts or circumstances to be taken into consideration by the Court in determining what is just and equitable under a *Matrimonial Property Act* claim. If the death or the contents of the Will were considered, this would frustrate the intent of the *Matrimonial Property Act*. If the surviving spouse would face hardship even after the *Matrimonial Property Act* claim was decided, then an additional application could be made under the *Dependants Relief Act*. In many cases, a joint *Matrimonial Property Act* and *Dependants Relief Act* claim is made right from the start.

Who May Make a Matrimonial Property Act Claim

The *Matrimonial Property Act* requires that a plaintiff must be married and establish: residency; marriage breakdown; and that the claim be brought within specified time limits.

The residency requirements necessary to establish jurisdiction are set out in section 3 of the *Matrimonial Property Act* and relate to either habitual residence or one of the parties having filed a statement of claim for divorce in Alberta.

A claim may only be brought in the event of marriage breakdown. The conditions which are evidence of a marriage breakdown are set out in section 5 of the *Matrimonial Property Act*, and include:
- a divorce judgment;
- a declaration of nullity or an order of judicial separation;
- the spouses have been separated for a period of one year, or less if there is no possibility of reconciliation;
- the spouses are living apart and one intends to or has transferred property intending to defeat the claim of the other; or
- the spouses are living apart and one is dissipating property.

If a surviving spouse does not fit within one of the categories listed in section 5 of the *Matrimonial Property Act*, then there is no right to make a claim against the estate of the deceased spouse.

The claim must also be brought within the time limits set out in section 6 of the *Matrimonial Property Act*. Calculation of the limitation period is very important.

If the surviving spouse had begun the action before the death of the other spouse, the action can be continued by the surviving spouse against the deceased spouse's estate. If the deceased spouse began the action before they died, and later died, the action may be continued by the personal representative of the estate of the deceased. The estate of a deceased spouse and his or her personal representative do not have the right to commence an action against the surviving spouse for division of matrimonial property.

Definition of Spouse

There was an issue as to whether the term "spouse" in the *Matrimonial Property Act* included a common law spouse. In *Walsh v. Bona*,[104] the Supreme Court of Canada decided that "spouse" in the *Matrimonial Property Act* does not include a common law spouse (opposite or same sex) and that the Charter was not offended by such an interpretation. The reasoning of the Court is that common law spouses can make a claim under the banners of unjust enrichment, *quantum meruit*, or constructive and resulting trusts.

Assets Subject to a Matrimonial Property Act Claim

Section 11(3) provides that:

> 11(3) When a matrimonial property order is made in favour of a surviving spouse, the Court, in addition to the matters in section 8 [of the *Matrimonial Property Act*], shall take into consideration any benefit received by the surviving spouse as a result of the death of the deceased spouse.

This provision contemplates a surviving spouse receiving benefits such as insurance or the right to jointly held property by way of survivorship.

Subsection 7(2)(e) of the *Matrimonial Property Act* exempts from a matrimonial property division "the proceeds of an insurance policy that is not insurance in respect of property, unless the proceeds are compensation for a loss to both spouses". For example, the proceeds of a life insurance policy on the husband, which named the surviving wife as a beneficiary,

---

[104] (2002) 221 D.L.R. (4th) 1.

was exempt, and was specifically found not to form part of the matrimonial property of the husband.

Where the matrimonial home is jointly held, but the mortgage is life insured, Madam Justice Trussler, in *Dunn v. Dunn Estate*,[105] held that the joint tenancy survived both the divorce and the filing of the *Matrimonial Property Act* claim, and that the home passed to the surviving wife by right of survivorship. The home did not form part of the estate of the deceased husband. The Court therefore ruled that because the house no longer formed part of the matrimonial property at the date of trial, it was not subject to division.

Debts

The Court is directed to divide non-exempt property having regard to the factors listed in section 8 of the *Matrimonial Property Act*, which factors include "the income, earning capacity, liabilities, obligations...(i) that each spouse had at the time of marriage, and (ii) that each spouse has at the time of the trial,"[106] and any income tax consequences which will result from the sale or transfer of property.[107] This is the basis on which debts are usually set off against assets, or used to reduce the overall value of the matrimonial property available for distribution.

Relationship of Dependants Relief Act and Matrimonial Property Act Claims, Dower and Intestacy

If a couple has separated, but not divorced, prior to the death of one of the spouses, the surviving spouse may have a claim for division of property under the *Matrimonial Property Act*, as well as the right to bring a claim under the *Dependants Relief Act*, the *Dower Act*,[108] and has an interest in the estate pursuant to the *Intestate Succession Act*[109] if there is no Will.

The *Matrimonial Property Act* confirms that both *Matrimonial Property Act* and *Dependants Relief Act* claims can be brought, and that the applications may be joined.[110] The entitlement of the surviving spouse

---

[105] [1994] A.J. No. 42 (Q.B.) (QL).
[106] Subsection 8(*d*).
[107] Subsection 8(*k*).
[108] R.S.A. 2000, c. D-15.
[109] R.S.A. 2000, c. I-10.
[110] See s. 18 of the *Matrimonial Property Act*.

under the *Matrimonial Property Act* is not affected by the existence of an *Dependants Relief Act* claim.[111]

Where there is a claim by a surviving spouse against the estate of the deceased spouse under both the *Matrimonial Property Act* and the *Dependants Relief Act*, the claim under the *Matrimonial Property Act* should be determined first. This is because section 15 of the *Matrimonial Property Act* deems that money paid or transferred to a surviving spouse under the *Matrimonial Property Act* does not form part of the estate of the deceased and is not subject to a claim against the estate by a dependent under the *Dependants Relief Act* or the *Matrimonial Property Act*.[112] Therefore, the terms of the matrimonial property Court Order will affect the order under the *Dependants Relief Act* because it reduces the size of the estate and increases the assets of the surviving spouse.

The success or failure of the surviving spouse under the *Matrimonial Property Act* will not necessarily govern the result under the *Dependants Relief Act*, as the purposes of the two statutes are entirely different. For example, in *Webb v. Webb Estate*,[113] where the spouses had entered into a separation agreement, and the husband had waived his right to bring a *Matrimonial Property Act*, *Family Relief Act* and dower claim in return for an agreed sum, the Court upheld the *Matrimonial Property Act* settlement, and dismissed the husband's claim under the *Matrimonial Property Act*. However, the Court went on to find that the husband was a dependent within the meaning of the *Family Relief Act*, and that he had not been adequately provided for, and that since a dependent could not contract out of his or her rights under the *Family Relief Act*, he should receive further provision from the estate of the deceased wife for proper maintenance.[114]

If only a *Dependants Relief Act* claim is brought, the Court considers the legal claim of the surviving spouse under the *Matrimonial Property Act* as part of the analysis process, a practice established by the *Tataryn* case.[115]

A surviving spouse may also have the right under the *Dower Act* to a life estate in the "homestead".[116]

---

[111] *Ibid.*, s. 18(1).
[112] See *Baker v. Baker Estate* (1992), 48 E.T.R. 261 at 278 (Alta. Q.B.).
[113] (1995), 28 Alta. L.R. (3d) 110 (Surr. Ct.).
[114] See *Zubiss v. Moulson Estate* (1987), 54 Alta. L.R. (2d) 167 (Q.B.), wherein the *Matrimonial Property Act* action succeeded, but the *Family Relief Act* claim was dismissed.
[115] See *Siegel v. Siegel Estate*, [1996] 3 W.W.R. 247 (Q.B.); and *Gow v. Gow Estate* (1998), 74 Alta. L.R. (3d) 279 (Surr. Ct.).
[116] Section 18.

Time Limitations

The time limitations set out in the *Matrimonial Property Act* must be strictly adhered to, because if the claimant is outside the limitation, the action will be statute barred. Section 6 of the *Matrimonial Property Act* sets out the time limitations within which the application for a *Matrimonial Property Act* order must be brought. If the action is brought on the basis that a Court has granted a divorce judgment, a declaration of nullity, or of judicial separation, then the action must be commenced within two years of the Court Order.

If the action is based on separation, the spouse must have lived separate and apart for at least one year before the action is brought, but must bring the action within two years of separation.[117] If spouses have been separated for many years, one of the spouses must file a statement of claim for divorce which will revive the right to a *Matrimonial Property Act* order.[118]

Where a grant of probate or a grant of administration is issued, any application by the surviving spouse under the *Matrimonial Property Act* must be brought within six months of the date of the grant.[119] This is consistent with the six month limitation under the *Dependants Relief Act*, although the *Dependants Relief Act* allows the claim to be brought later, with leave. The *Matrimonial Property Act*, however, does not.

Procedure

An action under the *Matrimonial Property Act* is commenced by a Statement of Claim, and as noted above, it may be joined with an application under the *Dependants Relief Act*.[120]

Estate Distribution in Light of a Matrimonial Property Act Claim

Section 13 of the *Matrimonial Property Act* provides that a personal representative is not permitted to distribute any portion of the estate without the consent of the living spouse, or Court Order. When an application for a *Matrimonial Property Act* order is made by the surviving spouse, the personal representative shall hold the estate subject to any

---

[117] *Matrimonial Property Act*, subs. 6(2).
[118] *Ibid.*, subs. 6(1)(a).
[119] *Ibid.*, subs. 11(4).
[120] See s. 4 and subs. 18(2) of the *Matrimonial Property Act*.

future order that may be made by the Court.[121] The effect of this is that a personal representative is taking a personal risk if he or she distributes any property without the consent of the surviving spouse or a Court Order if a matrimonial property action exists. Given the delays that often occur in these actions - it may be years before an estate is distributed - beneficiaries should ensure that the litigation is kept "moving" and that, where possible, an interim distribution, however minimal, is made.

BRITISH COLUMBIA

INTRODUCTION

Much of the discussion in this chapter also applies in British Columbia. The differences arise primarily with respect to dependant's relief claims and the rules and procedures related to estate actions and mediation.

DEPENDANT SUPPORT OR RELIEF CLAIMS IN BRITISH COLUMBIA

In British Columbia, dependant support or relief claims are made under section 2 of the *Wills Variation Act*.[122] Under that section, any spouse or child of a deceased can bring a claim on the basis that the Will does not "make adequate provision for the proper maintenance and support of the testator's spouse or children". Section 2 goes on to say that the Court then has discretion to order whatever provision it thinks is "adequate, just and equitable in the circumstances". The definition of spouse under section 1 of the Act includes a person who is "living and cohabiting with another person in a marriage-like relationship, including a marriage-like relationship between persons of the same gender" for at least two years. A child includes any natural child or adopted child of the deceased but it does not include a step-child. The claim must be brought within six months of the date of the grant of probate.

STEPS IN AN ESTATE ACTION IN BRITISH COLUMBIA

Rules 61 and 62 of the *Supreme Court Rules*[123] contain the rules and procedures related to estates. Rule 61 deals with non-contentious

---

[121] *Ibid.*, s. 14.
[122] R.S.B.C. 1996, c. 490.
[123] B.C. Reg. 221/90.

proceedings, whereas Rule 62 deals with contentious proceedings. The procedure which a charity might utilize will depend in part on whether it wants to take steps before or after the Grant of Probate has been obtained. This will depend on when it learns that there might be a problem related to the validity of the Will or the administration of the estate. Rule 62(2) provides that any person who has an interest in upholding or disputing a Will must be involved.

PROCEDURES BEFORE THE GRANT

Citations

When a charity believes that it may be a beneficiary under a Will, but has heard nothing with respect to it, there are several tools that can be used to move the matter forward.

If it appears that there is a valid Will, but the executor has not applied for a grant, under Rule 61(43), any interested person can cite the executor to accept probate by issuing a citation in Form 77 (Citation to Accept Probate as Executor). The executor can then either accept or refuse probate, or show cause why an Administration With Will Annexed should not be granted to the person who has cited the executor (the "citor") or to some other person named in the citation. The form requires the executor to apply for a grant within 14 days of service on him or her, or file an answer undertaking to apply within 14 days of the answer. The answer should also address why Administration should not be granted to the citor or to the other person named in the citation. If the executor does not file an answer, his or her right to be executor ceases.

A citation can also be used in circumstances where the charity is aware that there is an alleged last Will, but there are concerns about its validity (which all interested parties may share). Under Rule 61(45), a citation in Form 79 (Citation to Propound an Alleged Will) may be issued by any interested person who may want to apply for probate or administration ignoring the alleged last Will, requiring the executor and anyone named in the alleged Will to propound it as a Will. If neither the executor nor anyone named in the Will file an answer within 14 days, the Court may grant probate or administration to the person named in the citation. A citation and subsequent failure to file an answer under this Rule will preclude the Courts from having to pronounce against the alleged Will — a much shorter procedure than a proof in solemn form action.

A citation may also be used in circumstances where a person who has possession or control of a Will or other testamentary document (for example, a lawyer) will not release it or deal with it. In that case, under Rule 61(46), a citation in Form 81 (Citation to Bring in a Will) may be issued ordering the person to deposit the Will or other testamentary document with the Registrar's office at the Registry issuing the citation. The person cited must deliver up the Will or other document within 14 days of service of the citation. If the person cited does not have possession or control of the document, he or she must file an affidavit within 14 days saying so and setting out what knowledge he or she does have with respect to any testamentary document.

The person cited can also be examined under the provisions of the *Estate Administration Act*[124] and Rule 61(46)(c) of the *Supreme Court Rules* with respect to his or her knowledge of a Will or other document or asset relating to or belonging to an estate.

Once the Will or other document is deposited in the Registry, the citor can apply for the grant either by applying for a release of the Will or other testamentary document from the Registry or by making reference in the application to the Will or other document deposited in the Registry.

Caveats

A caveat is a document filed by a person who has an interest in the property of a deceased giving the Court notice that it should not grant probate or administration of an estate without first giving notice to the person who has filed the caveat. This means the caveator will be informed if an application for a grant is made. It allows the caveator time to decide whether or not to oppose the application for the grant. For example, a charity would file a caveat where it believed it was a beneficiary under a previous Will and not under a later Will, and where there were concerns about the validity of the later Will.

A caveat must be in Form 75 of the *Supreme Court Rules*. The caveator must declare his or her interest in the deceased's property and the grounds on which he or she files the caveat.

A grant cannot be issued while a caveat remains in force. In order to try to remove a caveat, any applicant for a grant can file a Notice to Caveator in Form 76 of the *Supreme Court Rules* stating that the caveator must file an appearance within seven days. If the appearance is not filed as required, the Registry on application by the applicant for the grant, will cancel the caveat. If an appearance is filed, the practice of the Registry is

---

[124] R.S.B.C. 1986, c. 122.

that the caveat can only be removed by Court Order or by consent of the parties.

A caveat also expires after six months unless it is withdrawn or renewed by Court Order. The practice is to simply file a new caveat rather than seeking a Court Order.

Generally, if a caveat does not lapse or is not withdrawn, the applicant for the grant must issue a writ under Rule 62 of the *Supreme Court Rules* (which govern contentious proceedings) seeking a grant and cancellation of the caveat.

PROCEDURES AFTER THE GRANT

Where a grant has already been made in common form of a Will which may be invalid, an action for revocation of the grant may be commenced. This action is commenced by writ of summons. The existing grant is called in pending resolution of the action. It must be lodged with the Registrar within seven days of service of the Writ.

Proof in Solemn Form

Where there is a dispute about whether the last Will is valid, it must be proved "in solemn form". As noted before, the most common bases of challenge are formal validity, lack of testamentary capacity and undue influence. Usually, these challenges are made under Rule 62 of the *Supreme Court Rules* by issuance of a writ of summons and the matter proceeds under the *Supreme Court Rules* like any other litigation. While Rules 61(11), (12) and (13) do allow a Will to be proved in solemn form by petition under Rule 10, this procedure would only be used where a caveat has not been filed and where the proceedings are not contentious.

The executor of the Will, or any beneficiary, can commence the action. All persons who have an interest in the validity of the Will must be parties to the action. This will include any beneficiaries under a previous Will, or if there is no previous Will, all persons who would be entitled on intestacy.

Once a writ of summons is issued, it will be served on the interested parties, who must file an appearance. The person commencing the action (the plaintiff) will also file a statement of claim setting out the interests of the plaintiff and the defendants as well as the facts which support the plaintiff's assertion that the Will is valid. Each defendant will file a statement of defence.

In a proof in solemn form action, under Rule 62(10), the defendant's statement of defence may say that he or she merely requires that the Will be proved in solemn form and that he or she only wants to cross-examine witnesses produced in support of the Will. A defendant who files this type of defence will not be liable for costs unless the Court finds that there was no reasonable ground for requiring proof in solemn form.

Even if a defendant does not file an appearance or statement of defence, the action must be proceeded with and heard by a judge. It cannot be discontinued nor can default proceedings be taken. Rule 62(13) specifically states, "No probate action shall be compromised without leave of the Court." Usually, once a probate action has commenced, an administrator *pendente lite* will be appointed to administer the estate until the judge in the probate action determines whether there is a valid Will and thus who is to act as executor.

There are production and exchange of document procedures and examination for discovery procedures in B.C. estate litigation similar to those discussed earlier in this chapter. It is possible, instead of having a full trial before a judge where witnesses are called and examined under oath, to have a summary trial under Rule 18(A) of the *Supreme Court Rules*. In this case, affidavit evidence is produced to prove proper execution in accordance with the formalities of the *Wills Act*,[125] knowledge and approval of the contents of the Will and testamentary capacity.

As earlier stated, if the parties agree to a compromise, it must still be approved by the Court. The Court must hear evidence and satisfy itself that the Will was valid.

Mediation

Mediation has become another tool in resolving probate and dependant's relief actions. The *Notice to Mediate (General) Regulation*[126] came into force February 15, 2001 under the *Law and Equity Act*.[127] Section 3 of the Regulation allows any party to a Supreme Court action to require the other parties to attend a mediation session by delivering a Notice to Mediate to every other party to the action and to the Dispute Resolution Office of the Attorney General. Under section 4, only one mediation may be initiated relating to the action. Section 5 states that a notice must be delivered no earlier than 60 days after the close of pleadings and no later than 120 days

---

[125] R.S.B.C., c. 489.
[126] B.C. Reg. 4/2001.
[127] R.S.B.C. 1996, c. 254.

before trial. Within 14 days of delivery of the Notice (or 21 days if there are more than four parties), under section 6 of the Regulation, the parties must jointly appoint a mediator. If they cannot agree on a mediator, then any party can apply to a roster organization for the appointment of a mediator.[128]

All parties must attend the mediation (unless relieved under certain sections of the Regulation) and they may be required to attend a pre-mediation conference. A party can sometimes attend by Counsel or send a representative and, of course, each party can have Counsel in attendance.

A mediation must take place within 60 days after appointment of the Mediator and at least seven days before trial. Each party must deliver to the Mediator at least 14 days before the mediation a Statement of Facts and Issues in Form 2 to the Regulation.[129] These Statements are distributed to the other parties by the Mediator.

Prior to the Mediation, a mediation fee declaration in Form 3 to the Regulation must be completed.[130] The fees vary depending on who the Mediator is. Form 3 will state the cost of the mediation services and that the parties will share the fee equally or on some other agreed basis.

If agreement is reached, the Mediator will prepare a memorandum of agreement for the parties to sign. These agreements are binding and subject to enforcement.

As Rule 1 of the *Supreme Court Rules* defines "action" to mean "a proceeding commenced by writ of summons", the Regulation does not apply to matters commenced by petition.

However, the parties to a proceeding (whether commenced by writ of summons or by petition) can always agree at any time to have a voluntary mediation which can occur at any time as determined by agreement of the parties. It should also be remembered that if there are parties under a disability, or if the dispute relates to construction of a Will or if it is a probate action, Court approval of the mediated settlement will likely still be required.

PRE-TRIAL AND TRIAL

In British Columbia, pre-trial is not mandatory in all cases but under Rule 35, any party "having delivered or received a notice of trial, may request" a pre-trial conference. In a pre-trial conference, the judge may order the

---

[128] Section 7 of the *Notice to Mediate (General) Regulation*.
[129] *Ibid.*, s. 26.
[130] *Ibid.*, s. 26.

parties to attend a mini-trial (where the parties attend in camera and without witnesses and the judge or Master gives an opinion on the probable outcome of the proceeding). A judge may also order the parties to attend a settlement conference where, in camera and without witnesses, all settlement possibilities are explored. Under Rule 66 of the Supreme Court Rules there is provision for a procedure called "Fast Track Litigation".

A trial date is very often reserved once the pleadings are filed to get the earliest possible date in case the matter cannot be resolved. If there are any persons under legal disability (minors or mental incompetence), a guardian *ad litem* will commence or defend the proceedings on behalf of that person. Rule 6(7) provides that the consent of the person who is to act as guardian *ad litem* must be filed before he or she can act. Any settlement of a claim where there is a person under disability must be approved by the Court.

Where there is a problem with a charitable gift, such as where the charity has ceased to exist or has been misnamed or where the purpose of the gift cannot be fulfilled, the office of the Attorney General must be served and will make recommendations to the Court with respect to any *cy-près* scheme with respect to the gift.

COSTS IN ESTATE LITIGATION

In British Columbia, costs are a matter of judicial discretion. Rule 57 of the *Supreme Court Rules* sets out the Rules with respect to costs. Rule 57(1) provides that costs should be payable as "party and party costs" under Appendix B to the Rules unless the Court determines that they should be paid as special costs (approximately, the parties' actual costs). Rule 57(3) sets out the matters which the Court should consider in assessing special costs.

Rule 57(5) states that where costs are payable for non-contentious business under Rule 61 (which contains the rules and procedures related to estates), they shall be assessed as special costs.

With the consent of the parties, the Court may fix lump sum costs under Rule 57(13).

Under Rule 57(16), where costs are paid out of an estate or property, the Court may order what part of the estate or property should bear the costs.

Estate litigation appears to be on the rise in British Columbia.

Appendix 1

ESTATE CHECKLIST — BRING FORWARD FORM

Estate of:_____   Date of Certificate:_____
Date of Death:_____   Date of Notification:_____
Estate Trustee:_____   Estate Solicitor:_____
Address:_____   Address:_____

Phone:_____   Phone:_____
Fax:_____   Fax:_____
Email:_____   Email:_____

Specific Bequest:_____
Legacy:_____
Residue:_____(Est.)
Life Tenant(s) Name/DOB_____

Other Charities: Name/Contact Person/ Telephone/Email
_____
_____
_____

Distributions

Accounts: Accounts:
Amount: Amount:
Release: Release:
Tax Receipt/Date Sent: Tax Receipt/Date Sent:

DATE REVIEWED (Initials)	ACTION (taken and required)

Appendix 2

RECEIPT BY LEGATEE

    I, [name], DO HEREBY ACKNOWLEDGE that I have received [amount] from [Name], Estate Trustee of the Estate of [Name], late of the City of Anywhere, in the Province of Ontario, deceased, in full satisfaction and payment of my share of the said Estate to which I am entitled under the Last Will and Testament of the late [name] dated [date].

    IN WITNESS WHEREOF I have hereunto set my hand and seal this [day] day of [month], [year].

SIGNED, SEALED AND DELIVERED)
In the presence of)
)
)_____
) [Name]
)
)
_____) per_____
(Witness)) [Authorized signing officer]

Appendix 3

ESTATE AUDIT CHECKLIST[1]

SECTION A

REVIEW WILL

1) Outright distribution   YES_____ NO_____
   _____   (go to **Section B**) (go to Number 2)

2) One or more trusts   YES_____ NO_____

        a) life interest   YES   NO   Beneficiaries_____

        b) vested interests   YES   NO   Beneficiaries_____

        c) contingent interests   YES   NO   Beneficiaries_____

        d) real property trust(s)   YES   NO   Beneficiaries_____

3) Restrictions   YES   NO

        a) investments   YES   NO
        b) capital distributions   YES   NO
        c) compensation   YES   NO

4) Other special instructions   YES   NO

if so, what: _____

---

[1] CAUTION: This is a fictitious case study created by Deborah L. Campbell for teaching purposes. Deborah L. Campbell, M. Jasmine Sweatman of Miller Thomson LLP. Copyright 2003.

SECTION B

REVIEW STATEMENT OF ORIGINAL ASSETS

Bank Accounts

Institution Name and Address _____

Held   Yes   No
Reviewed   Yes   No
Completely
Realized   Yes   No

Type of Account and Account Number _____

Balance at Date of Death _____

Interest to Date of Death _____

GIC's and CSB

Issuer & Certificate Number _____
_____

Held   Yes   No
Reviewed   Yes   No
Completely
Realized   Yes   No

Principal _____

Maturity Date _____

Interest Rate/frequency _____

Accrued Interest from Last Payment
to Date of Death _____

Bonds and Debentures

Issuer & Certificate Number _____

Held   Yes   No
Reviewed   Yes   No
Completely
Realized   Yes   No

Face Value _____

Maturity Date _____

Interest Rate/frequency _____

Market Value/$100 at Date of Death _____

Accrued Interest from Last Payment
to Date of Death _____

Mutual Funds

Name of Fund _____

Number of Units Held at Date of Death _____

Market Value Per Unit at Date of Death _____

Held	Yes	No
Reviewed	Yes	No
Completely Realized	Yes	No

Shares

Name of Corporation _____

Certificate No. _____

Number and Class of Shares _____

Market Value per Share at Date of Death _____

Private Corporation Shares _____

Ex-dividend _____

Held	Yes	No
Reviewed	Yes	No
Completely Realized	Yes	No

Foreign Currency Assets

Canadian Dollar Value at Date of Death _____

Held	Yes	No
Reviewed	Yes	No
Completely Realized	Yes	No

Insurance/Annuities

Company _____

Principal Outstanding at Date of Death _____

Accrued Interest (not always) _____

Held	Yes	No
Reviewed	Yes	No
Completely Realized	Yes	No
Action Req'd	Yes	No
Comments: _____		

Real Property

Address _____

Appraised Value at Date of Death _____

Outstanding Mortgage   YES   NO

    Balance Outstanding _____

    Interest Rate _____

    Monthly Payments _____

    Maturity Date _____

Held	Yes	No
Reviewed	Yes	No
Completely Realized	Yes	No

Mortgage Investments

Property Secured _____

Mortgagors _____

Principal Outstanding _____

Interest Rate (amortized payments) _____

Accrued Interest Payable _____

Payment Amount _____

Payment Date _____

Maturity Date _____

Held	Yes	No
Reviewed	Yes	No
Completely Realized	Yes	No

Chattel Mortgages/Promissory Notes/Outstanding Receivables

Debtor _____

Principal Outstanding _____

Interest Rate _____

Payment Date _____

Maturity _____

Held   Yes   No
Reviewed   Yes   No
Completely
  Realized   Yes   No
Action Req'd   Yes   No
Comments: _____

Miscellaneous Assets (usually includes unique items)

Income Tax Refunds _____

Subscription Refunds _____

Insurance Premium Refunds _____

Held   Yes   No
Reviewed   Yes   No
Completely
  Realized   Yes   No

Car _____

Furniture _____

Art _____

Jewellery _____

Personal Effects _____

Partnership or Proprietorship Interests _____

Estate or Trust Interests _____

Accrued Salary _____

Pension Benefits _____

Canadian Pension Plan Death Benefit _____

Canadian Pension Plan Payments _____

Old Age Security _____

SECTION C
REVIEW CAPITAL RECEIPTS

TASK	YES	NO	ACTION REQUIRED
Check descriptions against Statement of Original Assets to ensure that asset actually realized			
Accrued interest/ex-dividends reported?			
Realization of bonds/debentures (not necessarily face value unless bond matured)			
Shares • any stock splits before shares realized? • all shares realized? • partial realization? How many remaining? • broker's commission deducted?			
Mutual Funds • number of units? (if discrepancy, check for dividend reinvestment)			
Income tax refunds? (if for taxes paid by estate trustee, exclude from compensation)			
Principal portion of mortgage payments reported?			
Real property • value net of adjustments? • real estate commission deducted? • legal fees deducted? • outstanding mortgages discharged?			
Are all unrealized assets listed in Statement of Unrealized Original Assets?			
Capital gains on redemption of Trustee investments? (review Investment Account)			
Mathematics correct?			

SECTION D
REVIEW CAPITAL DISBURSEMENTS

TASK	YES	NO	ACTION REQUIRED
Calculate probate fees based on value of estate			
Funeral, cemetery, engraving expenses			
In specie distributions (should also be recorded in Capital Receipts)			
Legacies			
Estate Trustee expenses (details provided?)			
Income taxes • normally, only year of death and outstanding assessments for prior year returns • if for estate returns, check Original Assets and Trustee's Investments for capital gains			
Payments to life tenants — power to encroach on capital			
Is Estate Trustee the estate solicitor? • if yes, review accounts for legal services and accounts for executor's services (see duties)			
Payments to maintain asset (*i.e.*, real property) • if yes, what for? • should a portion be paid from income? (benefit for capital beneficiary, income beneficiary or both?)			

SECTION E
REVIEW REVENUE RECEIPTS/DISBURSEMENTS

TASK	YES	NO	ACTION REQUIRED
All income received on original assets until realized? • bank interest monthly • GIC interest — annually, semiannually or monthly? • dividends — usually quarterly? (sometimes less frequently or not at all)			
Mutual fund income distributions (can be monthly, annually, other) should also be reported in Investment Account showing additional units acquired			
Rental income			
Expenses to maintain rental property			
Payments to life tenants			
Payment of estate taxes			
Expense allocation re wasting asset (*i.e.*, cottage)			
Mortgage interest income/expenses			
Income on trustee investments • received regularly? • meets or exceeds payments made to life tenants? (check Cash Summary for revenue account balance)			

SECTION F
REVIEW INVESTMENT ACCOUNT

TASK	YES	NO	ACTION REQUIRED
Do investments selected maintain an "even hand"?			
Is investment income reported in Revenue Receipts?			
Is list of investments at end of accounting period included?			
Does investment total agree with investment total in Cash Summary?			

SECTION G
REVIEW TRUSTEES' COMPENSATION

TASK	YES	NO	ACTION REQUIRED
What percentages are used?			
Should percentages be adjusted? (re real property)			
Value used to calculate care and management fees			
Are care and management fees appropriate?			
Capital losses			
Transfers between accounts			
Adjusting entries			
Refunds			
Interim payments to trustees			
Solicitor and other professional accounts			

SECTION H
GENERAL REVIEW

TASK	YES	NO	ACTION REQUIRED
Asset realization cross-referenced to appropriate entry in capital receipts?			
Mathematics correct?			
Does list of unrealized original assets appear to include assets not cross-referenced on original list?			
Are there partial realizations? (See Capital Receipts for more detail)			

INDEX

A

Accounting. *See* Estate accounting
Accounts, passing. *See* Passing accounts
Administration. *See* Estate administration
Administration, letters of, 62
Administrator, 4
Administrator *ad litem. See* Litigation (Alberta)
Adult interdependent partners, 48, 55, 301, 303-304
Advertising for claims
    Alberta, in, 43
    Ontario, in, 31-32
Attorney
    described, 4
    for personal care or for property, 4
Audit
    estate audit checklist, App. 3
    generally, 130
    trust company accounts, 133-134

B

Beneficiary
    charitable. *See* Charitable beneficiary
    classes of, 33
    described, 3
    legatee vs. residual, 88, 112
    litigation
        effects on, 286-287
        involvement in, 299, 300
        parties to, as, 282
    minor, 148
    residual, 34
    right to inspect and investigate, 111
    trust, of, 4
    unborn, 53
    Will, distribution of copies to, 67
Bequest
    charitable, failure of, 251
    described, 7
    residuary, 29
    specific bequest beneficiary, 51
Bond, 7, 13, 40-41, 63

C

Capacity
    age, 254
    mental, 255-56
Certificate of appointment
    application for, 20-22
    described, 6, 7
    litigation and, 266, 269, 270
    obtaining, 18-19, 130

Cestui que, 7
Charitable beneficiary
    described, 6
    estate administration and. *See* Estate administration (Ontario)
    fiduciary obligations of, 6, 67
    income tax issues. *See* Income taxes
    notification of interest, 67
Charitable organizations
    complaints against, 293
    Court's inherent jurisdiction over, 293
    estate trustee, as, 18
    indemnity, power to give, 92
    intestacy and, 2
    litigation, involvement in. *See* Litigation (Ontario)
    obligation to scrutinize accounting, 128-130
Children. *See* Minors
    adopted, 50
    notice to, 56
Children's Lawyer, 7
Claims
    advertising for. *See* Advertising for claims
    creditors and claimants. *See* Estate administration
    liability of estate, as, 31-32
    litigation re. *See* Litigation
Codicil, 16
Compensation to estate trustee
    Alberta
        amount of, 94-98
        entitlement, 93-94
        out-of-pocket expenses, 98-99
        pre-taking compensation, 98-99
    British Columbia, 107-109
    Ontario
        accounting fees, 77 n19
        agreement prior to death, 78
        calculation of rate, 75-80
        care and management fee, 77
        case law re, 79
        corporate trustee practice, 74, 77, 78
        customary rate, 75, 76, 77, 79
        G.S.T., 77
        investment advisor fees, 77 n19
        legacy vs. compensation, 78
        multiple trustees, where, 75
        non-compensatory items, 76
        pre-taking compensation, 80-81
        review of, 81
        specified in Will, where, 78
        statement of compensation, 74
        three-step process to determine, 79
        Trustee Act provision, 74

Costs in estate litigation
  Alberta, in, 105-107, 301
  British Columbia, in, 109-110, 319
  Ontario, in, 92-93, 282-286
    administration cases, in, 285
    appeals, 285
    assessment of costs, 285
    dependants/spousal challenges, in, 284
    estate bearing costs, tradition re, 283-284
    factors, 283
    judicial discretion re, 282
    lump sum awards, 285
    Rules of Civil Procedure re, 283
    settlement offers, 286
    statutory provisions re, 282
    unsuccessful party as bearing costs, 286
    Will challenges, in, 284
Creditors. *See* Estate administration (Alberta)
Cy-près doctrine. See Litigation (Ontario)

D

Deed, 7
Dependants. *See* Estate administration (Alberta); Litigation
Devise, 7

E

Estate
  bring forward form, App. 1
  described, 1
Estate accounting (Alberta)
  oath of personal representative, 136
  passing accounts, 139-145
    Court applications
      dispensing with formal passing, 140-142
      formal passing, 142-145
    informal accounting and releases, 139-140
    persons entitled to receive, 135-136
    preparation of accounts, format, 136-139
      assets, listing, 138
      disbursements, 138
      inventory, 138
      reconciliation summary, 139
      Surrogate Rules re, 136-138
    statutory requirement re, 135
Estate accounting (British Columbia)
  compelling passing of accounts, 146-147
  "court format", 147
  formal passing of accounts, 148-151
    costs, 150, 151
    minor beneficiaries, 148
    reference to registrar, 149
    registrar's report, 150
    representation, 151
    service of documents, 149
  format, 147
  generally, 145-146
  Statement of Investment Account, 147-148
  Statement of Unrealized Original Assets, 148
Estate accounting (Ontario)
  account review, App. 3
  documents, of. *See* Testamentary documents, review of
  response to, 133
  auditing of accounts
    generally, 130
    trust company accounts, 133-134
  beneficiaries' right to inspect and investigate, 111
  charity's obligation to scrutinize, 128-130
    potential issues, 129-130
    Public Guardian and Trustee role, 128-129
  duty to beneficiaries, as, 111
  formal form of (Rule 74), 117-125
    cash summary, 124
    generally, 118
    Statement of Capital Disbursements, 121
    Statement of Capital Receipts, 121
    Statement of Estate Trustee's Compensation, 125
    Statement of Investment Account, 122-124
    Statement of Original Assets, 119-120
    Statement of Outstanding Liabilities, 125
    Statement of Revenue Disbursements, 122
    Statement of Revenue Receipts, 122
    Statement of Trustees' Investment, 125
    Statement of Unrealized Original Aassets, 124
  format, 116-117
    "court passing" form, 117
    "hybrid" form, 117
    "trust company" form, 117
  legatee vs. residual beneficiary's rights, 112
  passing accounts. *See* Passing accounts
  purpose of, 113
  release and indemnity, 126
  statutory requirement, as, 111
  testamentary documents. *See* Testamentary documents, review of
Estate administration (Alberta)
  advice and directions, applications for, 58-59
  children, notice to, 56
  creditors and claimants
    advertisement for, 43

Estate administration (Alberta) — *cont'd*
  notice to, 42-43
  notice of claim, 43
  time limitation on claim, 43
 Dependants Relief Act, notice of rights under, 54-57
  adult interdependent partners, 54-55
  children, 56
  spouses, 55
 generally, 37
 grant of probate
  application for, 38, 44-47
  documents filed, 38
  fees for, 47
  financial institutions, requirement by, 44-46
  hierarchy re, 39
  information collection, 47
  intestacy, where, 38
  preferences re, 38
  requirement to obtain, 44-46
  reserving right to apply, 39
 interpretation of Wills, 60
 Intestate Succession Act
  adopted children, 50
  "adult interdependent partner", 48, 54-55
  common law spouses, 48
  distribution rules, 48-50
  "issue", meaning of, 50
 Matrimonial Property Act, notice under, 57
 personal representative
  application for grant of probate. *See* grant of probate
  bonds, requirement re, 40-41
  conflict of interest, 40
  duties of, 41-42
  identification of, 38
  renunciation by, 39
 rectification of wills, 60
 spouse, notice to, 55, 57
 Surrogate Rules
  convicts, 53
  deceased persons, notice to, 52
  dependent adults, 53
  minor persons, 53
  missing persons, 52
  prescribed forms, 37-38
  residuary beneficiary, notice to, 51
  service of notices under, 54
  specific bequest beneficiary, notice to, 51
  unborn beneficiaries, 53
Estate administration (British Columbia)
 charitable beneficiaries, 67-68
  fiduciary obligations, 67
  notification of interest, 67
 documentation requirements, 64-65
 executor, appointment of, 64
 intestacy, 61-63
  application for letters of administration, 62
  bond, requirement of, 63
  distribution of assets, order of, 62
  "spouse", meaning of, 62
 probate, 65-67
  application by executor, 65
  copies of Will, distribution to beneficiaries, 67
  documentary requirements, 66
  fees, 67
  procedural requirements, 65-66
 Wills, 63-64
  formal requirements, 63
  holograph, 64
Estate administration (Ontario)
 advertising for claims, 31-32
  effect of, 31-32
  form of, 31
  statutory requirements, 31
 beneficiaries
  classes of, 33
  charitable beneficiary, 26-30
   death of testator, notice of, 27
   fiduciary obligations of, 28
   information, collection of by, 27-28
   interim distributions to, 34
   notice of application, receipt of, 27
   public relations considerations, 29-30
   real estate concerns, 36
   renouncement by, 36
   residuary bequests, 29
   status reports, requests for, 34
   statutory obligations, 28
   substitutional transactions, 36
   tickler system of, 28-29
   tax clearance certificates, 34
   value of estate, knowledge of, 29
   Will, provision of to, 26
 estate trustee
  appointment of, 16-18
  beneficiary's expectations of, 24-25
  certificates of appointment, 18-19
  charity as, 18
  charity's interests, 17
  division of labour with solicitor, 23
  documentary requirements for appointment, 18-19
  duties of, 23-24
  "executor's year", meaning of, 24
  legal requirements, 16
  renouncement by, 17
  retirement of, 17
  solicitor as, 25
  unreasonable delay by, 24
 final distribution, 37
 funeral arrangements, 11-12
 income taxes, 32-33

Estate administration (Ontario) — *cont'd*
   estate trustee's responsibility for, 32
   deadlines for, 32-33
   intestacy 13-14
      bond requirement, 13
      distribution rules, 13
      Estate Trustee without a Will, authority of, 13
   legatees, 34-35
   liabilities of estate, 30-31
      claims, 31-32
      debts of estate, 30
      legacies, payment of, 30
   non-contentious estate, tasks re, 19
   probate, 20-23
      certificate of appointment, application for, 20-22
         distribution of copies, 22
         filing of, 23
         material required, 21
         Rules of Civil Procedure re, 21
      estate administration tax, 22-23
      insolvent estates, 21
      inventory and valuation of assets, 22
      necessity for, 20
      survivorship, where right of, 20
      Will as public document, 22
   real property
      concerns of charity re, 36
      environmental concerns, 36
      vesting of in estate trustee, 35
   residual beneficiaries
      estate accounting details to, 34
   residue, distribution/investment of, 33
   solicitor
      division of labour with estate trustee, 23
      duties of, 25-26, 36-37
      initial meeting with, 12, 16, 19
      roles of, 12
   steps in, 6
   tax clearance certificate (CCRA), 33, 37
   testamentary documents, 14-19
      Codicil, 16
      holograph Will, formal requirements, 14-15
      Wills
         formal requirements, 14
         presumption of validity, 15
   winding up estate, 37
Estate trustee. *See* Estate administration; Personal representative
   authority of, source, 2
   certificate of appointment, 6
   charitable organization as, 18
   compensation. *See* Compensation to estate trustee
   described, 3
   functions of, 3
   income taxes, responsibility re, 81
   litigation, during, 274-275, 280-281
   professional, 70
   solicitor as. *See* Passing accounts
Estate trustee during litigation, 7
Estate Trustee with a Will, 3, 7
Estate Trustee without a Will, 3, 7

F

Fiduciary, 6, 28, 67, 299
Funeral, 11-12

H

Holdback, 8
Holograph Will. *See* Will

I

Income taxes
   capital gains, 83
   charitable beneficiary
      evaluation of gift and issuing of receipts by, 84-85
      review of income/capital distributions, 84
      review of taxes paid, 84
   clearance certificate, 33, 34, 37, 82
   distributions to charities, 83
   donation credit, 83
   estate returns, 83
   estate trustee's responsibility re, 81
   Income Tax Act provision re liability, 81
   indemnity, tax concerns re, 91
   life tenant income, 83-4
   tax returns, filing of, 82
Indemnity. *See* Release
   charity's power to give, 92
   described, 90
   inquiries by charity, 91
   need for, 90
   sample, 91
   tax liability concerns, 91
Insolvent estate, 21
Inter vivos, 8
Interpretation of testamentary instruments, 60, 245
Intestacy
   Alberta, in, 48-50, 311
   British Columbia, in, 61-3
   consanguinity, table of, 2
   described, 2, 8
   failure of charitable bequests under, 251
   grant of probate where, 38
   Ontario, in, 13-14, 251
Intestate Succession Act. See Estate administration (Alberta)
Issue, 8

J

Joint tenancy, 8

L

Lapse, 8
Legacy
  compensation vs., 78
  defined, 8
  payment of, 30
Legal and professional fees
  Alberta
    estate administration, for, 99-104
    solicitor's account
      assessing, 104-105
      form of, 104
  Ontario
    challenging, 71
    costs of, 70
    professional estate trustees, 70
    solicitor's accounts, 70-71
    tariff re legal fees, 70
Legatee
  defined, 8
  receipt by, App. 2
  rights of, 34-5, 88, 112
Letters of Administration, 62
Liabilities. *See* Estate administration (Ontario)
Life tenancy, 8
Limitations. *See* Time limitations
Litigation (Alberta)
  administrator *ad litem*
    appointment of, 296
    appropriate persons to act as, 297
    powers of, 296
  Adult Interdependent Relationships Act, 301
  beneficiaries
    as parties, 299
    involvement in litigation, 300
  contested claims procedure, 297-299
    chambers/summary applications, 298
    disputed material facts, where, 298
    statutory provisions re, 297-299
    time limitations, 298
  corroboration, 299-300
  costs, 301
  Dependants Relief Act applications, 301-307
    adult interdependent partners, 303-304
    agreements/releases, *etc.*, effect of, 307
    claims under, principles re, 302-303
    generally, 301
    limitation periods, 306
    Matrimonial Property Act claims and, 310
    procedure under, 306
    quantum meruit claims, 305
    spouses, 304-305
  evidentiary matters, 299-300
  examination for discovery, 300
  Family Relief Act, claims under, 304-305
  generally, 295
  Matrimonial Property Act
    assets subject to, 309-310
    debts, 310
    Dependants Relief Act claims and, 310-311
    Dower Act claims, 311
    effect of
      estate distribution, on, 312
      generally, 307-308
    entitlement to make claim under, 308
    intestacy and, 311
    procedure under, 312
    "spouse", meaning of, 309
    time limitations, 312
  parties, 299
  personal representative of estate
    fiduciary duties of, 299
    preconditions to litigation, 295
  settlement, 300
  time limitation considerations, 297
Litigation (British Columbia)
  costs, 319
  dependant support claims, 313
  steps in, 313-319
    post-grant, 316-318
      mediation, 317-318
      proof in solemn form, 316-317
    pre-grant, 314-316
      caveats, 315-316
      citations, 314-315
    pre-trial, 318
    Supreme Court Rules provisions, 313
    trial, 319
  Wills Variation Act claim, 313
Litigation (Ontario)
  beneficiaries, effects on, 286-287
  charities' involvement, 288-294
    factors re, 289-294
      ability to work with others, 292
      access to advisors, 292
      adequate representation, 290
      duties of charity, 290
      failure to meet obligations, 293
      number of residuary beneficiaries, 291
      public duties of charity, 290-291
      public relations, 291
      size of charity, 292
      timing, 292
    reasons for, 288
    roles, types of, 289
    special nature of charities, 288
    special nature of estate litigation, 293-294
  claims against estate, 258-264

Litigation (Ontario) — *cont'd*
  dependant support/relief claims, 260-261
  generally, 258-259
  services rendered claims, 261-264
    beneficiaries' involvement, 263
    charitable beneficiary's contribution, 264
    defence of, 262
    examples of, 261-262
    legal costs, 263
    procedure re, 262
    quantum meruit compensation, 262
  spousal election, 259-60
  confidentiality and privacy issues, 294
  conflict of interest, 287
  costs in. *See* Costs in estate litigation
  cy-près doctrine, 245-250
    administrative terms of charitable trust, 248
    costs of application, 250
    Court application procedure, 250
    Court's inherent jurisdiction over charities, 245
    limitations inconsistent with charity's objects, 248
    non-existent named beneficiary, 246
    omission in determining extent of gift, 247
    policy rationale, 246
    refusal to apply doctrine, effects of, 248
    successor beneficiaries, 247
    terms contrary to public policy, remedy of, 247
  effects of litigation, 286-7
  estate trustee during litigation, 274-5
  generally, 243
  interpretation of testamentary instruments, 245
  mediation, 277-279
  parties to, 280-282
    beneficiary, 282
    estate trustee, 280-281
    mentally incapable persons, 281
    minors, unborns and unascertaineds, 281
  settlement, 277
  sources of, 243
  special nature of, 293-294
  steps in estate action, 264-280
    certificate of appointment
      objection to issuing, 269
      order to accept or refuse, 266
      return of, 270
      revocation of, 270
    directions, application or motion for, 271-273
    examination for discovery, 276
    formal proof of testamentary instrument, 269
    generally, 264-265
    interlocutory procedures, 275
    mediation, 277-279
    notice of appearance, 273
    notice of commencement of proceedings, 268
    notification, 265
    Order for Assistance, 265
    Order for further Particulars, 268
    Order to Beneficiary Witness, 267
    Order to File Statement of Assets, 267
    Order to Former Spouse, 267
    Order to Pass Accounts, 268
    pre-trial, 279
    production of documents, 275-276
    statement of submission of rights, 273-274
  types of, 244
  Will
    challenges. *See* Will challenges
    lost or destroyed, proving, 244
    validity of, 243, 244
  Will challenges, 251-258
    age capacity, 254
    fraud, 258
    generally, 251, 254
    intestacy, failure of charitable bequests under, 251
    mental capacity, 255-256
    proper execution, 252-254
      holograph Wills, 254
      typed or processed Wills, 252-253
    suspicious circumstances, 256-257
    undue influence, 257-258

M

Matrimonial Property Act
  claims under. *See* Litigation (Alberta)
  Dependants Relief Act applications and, 310
  notice under, 57
Minors, 53, 148, 281

N

Next-of-kin
  defined, 9
  intestacy and. *See* Intestacy

P

Passing accounts. *See* Estate accounting
  compelling, 114-116
  "court-format", 114
  orders for assistance, 115-116
  Rules of Civil Procedure re, 115

Passing accounts — cont'd
    compensation. See Compensation to estate trustee
    described, 112
    effect of, 117
    formal passing, 126
    generally, 69
    income taxes. See Income taxes
    indemnity. See Indemnity
    initiation of, 112
    legal and professional fees. See Legal and professional fees
    "over the counter" passing, 126-128
        procedure, 126-127
        solicitors' costs, 127-128
    release. See Release
    review by counsel, costs of, 69
    solicitor as estate trustee, where, 25, 72-74
        compensation, charge for, 73
        delegation of functions, 73
        "double dipping", 72
        estate trustee vs. solicitor's work, distinguishing, 72-73
        professional services, charges for, 72
        provision in Will re, 73
    timing of, 113
Per capita, 9
Per stirpes, 9
Personal representative. See Estate trustee
    defined, 4
    estate administration and. See Estate administration (Alberta)
    litigation and. See Litigation (Alberta)
    oath of, 136
Power of attorney. See Attorney
Probate
    certificate of appointment, 6
    described, 5
    grant of. See Estate administration
    intestacy and, 38
Public Guardian and Trustee, 9, 128-129
Public policy
    acceptance of gifts and, 27, n21
    terms of Will as contrary to, 247

Q

Quantum meruit, 9, 262, 305

R

Real property, 35, 36
Rectification of Will, 60
Release. See Indemnity
    acknowledgment, 86
    administration of estate issues and, 89-90
    content of, 87-88
    described, 86
    distribution vs. release, 89-90

drafting by charity, 88
effect of, 88
form of, 87
receipt vs. release, 88
residuary vs. legatee beneficiaries, 88
review of, importance of, 89
signature section of, 87
wrongdoing, from, 87
Residual beneficiary
    estate accounting details to, 34
    notice to, 51
    rights of. See Beneficiary
Residue
    bequests, 29
    defined, 9
    distribution/investment of, 33
Right of survivorship, 9, 20

S

Service of documents, 54, 149
Services rendered claims, 261-4
Solicitor
    division of labour between estate trustee and, 23
    estate administration and. See Estate administration (Ontario)
    estate trustee, as. See Passing accounts
    fees of. See Legal and professional fees
Spouse
    claim by, 55, 57, 304-305
    common law, 48
    defined, 62, 309
Sui juris, 10
Surrogate Rules. See Estate administration (Alberta)
Suspicious circumstances, 256-257

T

Taxes. See Income taxes
Tenancy in common, 10
Testamentary documents, review of
    capital disbursements, 132
    capital receipts, 131
    certificate of appointment, obtaining, 130
    compensation calculations, 133
    general review, 133
    investment account, 132
    questions on review, 130-133
    revenue receipts/disbursements, 132
    statement of original assets, 131
Testate, 10
Testator/testatrix
    described, 3, 10
Time limitations
    Alberta, in, 297
    contested claims, 298
    creditors claims, 43

Time limitations — *cont'd*
   Matrimonial Property Act, under, 312
Title, 10
Trust
   beneficiary, 4
   charitable, 248
   described, 5
   types of, 5
Trust company, 70, 74, 77, 78, 133-134
Trustee
   described, 4
   estate. *See* Estate trustee

U

Unborn beneficiaries, 53
Undue influence, 257-258

W

Will
   absence of, 2
   Codicil, 16
   copies to beneficiaries, 67
   described, 1
   formal proof of, 269
   formal requirements, 14, 63
   holographic, 2, 8, 14-15, 64
   interpretation of, 60, 245
   litigation re. *See* Litigation (Ontario)
   presumption of validity, 15
   public document, as, 22
   public policy, 27, n21, 247
   rectification of, 60
   validity requirements, 2
Wills Variation Act claim, 313
Winding up estate, 37